INVENTIONS
THAT CHANGED THE WORLD

FOREWORD

As the new millennium begins, **THE EVENTFUL CENTURY** series looks back at the vast panorama of the last hundred years—a century which has witnessed the transition from horse-drawn transport to space travel, and from the first telephones to the information superhighway.

THE EVENTFUL CENTURY chronicles epoch-making events like the outbreak of the two world wars, the Russian Revolution and the rise and fall of communism. But major events are only part of the glittering kaleidoscope. It also describes the everyday background—the way people lived, how they worked, what they ate and drank, how much they earned, the way they spent their leisure time, the books they read, and the crimes, scandals and unsolved mysteries that set them talking. Here are fads and crazes like the hula hoop and Rubik's cube ... fashions like the New Look and the miniskirt ... breakthroughs in entertainment, like the birth of the movies ... medical milestones like the discovery of penicillin ... and marvels of modern architecture and engineering.

INVENTIONS THAT CHANGED THE WORLD traces the technological innovations that are now accelerating at such a pace that the sum of human knowledge is doubling every decade. More inventions have been devised and put to use since 1900 than in the rest of human history put together. A child born in 1900 entered a world where no one had yet flown in an airplane, used a vacuum cleaner or seen a television program. Even a child born half a century later, in the aftermath of World War II, was coming into a world where computers were known only to a handful of research scientists, the transistor had yet to be invented, and the vast majority of the people who crossed the Atlantic each year still did so by ship, not plane.

INVENTIONS THAT CHANGED THE WORLD explains what these key inventions were, illustrates how they worked, and describes how they have transformed our daily lives.

INVENTIONS
THAT CHANGED THE WORLD

 Reader's Digest

The Reader's Digest Association, Inc.
Pleasantville, New York/Montreal

INVENTIONS THAT CHANGED THE WORLD
Edited and designed by Toucan Books Limited
Written by Richard Walker, Richard Tames, John
Man, Charles Freeman
Edited by Robert Sackville West and Mandie
Rickaby
Designed by Bradbury and Williams
Picture research by Julie McMahon

FOR THE AMERICAN EDITION
Produced by The Reference Works
Editor-in-Chief Harold Rabinowitz
Managing Editor Ross Mandel
Editor Ben Soskis
Production Bob Antler/Antler Designworks

FOR READER'S DIGEST, US
Group Editorial Director Fred DuBose
Senior Editor Susan Randol
Senior Designer Judith Carmel

READER'S DIGEST ILLUSTRATED REFERENCE BOOKS
Editor-in-Chief Christopher Cavanaugh
Art Director Joan Mazzeo

Printed in the United States of America 1999

Library of Congress Cataloging in Publication Data

Inventions that changed the world.
        p.   cm. — (The Eventful 20th century ; 4)
    ISBN 0-7621-0269-1
    1. Inventions — History.
    I. Reader's Digest Association. II. Series.
    T15. I58   1999
609 — dc21   99-38516

Front Cover
From Top: Ford Model-T; Candlestick telephone;
Personal computer

Back Cover
From Top: Radio telescope at Jodrell Bank in
England; French vacuum cleaner, 1911; Artist's
vision of steam power

Background pictures:
Page 9: Neon lights in Piccadilly Circus, London
Page 35: Microcircuit on a silicon chip
Page 53: Optical fibres
Page 67: Scan of normal brain
Page 81: Solar reflectors at an experimental solar
power station in New Mexico
Page 93: Aerial view of airport terminal
Page 121: Parachutists of the 82nd Airborne
Division, U.S.A.
Page 133: A collection of old 78 rpm records
Page 150-1: Autogyro in flight
Page 152-3: HMS *Starfish*, 1937
Page 154: Computer memory chip
Page 155: Contac 400 sustained release capsule (for
common cold)

CONTENTS

GIANT LEAPS FOR MANKIND

A SINGLE CENTURY HAS TAKEN US FROM TRAVEL BY STEAM TRAINS TO LANDING A MAN ON THE MOON

Technological innovation and expertise were accelerating at such a pace by the end of the 20th century that the sum of human knowledge was doubling every decade—bringing about an extraordinary transformation. A single lifetime has seen humankind advance from clockwork to space travel and the information super-highway.

The Stone Age lasted 2 million years; the Copper, Bronze, and Iron Ages spanned 5,000 years; the age of water and wind

THE BIRTH OF A CENTURY Who could have foreseen such unimaginable changes at a time when horsepower was taken literally?

power occupied a further 1,000 years until it was completely shaken apart by the coal-fired, steam-powered Industrial Revolution in the space of a mere 150 years.

Into the subsequent 100 years were crammed two discernible "ages," electric and electronic, as well as the beginning of a third—our current era—whose limits seem boundless. Now, we find ourselves at the forefront of the Information Age, where the most precious commodity is data—capable of being processed into an infinity of new ideas and devices.

The 20th century sprang in essence from the 1880s and the achievements of a few famously inspired late-Victorian inventors. By 1900, electric power and light and the telephone, the steam turbine and the internal combustion engine were all in place, as

were processes to make steel and aluminum cheap and plentiful. Over the same period, organic chemistry blossomed from unlikely beginnings in the dye industry in Germany.

There, manufacturers had started to seek synthetic substitutes for natural materials they could no longer acquire from colonial sources. In the process, they opened up an Aladdin's cave of wonders, including the first plastics. Major companies, determined to exploit the new technologies, then opened research laboratories to further their development. For whereas previous generations of inventors (exemplified by the self-taught Thomas Edison) depended upon inspired guesswork, it was now down to the disciplined team efforts of highly trained and specialized scientists. One single breakthrough could lead in many surprising directions. Defining and particularizing key acts of creation become increasingly difficult and subjective as the efforts of so many converged and fed upon one another.

The impulse for change

Electricity was the key that turned the lock on technology, making it a part of everyone's life for the first time. From the first electric power stations able to illuminate a few thousand light bulbs in New York and London in 1882, this efficient way of packaging energy and providing it on demand resulted in a spate of electromechanical inventions by the turn of the century. With the advent of turbine generators, it was providing power to spare for exciting new industries. Electricity also brought

about communication by electromagnetic waves. With the development in 1907 of the vacuum tube amplifier, or radio valve, it brought the world together through broadcasting and, later, television.

At the same time, personal mobility increased out of all recognition through the speedy development of the automobile. The internal combustion engine had still to prove itself in 1900. The car industry was minuscule and more vehicles were powered by steam or electricity than gas. Lightweight steam engines were even fitted to experimental aircraft before the Wright brothers flew in 1903, powering their aircraft with an internal combustion engine. It was efficiency-obsessed Henry Ford who, with his Model T, set an irreversible course for motor transport and mass production in general—to such an extent that Ford later felt able to lay claim to inventing the 20th century.

The motor industry was soon driving the economies of industrial nations and literally reshaping the world. It set a fast pace of industrial growth and its needs fostered further invention—machine tools for its production lines, high-speed cutting steels and innumerable humbler yet profound advances, such as spray paints. From powering cars, the oil industry began to challenge coal-mining as the prime energy source, and it provided the base substance for more new plastics and other petrochemical products.

Just when the economic depression of the 1930s threatened to slow the rate of technological advance, the demands of the Second

HOME FROM HOME The invention of the automobile brought about personal mobility and a whole new concept—caravan vacations.

World War redoubled it by stirring an inventive frenzy. The space rocket and the jet engine, nuclear energy, electronics, the computer and a welter of new materials—all owe their early development to the desperation of that time. The transition from electric to electronic technology occurred just two years after the end of the war, and sprang from the invention in 1947 of the transistor. This replaced the bulky, unreliable and

HIGH SOCIETY A view from one of the 16,100 windows in the Sears, Roebuck & Co. headquarters in Chicago. Completed in 1973, it was the tallest office building in the world at 1,454 feet.

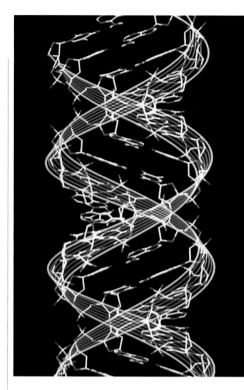

THE CODE OF LIFE It took until the middle of the century for scientists to understand DNA and heredity. Within 30 years, doctors would embark on genetic engineering.

power-consuming vacuum tube. However, electronics would not achieve its full impact until the 1960s with the development of cheap and ever tinier and more complex transistor-based integrated circuitry.

Culminating in the microprocessor chip, electronics brought about a technological revolution by facilitating industrial automation and the emergence of the computer as a universal tool. The development of the laser put light to companion use in such devices as optical scanners and compact storage disks.

Allied with a network of communications satellites, the computer brought about an explosive expansion in the capacity to amass, manipulate and transmit information. Virtually everything from business practice to military strategy and fundamental research was transformed. No image, concept or object was too complex to be digitized into the ones and zeros of pure data. The very stuff of life, deoxyribonucleic acid (DNA), was reduced to a string of codified information and the complete gene-mapping of the human organism was embarked upon.

Time and space in this new Information Age lost much of their meaning. Data exchange became instantaneous through faxes, modems and e-mail; entertainment could be scheduled to the user's wishes through the video recorder and similar devices; business could be conducted from remote locations with no appointment necessary, just as banking hours were made meaningless by automated teller machines.

The health of nations

Nothing benefited more from a convergence of technologies than medicine, which at the start of the century was only beginning to comprehend the nature of disease. By the 1990s, the innermost workings of the body could be probed and problems diagnosed without so much as a pinprick. Organs could be replaced or restored artificially, while genetic engineers had begun to address ways of "programming out" hereditary ailments.

More people were living longer, eating better, and enjoying qualities of health and leisure opportunities unimagined in the past. But technology, which had supplanted religion in the minds of many people, proved to be as wrathful and intolerant a god as the one in the Old Testament. The dropping of the atom bomb on the Japanese cities of Hiroshima and Nagasaki in 1945 was a stark intimation of this: numbers of the bomb's inventors were appalled at the consequences of their own creation. The Union of Concerned Scientists—which this group formed in 1946—was the first organized protest against irresponsible progress.

Fear of the future

Apart from fears of nuclear annihilation whipped up by the postwar Cold War, alarm began to be raised over more insidious effects of headlong "progress." The Club of Rome, a panel of leading economists and scientists, startled the world in 1972 with an alarmist report entitled *The Limits of Growth*. Their conclusions were based on computer models that predicted widespread shortages and famine because of the depletion of non-renewable natural resources.

Ecology movements were formed to reverse the trend, but the range of concerns multiplied. The false promise of cheap, clean nuclear energy became buried under mountains of radioactive waste and calamitous reactor accidents. The bounty of agriculture's herbicide- and pesticide-propelled green revolution bore a price in polluted rivers and contaminated foodstuffs. The over-prescription of "wonder" drugs resulted in virulent new strains of diseases which were thought to have been conquered. Warnings about acid rain and global warming carried a ring of doom previously associated only with nuclear holocaust.

Much inventive energy turned to seeking substitutes for toxic chemicals and to finding ways of cleaning up the environment. The recycling of waste materials became a major technology in its own right. Retrotechnology—finding simple old-fashioned means of achieving an end—gained new respect. Developing clean, cost-effective alternatives to fossil fuels—such as solar, wind or geothermal power—became an increasingly urgent challenge. In tandem, there came the quest for a means of electric propulsion efficient enough to end the air-fouling tyranny of the internal combustion engine.

Progress, it was ruefully realized, had negative aspects. "Future shock"—technology changing faster than the human mind can accommodate—resulted in heightened emotional stress as millions of jobs were lost to automation and computerization.

With each new invention, skills of a lifetime were rendered obsolete. Making and doing things depended upon fewer and fewer people, so what was to become of the rest of us? As the century of runaway invention drew to its close, the prospects for the future were never greater—nor were they more fraught with uncertainty.

POCKET REVOLUTION Now as common as the ball-point pen—also a 20th-century invention—electronic calculators were made possible by transistor technology in 1947.

Transforming The World Around Us

THE COMING OF ELECTRICITY HAS RELEASED EVERYDAY LIVING FROM SOME OF THE CONSTRAINTS OF NATURE—IN PARTICULAR, FROM THE RHYTHMS OF LIGHT AND DARK, HEAT AND COLD. IT HAS ALSO POWERED NEW MACHINES THAT HAVE BROUGHT RELIEF TO DOMESTIC DRUDGERY. IN THE PROCESS, CONVENIENCE HAS BECOME THE WATCHWORD OF THE CENTURY—IN EVERYTHING FROM SHOPPING TO FAST FOOD.

BUILDING A NEW AGE

IMPROVEMENTS IN STEEL AND CONCRETE HELP TO RESTRUCTURE THE WORLD

Before the second half of the 19th century, the walls of the ground floor of a building had to bear the load of the floors above. If these walls were not to be unrealistically thick, the height of a building had to be limited to around five stories. Steel-frame construction, in which a skeletal steel frame carries the weight of the building, while lightweight walls simply act as curtains against the elements, freed builders from such limitations, and inspired turn-of-the-century American architects to feats of daring. Hydraulic elevators of the time were effective only to about 20 stories, but in 1903 the Otis company perfected the electric elevator by offsetting the weight of the car with a sliding counter-weight. Conservative architectural attitudes curbed experimentation in Europe, however. The first steel-framed building, equipped with an elevator, was not completed in London until 1904.

LIFTOFF Elisha Graves Otis demonstrates the safety elevator which made tall buildings practical.

Reaching for the skies

Toward the end of the 19th century, as America gobbled up its frontier land, one had to look upward for a new undiscovered territory. Indeed, in cities across the country, the skyline soon became as crowded as the booming American west. The first phase of skyscraper construction in the U.S. culminated in the 60-story Woolworth Building, completed in 1913. Hailed as The Cathedral of Commerce, and rising 792 feet into the air, it held the record for the next quarter century—the era in which concrete began to dominate the world's buildings.

One of the problems with concrete is that it cracks under pressure. However, when steel rods are embedded in concrete slabs, they take the tension and reinforce the concrete. This technique was pioneered by German and French engineers, notably François Hennebique, who by 1900 had completed the world's first bridge of concrete trussed with iron bars. But it was in the United States that the world's first office block of reinforced concrete was built—the 16-story Ingals Building in Cincinnati.

To meet the burgeoning demand for big buildings, the motor-powered concrete mixer was devised; the truck-mounted transit mixer followed in 1926. Large automatic concrete-mixing plants were devised for such giant enterprises as the Grand Coulee

SCRAPING THE SKY

The soaring skyscraper put the exclamation mark on the 20th century. But like many of the century's achievements, it drew its inspiration from a 19th-century innovator, Chicago architect William Le Baron Jenney. On a trip to Southeast Asia, Jenney had been struck by the traditional homes made of reed matting strung on a framework of tree-trunks. He envisioned "an internal steel frame on which the fabric would be strung like flesh upon a skeleton." The result in 1885 was the 10-story Home Insurance Company Building, ancestor of all high-rise structures.

Another Chicago architect, Louis Sullivan, pioneered the clean, functional lines of the modern skyscraper, but his designs proved too much for early 20th-century taste. Most property developers at first preferred structures to imitate the architecture of earlier ages, such as the neoclassical Flatiron Building and the neo-Gothic Woolworth Building, both in New York City.

The 1920s were the heroic age of the skyscraper, when corporations vied with each other to construct ever-higher buildings, and Manhattan became a canyoned island with their efforts. In 1929, however, the Wall Street stock market crashed and for the time being all construction ceased—except for one gargantuan enterprise which became a beacon of hope in the Depression years. This was architect William Lamb's handsome 102-story Empire State Building, completed in 1931. The Empire State became the most romanticized of all skyscrapers, the setting of numerous movies from *King Kong* onward and of real-life dramas. In dense fog, on July 28, 1945, a B-25 bomber piloted by Lt.-Col. William Smith plowed into the 79th floor at 200 miles per hour. Fourteen people were killed and 25 were injured in the tragic accident, but the building's frame was barely dented. Able to brush aside more than 6,000 tons of wind pressure on a gusty day, the structure incorporated three times as much steel as its design required.

SKY-HIGH The Woolworth Building of 1913 in New York fused new technology with traditional architecture. It has endured as a much-loved monument.

1903 Counterweight elevator designed

1913 Woolworth Building in New York completed

1924 The first hardboard, Masonite, is invented

1931 The Empire State Building in New York

Dam in the United States, which began in 1933 and consumed more than 19 million tons of concrete in its 550 foot high wall.

Prestressed concrete, made practical by the development of high-strength steel wires, now came into widespread use. Conceived in Germany, it was perfected from 1904 onward by the French civil engineer Eugène Freyssinet, who stretched the steel wires running through a slab of concrete while the concrete was still wet. Once the concrete had set, he released the tension, which compressed—or "prestressed"—the concrete, thereby strengthening it. This new building material made for far lighter load-bearing beams and for stunningly slender bridges; it also used about 70 percent less steel and 40 percent less concrete than reinforced concrete.

New building materials

Other materials also made their appearance in the early decades of the century. Plasterboard, a sandwich of plaster and paper used for covering walls and ceilings, originated in the United States, where it was being widely used by 1910. In 1924, American inventor William Mason chanced upon the first hardboard, when a leaky steam valve cooked compressed sawmill waste into a dense, tough, weather-resistant sheet; Masonite was on the market within a year.

For 40 years, until the completion in the early 1970s of the World Trade Center in New York and the Sears Tower in Chicago, the Empire State Building was the world's tallest building. It was to be the last and the grandest of the big-boned, steel-framed giants. Architects now turned to lighter cladding materials, including glass. The fusion of

HIGH HARMONICS The New York skyscraper boom between the wars created an elite breed of fearless construction workers. This 1930s team has just added ten floors in a record ten days.

EXTRA-STRONG STRUCTURES

Visionary architect Buckminster Fuller captured world attention in the 1960s with his geodesic domes—habitable spheres with the segmented geometry of a soccer ball. A decade later, scientists used soot to create molecules of an unsuspected kind of carbon that mirrored the geodesic design and shared its strength and resilience. In honor of Fuller, they called them Fullerenes, or Buckyballs.

steel and glass was perfected by German-born Mies van der Rohe, whose shiny "curtain" wall structures became a signature image of the 1950s.

Mass-production techniques borrowed from industry were applied to meet the post-Second World War housing demand. Results ranged from Britain's factory-built asbestos or aluminum-clad "prefabs" to the 17,447 simple, identical homes of Levittown, built by developer Bill Levitt on 19 square miles of potato fields, an hour's drive from New York City. "Housing schemes" and blocks of high-

LIGHT FANTASTIC A helicopter transports its own hangar. The geodesic dome was a 1960s experiment in low-cost lightweight construction.

rise flats proliferated in the 1960s and 1970s, many using prefabricated concrete components fixed to a steel frame.

With the development of stronger steels from the 1950s, skyscrapers became vast, hollow tubes. The structural backbone at the heart of the building—a series of steel cross-braces—was abandoned in order to liberate the internal space; instead, engineers created the "exoskeleton," a resilient outer frame that swayed, like a tree, with the wind so that the pressure never became such that the building toppled. However, the full potential of skyscraper sway was limited by the discovery in the early 1970s that even an imperceptible movement could induce nausea in people. The effect was compounded at the

THE NINETIES LOOK The NEC Super Tower in Tokyo (right) was designed to meet environmental concerns. Below: The Dallas skyline at sunset, a classic 1990s cityscape.

1900

1903 Counterweight elevator designed

1913 Woolworth Building in New York completed

1924 The first hardboard, Masonite, is invented

1931 The Empire State Building in New York

1950

top of the twin towers of New York City's World Trade Center, each rising 1,353 feet in the air and each swaying independently—and therefore visibly.

Buildings of the future

A high-tech architecture, with buildings turned inside out to expose their pipes, shafts and other working parts, was pioneered in the 1977 Georges Pompidou Center in Paris, and later in London by the Lloyd's Building. But environmental concerns also stimulated the development of a "green architecture" movement that found

FULL EXPOSURE The Pompidou Center in Paris, designed by Richard Rogers and Enzo Piano, pioneered "inside-out" architecture to stunning effect.

early expression in New Orleans' Chevron Plaza Building of 1979. This reinforced concrete structure was designed specifically to save energy in its heating, ventilation and air-conditioning systems. By 1987, the movement had flowered to produce the likes of the Nederlanden Bank headquarters in Amsterdam, whose ten glass-topped towers collected solar heat and optimized the use of natural light. Solar panels were also being used increasingly in domestic buildings.

Aided by computer technology, this approach has led to intelligent buildings that combine automated efficiency with a pleasant working environment. In Tokyo, the electronics company NEC invested in a 43 story "Super Tower" for its headquarters staff of 6,000. Nicknamed the Space Shuttle for its profile, the building has a huge atrium that soars up to the 12th floor and a roof that opens in good weather. All functions from lighting to security are managed by computer, with sunlight absorption controlled to maximize energy efficiency. The building's electronic brain notes the location of every staff member to eradicate fruitless searching, and links them by video with 35,000 colleagues worldwide.

From the 1990s, architects were looking skyward once more as a means of providing much-needed office space in the crowded major cities. In Paris, work began on the Tour Sans Fin (Tower Without End); in Kuala Lumpur on the twin 1,464-foot Petrona Towers; and in Hong Kong on the 1,594-foot Nina Tower.

TURNING ON THE POWER AND LIGHT

ELECTRICITY HAS BEEN THE CATALYST FOR MASSIVE CHANGE IN EVERYDAY LIVES

Electric light, which has so radically transformed the quality of our daily life this century—in the home, at work and on the streets—spread more slowly than is often assumed. Power distribution was fairly chaotic at first; by the end of the 19th century, New York City had 92 franchises for the provision of electricity, and up until mid 1920, Britain had some 600 independent operations in all.

The quality of light

The quest for the right type of light was equally prolonged. Swan and Edison vacuum lamps, dating from the early 1880s, had carbon filaments that burned, albeit briefly, in a vacuum. What was needed was a metal with a high melting point that gave a brighter, whiter light.

By the beginning of the century, the Austrian chemist and engineer Carl Auer von Welsbach was making filaments of a metallic element called osmium, and in 1905 a Berlin firm experimented with tantalum; but osmium was rare and expensive, and tantalum light was not bright enough. The solution was tungsten, with the highest melting point of all, but so hard and brittle that it was some years before it could be made into fine wire.

The breakthrough came in the United States, when William Coolidge compressed tungsten powder into a rod-shaped mold, which could then be drawn into a filament under intense pounding and heat. One of the problems with the tungsten light bulb, however, was that, as it glowed, atoms evaporated from the filament under the heat. Not only did this thin the wire filament itself, reducing its life, but it also caused condensation on the sides of the glass bulb, thereby dimming the light. Another American, Irving Langmuir, solved this problem by winding the tungsten filament in a tight coil around a supporting bar, which reduced heat loss and improved the efficiency

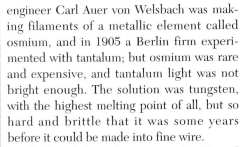

THE BETTER LIGHT BULB Ever since Edison's first lamp in the 19th century (below left), the quest for improved domestic lighting has continued: from an incandescent bulb of 1929 (top), to an ultra-modern filament-free light bulb (below), lasting 60,000 hours.

of the bulb, and by filling the bulb with an inert gas, which slowed down the process of evaporation but did not react with the filament. The result in 1913 was the incandescent light bulb in its familiar form.

Neon was a by-product of the race for the better light bulb. French chemical engineer Georges Claude passed an electric current through neon gas and found that the gas glowed bright red. As a source of light, it disappointed Claude—but not Jacques Fonseque, an advertising agent. Fonseque noted that with no need for a filament, the containing tube could be looped into letters that glowed in the night. The first neon sign graced a Montmartre hairdressing salon, and the first neon advertisement promoted Cinzano vermouth, both in 1912.

Other electrically charged gases were put to use. Sodium vapor lamps produced a smog-piercing orange-yellow glow that proved effective for street lighting from 1935. And mercury vapor lamps generated a bluish light loaded with harmful ultraviolet rays that limited its application until the 1930s. Scientists then discovered that, by coating the inside of the tube with chemical compounds called phosphors, it gave out safe, visible fluorescent light with a quarter of the electricity consumption of an incandescent bulb. Fluorescent lighting was a hit at the 1939 New York World's Fair, by which

Fluorescent powder coating on inside surface

Visible light

Visible light

Induced secondary current

Glass bulb containing inert gas with a small amount of vapor

Electric current causes the electrons in the gas filling to excite metal vapor atoms, giving rise to ultraviolet radiation

Power coupler

> ## ELECTRICITY FOR EVERYONE
>
> Electricity for all was no more than a vision at the dawn of the century. But, as the French novelist Emile Zola wrote in 1901, "The day must come when electricity will be for everyone, as the waters of the rivers and the wind of heaven. It should not merely be supplied, but lavished, that men may use it at their will, as the air they breathe."

1900

1908 William Coolidge demonstrates the tungsten filament
1912 First neon advertisement

1935 Sodium-vapor street lights
1939 Fluorescent lighting demonstrated at New York's World's Fair

1950

pioneered by American physicist Don Hollander and developed by the Philips Corporation in the 1990s. This produced the E-Lamp, a virtually indestructible bulb that consumed very little power. In place of a filament, a high-frequency radio signal excited gas to emit light.

NEON JUNGLE Early neon signs (right) gave little hint of the kaleidoscope to come. Neon glowed in 150 hues by the 1980s, and casinos in Las Vegas (below) throbbed beneath signs containing 8 miles of tubing per sign.

LIGHTING THE WAY The lighting provided on highways increased the hours and the safety of long-distance automobile travel.

time tubes in three sizes and half a dozen colors had been launched on the American market. Low-voltage fluorescent lights, with many times the life span of filament bulbs, met the bulk of business and industrial needs by the 1970s, when annual tube production reached 1,000 million. A new approach to lighting—by radio waves—was

POWER SET FREE

The Dutch physicist Heike Kamerlingh Onnes discovered in 1911 that some metal alloys lose all resistance to electricity at very low temperatures—that they become "superconductors," conducting electricity without any loss of heat or energy. The phenomenon occurs near absolute zero (–460°F) and can only be achieved by bathing the metal in costly liquid helium, which limits the use of superconductors. In 1987, however, two Swiss-based scientists won a Nobel prize for their discovery that certain ceramic materials become superconductive at more achievable temperatures. By 1993, researchers in Zurich had a material that worked at a "balmy"–140°F. This raised the prospect of a world released from the stranglehold of high-voltage cables; of easy, underground storage of limitless energy in magnetized ceramic coils; and of more powerful, yet smaller, motors and generators.

1987 Nobel prize for Swiss-based scientists who discover that ceramics can be superconductors

1990s E-Lamp pioneered by Philips

COMFORTS OF HOME

NEW INVENTIONS BRING A WARM GLOW AND MANY MORE MODERN CONVENIENCES

In 1900, electricity was expensive and available only in urban centers; it took decades for many rural communities to receive electricity, and many homes depended on gas-fire heating and lighting until after the Second World War. From then on, most of the changes in the home were driven by the increased availability of electricity.

A much-improved gas fire was introduced in 1900 by British manufacturer John Wright, who used fretted columns of fire clay, rather than tufted asbestos, to radiate

ELECTRIC HEATING The Belling "Standard" electric fire of 1912 was portable and had a hinged flange to support a kettle or pan.

the heat; the Wright design would endure throughout the century. At the same time, however, electric fires were improving. An electric fire had been patented in London in 1892, but in 1906 American Albert Marsh made a significant contribution by inventing nichrome, an alloy of nickel and chrome, which glowed red hot without disintegrating under heat, and was therefore ideal for electric fire elements. The first really effective electric fire was developed in 1912, in a garden shed in Enfield, a town near London, by Charles Reginald Belling who wound nichrome wire around a bar of fireclay. Manufacture of six-bar Belling "Standard" heaters with knob controls began immediately, with a design that became standard worldwide. Electricity was still alien and mysterious enough for early models to come with the warning, "DO NOT USE A POKER."

New materials in the home

The domestic environment was by now being transformed by the development of scores of materials and processes which gave new shape and serviceability to furniture, furnishings and appliances. In the early years of the century, plastic existed only as Celluloid. By 1900 it was being put to myriad uses, from mass-manufactured buckles, combs, eyeglass frames and piano keys, to objects faked to look like ivory or mother-of-pearl. There were wipe-clean Celluloid tablecloths; Celluloid collars and cuffs; even Celluloid false teeth. But Celluloid had drawbacks. It was prone to cracking and to catching fire, and it melted under the slightest heat, so that it was not advisable to wear dentures while sipping hot tea.

The modern plastic age was born in 1909, when Leo Baekeland announced to the American Chemical Society his invention of Bakelite, "the material of a thousand uses." Bakelite was hard, impervious to heat, and could be dyed in bright colors; it was also an ideal insulator. By the 1920s, Bakelite was used for everything from knife handles and door knobs to telephones and radios.

BATH TIME An advertising card promotes the use of a Sadia electric water heater in a bathroom of the 1930s.

The success of Bakelite stimulated research that produced a universe of new materials for the home. Paints became tougher, easier to apply and more colorful with the development of petroleum-based alkyd paint resins and—from 1927—of aniline dyes. Hard, resistant polyurethane paints were pioneered by the German chemist Otto Bayer in 1939, and the wartime German development of polyvinyl acetate (PVA) provided the medium for the first emulsion paints.

The spread of the plastics revolution was gradual, as builders and decorators learned and experimented, but the flow of new materials was unabated. Polypropylene, a

TIME FOR A HOT TUB

The whirlpool bath that became a cult appliance in California in the 1960s—and later worldwide—was invented by an Italian immigrant family who made farm pumps. Roy Jacuzzi built his first "hydromassage bath installation" to try to ease a cousin's arthritis. In June 1968, he staged a demonstration at a fair in Orange County, near Los Angeles. By the 1980s, "Jacuzzis" with underwater lighting and room for six were on the market.

strong plastic whose uses ranged from domestic appliance casings to carpeting, was perfected in 1954 in Italy, which succeeded the United States as a design leader. Washable wallpaper, however, was an American innovation, first produced by Du Pont in 1968; it was made from polythene.

Securing a constant, ready supply of domestic hot water took more than 60 years of trial and error. Nineteenth-century gas "geysers"—a term coined by an early inven-

1900 John Wright's gas fire

1909 Bakelite invented

1912 The first effective electric fire

1927 Thermostats used in central heating systems

1939 Polyurethane paint pioneered

AUTOMATED GARDENING

The smartly striped lawns of the 20th century would not have been possible without the motorization of the lawn mower. Although horse-drawn mechanical mowers had been mass-produced since the first half of the 19th century, the development of the internal combustion engine eased the gardener's workload.

A mower with a gas motor was produced by the British Ransome company in 1902. The same company patented the first electric-powered mower in 1926, although it was not until 1969 that Black and Decker produced the first successful lightweight electric model. Another major breakthrough was the mobile "hovercraft" mower that skimmed the grass on an air-cushion, developed by Flymo in 1963. Night mowing without disturbing the neighbors was possible from 1990 with the advent of the silent Mulchinator, a battery-powered machine that pulverized the harvested grass into mulch.

MOWING MACHINE The Ransome lawn mower of the early 1900s was cumbersome; it would be 60 years before more manageable models were made.

tor—filled the air with noxious fumes and contaminated the water.

In 1912, however, Charles Belling also invented an electric geyser that boiled a gallon and a half of water in a minute. One of the problems with this device was that the temperature could not be controlled.

Hot water in the home

A Scotsman, Andrew Ure, had proposed a solution in 1830, but it was not applied to electrical equipment until the 1920s. This was the thermostat, a bonded strip of two metals with different expansion rates, which bent to switch the current off and on according to the temperature. Thus equipped, the immersion heater—and automatic central heating systems from 1927—became a practical reality in developed countries.

BEDTIME COMFORT The influence of the hot-water bottle is evident in the molded Bakelite casing of this electric bed warmer (right) of 1949.

A gas thermostat, consisting of a valve-controlling rod of invar (a heat-resistant nickel-steel alloy) and brass, was patented in 1923, but it was not until 1931 that Bernard Friedman and the Junkers company in Germany put everything together in the Progas, the first efficient gas water heater, known to much of the English-speaking world as the Ascot.

About the same time, dual electric immersion heaters, supplying both bath and sinks, were produced by several companies. Their basic design proved as enduring as that of the Ascot.

The intelligent home

The first instantly adjusting central heating system using ultrasonics was produced by Matsushita in Japan in 1972, and for the next quarter of a century the challenge of remote control and automation was increasingly met by microelectronics and computers. Honeywell in the United States developed a "Total Home System," which offered a keypad selection of 15 customized modes. Security, temperature, and lighting could all be checked and reprogrammed over the phone. Pacific Gas & Light in Sacramento built a prototype "smart" house that cut power consumption in half through the use of temperature-responsive glass, automated louvered shading, and a "home automation system" programmed to exploit cheap, off-peak rates.

In Tokyo, the Tron "Intelligent Home" was an open-ended project of the 1990s backed by Mitsubishi. The prototype incorporated 1,000 microcomputers and hundreds of sensors and actuators, to provide whatever the owner desired. Its automated kitchen could tackle more than 300 recipes, and the health-conscious bathroom checked pulse and blood pressure at the touch of a finger.

ADJUSTABLE HEATING In a thermostat, mercury in a tube is attached to a bonded strip of two metals with different rates of expansion under heat. As the strip bends, the mercury slides onto electric contacts.

Cleaning up was also automated: a video selector and elevator retrieved and returned items to an underground store. The long-term goal was to create a home that would sense when it was time to clean itself.

THERMOSTAT ON

Mercury

THERMOSTAT OFF

Bi-metallic strip

THE DREAM KITCHEN

AMERICAN MASS-MARKETING MAKES THE MODERN KITCHEN AN OBJECT OF UNIVERSAL DESIRE

In the late 19th century, many Americans and Europeans had recognized the potential of electricity in freeing food preparation from the smoke, dirt and drudgery of the coal-fired range or the cumbersome limitations of gas. The Bernina, a hotel in the Swiss Alps, had powered its oven off a waterfall from 1889 and Rookes Evelyn Bell Crompton, a retired English colonel, had wired an iron plate creating a crude heating element in the early 1890s. An "electric rapid cooking apparatus" was manufactured in Britain and shown at a Chicago exhibition, but this ancestor of the electric kettle was unreliable as well as painfully slow: it took 12 minutes to boil a pint of water.

By the early 1900s, the kettle and similar "hot plate" appliances were on the market.

ELECTRIC COOKER The massive Carron range of 1912 was one of the first electric cookers to be installed in an English home.

DOING THE DISHES The German hand-cranked dishwasher of 1929 called for plenty of patience. Heat-resistant Pyrex glassware (inset) was developed in the U.S. in 1915.

In the United States, General Electric grouped all these devices together in 1906 in its first electric range, a piece of equipment with 30 plugs and switches embedded in a wooden table, powering an oven, boiler, pots, pans, and even a waffle iron.

The electric kitchen

By 1910, range designs had developed their now familiar appearance, with heat-resistant, glass-panelled oven doors. Wall-mounted control panels, featuring a fearsome array of switches and fuses, provided basic temperature options of low-medium-high. By this time, a primitive electric toaster, with bare wires wrapped around strips of mica, was also on sale, and an electric frying pan soon followed. Electric mixers began modestly when a small motor hitched to an egg beater

RECYCLING TRASH

Kitchen waste makes up the bulk of domestic trash. An electric waste disposal that fit into the sink outlet had been invented by General Electric in the United States in 1929 but, like the flush toilet, it simply dispatched the problem elsewhere. As the use of waste disposals grew, they were banned in Japan, where a solution was devised in the environment-conscious 1990s. The Home Garbage Drier consisted of a bin with a hot-air unit and fan. This reduced organic waste to a compact, fresh-smelling residue that made an ideal garden fertilizer.

1910 First domestic
electric food mixer

1926 Pop-up
toasters in USA

1931 Mass production
of "Electrolux"
refrigerators

1939 Electric
carving knife

1947 The
Kenwood Chef food
processor designed

was offered by George Schmidt and Fred Osius of Wisconsin to ice cream parlors, then all the rage. The product was improved from 1910 by engineer Chester Beach, who designed, for domestic use, a universal electric motor that was compatible with both alternating and direct current and drove a food mixer on a stand.

With its lack of domestic servants, America raced ahead of Europe in pursuit of kitchen sophistication. In Britain, for example, the forces driving innovation were slightly different. The first electric mixer was marketed by a scientific equipment supplier for laboratory use, and the country's first practical electric cooker was developed for Royal Navy submarines—before it reached the domestic market after the First World War as the Belling Modernette.

Pop-up toasters were appearing from 1926, thanks to the inventive mind of American Charles Strite, and spinning-blade mixers and blenders with built-in motors were in action by the mid-1930s. Precise temperature control of ovens and other appliances was achieved through the gradual introduction of various types of thermostat. And by 1939, the up-to-the-minute American host could even carve the roast with an electric knife.

FIRST FRIDGE Stoutly boxed in wood, the first Frigidaire was made in the United States in 1921 by a subsidiary of General Motors.

From the mid-19th century, Americans had tried to ease the chore of dishwashing by mechanization, and by 1900 Josephine Cochran, a housewife from the American Midwest, had commercialized a hand-cranked machine that sprayed water over dishes in a covered cauldron set on a tripod stand; there was also a large steam-powered version. Hardware merchants Willard and Forrest Walker offered the choice of gas-powered or electric motor drives in 1912—at six times the price of the manual model.

Leakage was high, reliability low, and development stalled until General Electric bought out the Walkers' machine, and an effective dishwasher detergent called Calgon

was discovered in 1932. The first fully enclosed dishwasher appeared in 1936 and automatic machines with rinse cycles were on the American market by 1940. They were not introduced in Europe until 1960.

Keeping cold

The refrigerator also evolved gradually. The icebox was the first practical means of coping with the hot American summers; it was serviced by door-to-door icemen who delivered slabs from ice-making plants. Domestic refrigeration was held back, however, by the hazardous nature of the chemicals used—ammonia or sulphuric acid, which was subjected to a repeated cycle of compression and condensation, followed by evaporation during which it cooled the refrigerator. Only a few thousand home units were being produced in the early 1920s.

Swedish engineers Balzar von Platen and Carl Munters were pivotal in the development of the first practical, quiet-running refrigerator with an electric motor to drive the compressor. They sold their Electrolux patents to the U.S., where in 1930 Thomas Midgley and Albert Henne concocted the first fluorocarbon—known scientifically as dichlorodifluoromethane but renamed Freon 12—for use as a non-toxic refrigerant in air conditioners and refrigerators.

Transforming the kitchen

Porcelain enamelling, in which a thin layer of glass is fused onto metal to prevent corrosion and scratching, appeared in 1926, and pure white—the epitome of cleanliness—dominated the design of kitchen appliances

FOOD MIXERS An American mixer from 1918 (left) consists simply of an electric motor lashed to two rotary beaters. By the 1960s, food mixers had more features; a German housewife demonstrates pasta-making (above).

POP-UP PRIDE This toaster of 1951 was promoted in the U.S. as "part of the family . . . a cherished possession for which no substitute is ever completely satisfying."

by the 1930s. Manufacturers hired French-born Raymond Loewy and other top designers to streamline their products, among which the refrigerator became the supreme status-symbol: the "sleek, sanitary monolith" that began to reign over American domestic life. Models were offered in series of ascending prices and changed annually, with heavy advertising and optional extras, such as lettuce crispers, meat savers, and automatic reset defrosters.

Fifty years in the kitchen

The First World War forced a temporary halt to innovation. But afterwards, the American dream kitchen became an object of universal desire around the world, and one that was increasingly attainable due to the economies of mass production. Fitted cupboards and plastic-laminated surfaces became the norm, as kitchen design tended toward ever more functional, hygienic and modish layouts.

The gap between North America and the rest of the developed world dwindled. The multiple-use food processor, with its sturdy motor, stemmed from a British design of the late 1940s—Kenneth Wood's Kenwood Chef. Domestic deepfreezes appeared on both sides of the Atlantic around 1955, as did the microwave oven (first patented in 1945), which was cumbersome, costly and

STATE OF THE ART A kitchen of the 1980s features the latest in stainless steel fittings: cupboards, oven and hood.

unpredictable. An electric vegetable shredder was the talk of 1957, and the nonstick frying pan—developed by Frenchman Marc Grégoire from 1954—the hit of 1960.

The accidental invention, when a test oven overheated, of a "pyro-ceramic" resulted in a new class of ovenproof cooking ware and—in 1966—an electric cooker with a smooth ceramic heating surface in place of metal hobs.

The kitchen in the computer age

The kitchen entered the computer age, with microchips automating such processes as defrosting and cooking cycles. Energy efficiency became a selling factor, too: in 1982, one U.S. refrigerator manufacturer boasted of having cut the electricity consumption of its models by almost 50 percent.

By the 1990s, a new approach to cooking was in prospect with the development of magnetic induction. A magnetic field between the slim cooking "table" and the metal pan above heated the pan and its contents, but not the table surface; through "smart" computer technology, a prototype table could distinguish between utensils and not heat any knives or forks resting on it.

THE 60-SECOND HAMBURGER

Raytheon was engaged in making radar equipment in 1945 when its top researcher, Percy Spencer, paused in front of a magnetron, radar's power drive, and found that a chocolate bar in his pocket had begun to melt. Spencer sent for a bag of popcorn and, sure enough, the kernels began to pop under bombardment from the magnetron's microwaves. Having established that they had developed a device which, by agitating the water molecules in food, cooked at astonishing speed (a hamburger in 60 seconds), Raytheon patented it as a "high frequency dielectric heating apparatus." Under advice from Raytheon's marketing department, the device was launched as the Radarange, which by popular consensus became known as the microwave oven. Early models weighed 750 lbs., cost $3,000, and dished up unappetizingly pallid meats and flaccid chips. Their tendency to leak radiation also caused alarm.

The spirit of innovation never rests, however. A pan that can fry an omelette in 20 seconds is in production; its secret lies in a heat-conductive coating, extracted from a manganese-aluminum alloy. And, at century's end, a refrigerator that cools by sound waves is under development.

CAPTURING TIME

TIMING KEEPS PACE WITH THE CENTURY'S ACCELERATED TEMPO

As time became an increasingly precious commodity throughout the century, it was calculated with ever-growing precision. Men, in particular, may at first have resisted conversion from the pocket watch to the wristwatch, but the rigors of the trenches during the First World War soon led to its general adoption.

The self-winding watch, with a mainspring that was rewound by the wearer's arm movements, was invented by London watch-

WATERPROOF WATCH

The reliability of the world's first waterproof watch was demonstrated spectacularly in 1927 by a young London office worker named Mercedes Gleitz, who swam the English Channel with one strapped to her wrist.

maker John Harwood in 1924, and manufacture began in Switzerland four years later. By then, Rolex had launched the first waterproof model, calling it the Oyster. In the late 1930s, the first battery-powered watch was produced by Lip, a French company; it ran on a two-cell battery, was lighter than a mechanical watch, and—as owners proudly demonstrated—it did not tick.

Similar developments were happening to clocks. Battery-powered clocks were introduced in 1906, and clocks running off household electricity in 1918. In the 1920s, however, work began on a new approach that would eventually transform the world of clock and watchmaking. The idea was to mark time by the natural vibrations of a quartz crystal subjected to an electric current. The technology was in place by 1929, when Warren Alvin Marrison built the first quartz clock. Accuracy within a thousandth of a second was claimed, though early models often ran wild or stopped suddenly.

Time for a new age

Down-sizing the quartz vibrations to create a watch was not achieved until 1969, when Seiko of Japan launched the first quartz watch. The digital watch followed two years later. Named the Pulsar and designed in Dallas, Texas, by George Theiss and Willy Crabtree, it wedded a quartz movement with new microelectronic technology and a light-emitting diode (LED) display. This consisted of lines of a chemical that glowed to form the appropriate numbers when an electric current was passed through it.

Demand for these high-tech wonders was immediate, and by 1975, when digitals with liquid-crystal displays (LCD) began to appear, prices had plummeted. Easier on the battery, the molecules of the LCD (first produced in Switzerland in 1971) rearranged themselves in response to an electric current. Besides hours, minutes and seconds, displays typically included the day of the week, a stopwatch, an alarm clock, a calendar and even—by 1978—a calculator.

WATER WATCHES The Rolex Oyster watch pioneered waterproofing in the late 1920s. The Japanese electronic stopwatch for swimmers (right) is typical of advances made by the 1970s.

ACCURATE TIMEKEEPING

TIME BEGINS HERE A youngster checks his watch against a 24-hour clock outside the Royal Observatory, Greenwich.

Time varied from place to place until the coming of the railways, causing confusion when timetables were drawn up. An international time standard was therefore set in 1884, keyed to the meridian, or line of longitude, that passes through Greenwich, on the Thames in London—hence Greenwich Mean Time (GMT). It is a "mean time" because it is based on the solar day, which varies with the Earth's elliptical orbit, and so has to be averaged.

GMT was redesignated Universal Time in 1935 and a quest for greater precision began. The best timekeeper then available was a remarkable electromagnet clock, built in 1921 by W.H. Shortt, a British railway engineer. Shortt's clock was accurate to one second in ten years and was able to identify slight irregularities in the Earth's orbit. Advances in physics in the wake of the Second World War led to proposals for an atomic clock, scaled to the radiation vibration of certain atoms. By June 1955, a caesium atomic clock, with an accuracy equivalent to one second in 300 years was working reliably at the British National Physical Laboratory. Using it, an exact definition of the second was arrived at: 9,192 531,770 caesium vibrations.

In 1969, using a clock that counted the vibrations of the ammonia atom, the U.S. Naval Laboratory in Washington narrowed the accuracy to one second in 1.7 million years. Microelectronics worked their usual miracle, and by 1978 atomic clocks the size of radios were on the market.

1924 Self-winding watch invented
1929 First quartz clock

1955 First atomic clock

1969 First quartz watch
1971 First digital watch

THE CLEANING REVOLUTION

**DUST-SUCKERS, ELECTRIC WASHERS AND
DETERGENTS ELIMINATE ELBOW GREASE**

When the century dawned, soap and elbow grease, mops, brushes and brooms were the main weapons in the war against dirt. Their limitations help to explain why domestic service was second only to farm labor as a source of employment in countries such as the United States.

In the first decade of the 20th century, however, there were developments on several fronts. In 1901, civil engineer Hubert Cecil Booth was unimpressed by a demonstration of a machine that raised a cloud of dust, which was then captured in a container. Booth had a better idea: why not set the machine to suck instead of blow? He experimented by placing a handkerchief over his mouth and then sucking from the surface of a dusty chair; the handkerchief was blackened with grime. The same year, he patented the vacuum cleaner, which used an electric pump to suck air into a hose, and set up in business as the Vacuum Cleaner Company. His machine was so large that it had to be hauled about in a horse-drawn cart; 800 feet of hose snaked from the cart to the inner recesses of noble homes, where some hostesses took to marking the occasion with a tea party.

In 1906, Booth scaled down his apparatus to create an 88-pound "Trolley Vac," but he was overtaken by developments in the United States. In 1907, a janitor named Murray Spengler assembled an old box which he sealed with tape, a pillowcase, an electric fan, a broom handle, a stove pipe, and a roller that he built into a brush by attaching goat bristles. Spengler sold the rights to his lightweight contraption to relatives who ran a firm called Hoover, which launched its epoch-making Model "O" in

AUTO WASH In this 1920 machine, electricity was used to drive a washtub and wringer. The bottom-mounted motor was dangerously exposed to slopping suds.

1908. Later, a vacuum cleaner with a horizontal canister and a nozzled hose was designed in Sweden in 1913 by Alex Wenner-Gren to provide dexterity in tackling stairs, upholstery, and car interiors.

Washing and ironing

Also in the early years of the century, Alva Fisher of Chicago was designing a motorized tub that turned, stirring the washing. Her rotary-tub electric-powered washing machine was on the market by 1906, and others soon followed. In 1911, the Maytag company launched the first washer with an electrically driven wringer. And in 1924, a primitive washer-dryer was produced by the Savage Arms Corporation of Utica, New York; the tub had to be lifted and placed on a separate faster-spinning drive shaft to extract the water by centrifugal force. In 1937 Rex Bassett, a mechanic, made the first attempt at an automatic washing machine, called a Bendix after the man who provided the factory space. It was received with excitement,

DUST BUSTERS Early vacuum cleaners for carpets, such as the French example (above) from 1911, were extremely cumbersome and could barely fit in the home. By the 1930s, however, GE was using dancing stars like Ann Miller (shown with GE "cleaner specialist" Herman Rose) to show how easy vacuuming was.

1901 First vacuum cleaner

1906 Electric-powered washing machine
1908 Hoover's Model "O"

1917 First artificial soap, or detergent
1926 Electric steam iron

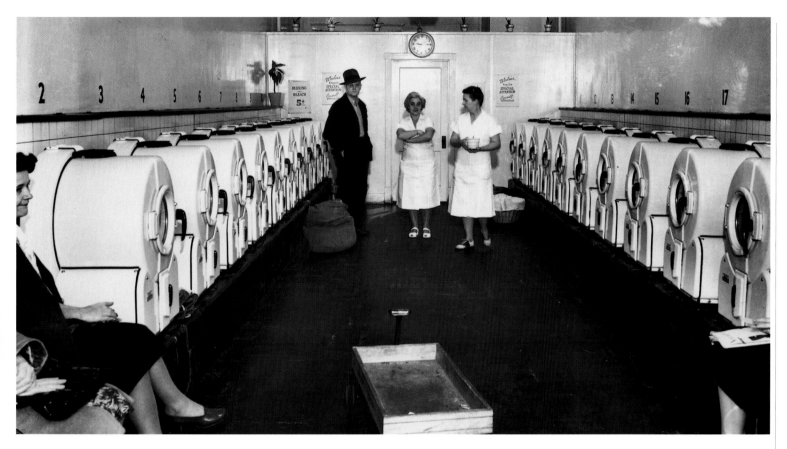

but was so unstable at high speed that it had to be bolted down. The Westinghouse company remedied this problem with the use of spring-mounted shock absorbers, but true automatics with electric water heaters and pumps were not developed until the late 1940s. Tumble driers blowing hot air through a spinning drum appeared in the 1950s, and the twin-tub housing a washer and a spin-dryer in one cabinet in 1957.

Irons had been among the first appliances to be electrified, and in 1926 the electric steam iron was introduced in the U.S. by the Eldec Company. A thermostat-controlled iron with temperature settings for different fabrics appeared 12 years later and proved more suitable for domestic use.

The whiter wash

Soaps were often home-made from animal fat and ash until well into the 20th century. During the First World War, however, there was a shortage of natural fats, and German scientists were driven to produce the first artificial soap, or detergent. Available from 1917, it was called Nekal and required a lot of rubbing for mediocre results.

In response to a sharp decline in domestic servants, Unilever in Britain developed the world's first effective detergent in 1921. Marketed as Lux, it was an improvement on ordinary soap because it did not leave an insoluble scum and did not yellow during ironing. "Whiter than white" washing was now increasingly promised by detergent manufacturers—through the addition of fluorescent brightening agents. Omo was launched in 1952, and Wisk, the first liquid laundry detergent, appeared in 1957.

Detergents next went "biological" with the introduction of enzymes—chemicals that break down difficult protein stains, such as egg. Procter & Gamble patented a process in April 1967 and launched enzyme-enriched Ariel within a year.

By the end of the century, there was even a prospect of washing systems without detergents. A cold-water cleaner that used ozone to break down dirt molecules was patented by a Florida company, Tri-O-Clean;

IRONING OUT PROBLEMS Inventors were constantly improving the electric iron. This scorch-proof design of the 1950s has a weighted "cold head" on which it rests whenever the hand is removed.

READY TO ROLL The world's first launderette opened in Texas in 1934, but even in 1946 an "automatic laundry" in Chicago with 20 new machines was worthy of press coverage.

research also focused on ultrasonics—cleaning by high-frequency sound waves. In Japan, there were even machines that determined how much cleaning a load of clothes required. Washing was by bubble action instead of agitation: the dirtier the wash, the busier the bubbles.

1957 Twin-tub washer and dryer
1957 First liquid laundry detergent

1967 Launch of enzyme-enriched Ariel

NEW FABRICS, NEW FASHIONS

EXOTIC FIBERS CONJURED FROM CHEMICAL LABORATORIES CHANGE THE FACE OF FASHION

Whalebone corsets and Celluloid collars cramped self-expression in 1900. Dark shades of dress were the rule, because they hid the dirt; and fast, synthetic colors were only just being developed.

Synthetic fibers

The foul smell and occasional explosions that rocked Station Road in western London in the 1890s gave notice of enormous changes at hand. Intrepid workers at a small pilot plant were learning by trial and error how to spin the first artificial fiber, using a process patented by chemist Charles Cross and two colleagues. This was rayon, derived like Celluloid from chemically treated plant pulp (however, they called it "artificial silk"—"rayon" was coined in the United States in 1924).

The development of synthetic fabrics enabled many people to buy silky clothes that would previously have been too expensive. Rayon stockings were developed in Germany in 1910; and by 1913, "artificial silk" stockings were all the rage. Cellulose acetate, a cousin of rayon developed in Switzerland shortly before the First World War, had first been used to make strengthening "dope" for the fabric wings of warplanes, but at the cessation of hostilities, it was transformed into silky Celanese: from 1921, any woman could have "silk" underwear.

Nylon, the first wholly synthetic fiber, was invented in 1935 by Du Pont researcher Wallace Carothers. It was strong, elastic, and did not absorb moisture. Nylon was tried

STOCKING SUCCESS First came rayon, and then the miracle of nylon. During the 1940s, nylon stockings became a luxury that more and more women could afford.

first as a toothbrush bristle, and then as a sheer yarn for stockings, tested on Du Pont staff in 1939. Word spread, and when "nylons" went on sale in New York on May 15, 1940, they were an immediate success.

Nylons became a valuable barter item of American soldiers during the Second World War and a post-war global phenomenon, along with drip-dry, non-iron nylon shirts. The war in Europe delayed the introduction of polyester, the second major polymer fiber, invented by Briton John Whinfield; more durable than rayon and more heat-resistant than nylon, it was launched as Dacron in the United States and Terylene in Britain.

New fibers, each with unique properties, now poured from the laboratories. In the United States, Dow Chemical contributed shimmering, aluminum-based Lurex in 1946; Du Pont produced Orlon, a soft acrylic alternative to knitting wool that was being made into garments by 1951, and clinging Lycra from polyurethane in 1952. Acrilan, an acrylic cloth fiber, appeared in 1952 and tri-acetate fibers such as Arnel were beginning to challenge the luxury-feel of the best natural materials by the mid-1950s. A process to pleat woollens permanently was developed in Australia, and permanent-press polyesters followed in 1964. And in 1969, out of the same Teflon technology that produced the non-stick frying pan, came Bob Gore's Gore-Tex, a "breathing" fabric that provided unique weather insulation.

Supporting technologies kept pace. Research by ICI chemists in Britain led to

MAN-MADE FIBERS Scientists this century have created synthetic polymers, or giant molecules, by stringing smaller molecules together in chains. Some of these (right) are based on cellulose, the main constituent of plant cell walls, and others on oil.

WOMEN'S LIBERATION

The extraordinary devices invented by men to improve—in their eyes at least—the charms of women have included a "dimple-maker," a "nose-shaper," and a "breast developer." There are, for example, mosaics from an ancient Roman villa in Sicily which show female gymnasts dressed in what look very much like bikinis. In our own century, one of the earliest examples of innovative female undergarments designed by men is the "Bust Supporter" patented in 1907 by Johannes Bree of Charlottenburg, Germany. A strangling harness of straps, girdles and back-plates, it was an improvement on the corsets of the time, he maintained, "in that it favorably assists in the working of the intestines."

However, by now women were assuming command of themselves. Kate Morgan in London had patented a modified corset with a soft top in 1903, and in 1909 the American edition of *Vogue* magazine carried an advertisement for a separate bust-supporter that looked like a modern bra. Such developments did not deter Mary "Polly" Jacob, a 19-year-old New York socialite, who in 1913, with the help of her maid, Marie, stitched together two handkerchiefs and pink ribbon, and filed a patent for what she called a "backless brassiere." The patent was granted in 1914.

BRA AND BEYOND This advertisement for a German "Büstenformer" dates from 1950.

Polly, who claimed descent from Robert Fulton, inventor of the steamboat, hired two immigrant girls to sew samples, but when the leading stores turned her away she sold the rights to the Warner Brothers Corset Company for $1,500. Warner turned its investment into an estimated $15 million and Polly went on to lead a full, flamboyant life as the much-publicized inventor of the bra. She changed her name to Caresse Crosby, married twice, and once rode naked down the Champs Elysées on an elephant to publicize an arts ball.

The word "brassiere" is derived from Old French for "upper arm." A Frenchman named de Brassière tried to claim rights to the name in 1929, but the courts rejected his claim. The Caresse bra was superseded in the 1920s by the cup-support, designed by Russian-born Ida Rosenthal, a New Jersey dressmaker. Bra-sizing came a decade later.

1900   1950

1905 Artificial silk, or rayon, produced commercially   1914 Backless brassiere patented   1921 Synthetically silky Celanese underwear on sale   1935 Nylon invented   1941 A polyester, called Terylene, is produced   1946 The first bikini

the production in 1956 of a wider, brighter array of color-fast dyes for artificial fibers and cottons. From Germany came automated, shuttleless looms which, by 1959, were able to weave up to four colors simultaneously. From the mid-1960s, the spinning process was streamlined with the introduction of Czech-designed rotor machines that cleaned, carded, and spun natural and synthetic fibers five times faster than before. The 1970s witnessed the launch of computerized knitting machines, which created dazzling patterns. And computer-aided design and production in the 1980s facilitated the emergence of high-quality designer labels.

New trends

Fashion was also playing fast and loose with the old order of things. On July 5, 1946, French swimsuit designer Louis Réard unveiled the two-piece bikini. Considered so improper that the term was not included in

French dictionaries until 1956, the bikini was not accepted in the United States until the 1960s. By this time, minimalism had reached its logical conclusion in the miniskirt, created by London designer Mary Quant in 1965.

By the 1990s, science was improving upon nature by "engineering" new natural textile fibers. Using cross-pollination and wild plant strains, an American entomologist named Sally Fox developed cottons for jeans manufacturers that were not only pest-resistant, but came in natural shades of beige, brown, and green. In 1992, Agracetus, a technology company based in Wisconsin, patented a method of inserting alien DNA into cotton plants with a view to producing a natural fiber that was stronger and wrinkle-proof.

In Lyon, the French Textile Institute pioneered a molecular grafting technique to create a new breed of bio-textiles with remarkable properties. These included a fluorine-charged cotton resistant to all stains and dyes, and a copper-charged "antiseptic" cotton resistant to bacteria—all of which proving that the era of textile innovation was far from over.

MAGIC REVEALED An electron microscope view of Velcro: the two surfaces, one carpeted with hooks and the other with loops, form a strong bond when brought together.

SWIMSUIT EXPOSURE Daring baring of the midriff in 1940 predated the bikini bombshell by six years.

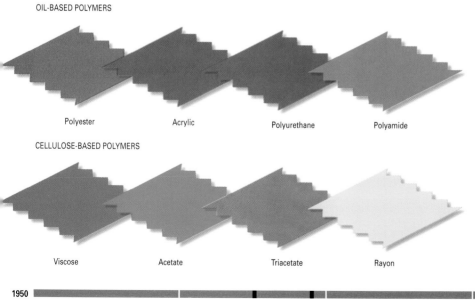

OIL-BASED POLYMERS

Polyester   Acrylic   Polyurethane   Polyamide

CELLULOSE-BASED POLYMERS

Viscose   Acetate   Triacetate   Rayon

1965 Mary Quant creates the miniskirt

1969 Gore-Tex

1990s Genetic engineering of natural textile fibers

LOOKING GOOD

ARTIFICIAL ENHANCEMENTS ENABLE PEOPLE TO PUT ON A BRAVE NEW FACE AND BODY

In 1900, men still scraped their faces with "cutthroat" razors, and women toiled with hot tongs to frame theirs in curls. However, an American travelling salesman and a cobbler's son from the Bavarian Alps were working on better ideas.

The salesman, King Camp Gillette, had conceived the disposable-blade safety razor in 1895, but it took him six years to realize his vision with the assistance of engineer William Nickerson. They filed a patent in 1901 and began manufacture in Boston in 1903; in their first year, they sold only 51

A CLOSE SHAVE There was no stopping the safety razor after troops returning from the First World War spread word of its virtues.

razors and 168 blades.

The cobbler's son, Karl Nessler, was by then a fashionable hairdresser obsessed with the creation of a "scientific everlasting wave" machine. He moved from Paris to London, changed his name to Nestle, and ploughed his profits into the machine project. On October 8, 1906, he rented a hall to demonstrate the prototype—an intimidating arrangement of hot gas pipes and asbestos tubes suspended over the head like a giant spider.

Electricity replaced the gas pipes in 1909, and by the outbreak of the First World War members of the British royal family were patronizing Nestle. The process was patented, but this provided little protection in the U.S., where the term "permanent wave" was coined. Nestle arrived in New York in 1915 to find more than 600 imitators already established.

FACE SAVERS Cosmetics were big business by the 1920s. The harlequin figure used to promote a Parisian face powder of the period typifies a saucy new spirit.

Gillette was more fortunate. When America entered the war, the U.S. Army ordered more than 4 million safety razors for its troops, and with such an endorsement, the shaving revolution was soon complete.

American army colonel Jacob Schick marketed an electric razor in 1931, but general acceptance was slow; it was expensive and many men still preferred the feel of wet shaving. In 1937, Philips in Holland developed a circle-action cutter, launched as the Philishave. The battery-operated "cordless" razor was introduced by Remington in 1960, but most subsequent effort was directed at traditional "wet" shaving. Twin-bladed safety razors were developed by Gillette in 1971 and swivel-heads in 1975.

Face savers

The First World War had put millions of women to work and given them far greater independence. Combined with the influence of Hollywood movies, it broke the traditional taboo against make-up and helped to create the cosmetics industry. After a tentative start—with lotions and creams imbued with flattering color—Hamburg chemist Paul Beiersdorf invented a snow-white skin cream, Nivea, in 1911. As the century draws to a close, "youth creams" to wipe away the ravages of aging are in prospect with the development of Tretinoin, a drug derived from vitamin A. First tried as a prescriptive acne treatment, it was approved for controlled use in certain skin creams in 1995,

FOODS TO MAKE US LOOK GOOD AND FEEL EVEN BETTER

The 20th century has been characterized by an increasing preoccupation with personal health, and with ways of preventing disease and promoting a healthy appearance. Many of these have revolved around the foods that we eat.

Decaffeinated coffee, for example, was invented by Dr. Ludwig Roselius in 1903; he called it "Sanka," a contraction of the French "sans caffeine." Dietetics soon emerged as a science, with a fruit-intensive diet plan of 1910 leading to the invention in Switzerland of muesli. Non-dairy coffee creamer appeared in 1961.

Calorie-free chemical substitutes for sugar, such as saccharin (from the 19th century) and cyclamate (from 1950), fell from grace in the 1970s when they were suspected of causing cancer if consumed in exceedingly large quantities. But science rose to the crisis. A chance lick of the fingers in a Searle laboratory led to the discovery of aspartame, first marketed in the United States as Nutrasweet.

The dieter's dream of fat-free food was answered by Olestra, a "fake fat" compound developed by Procter & Gamble. In January 1996, the U.S. health authorities gave approval for its use in snack foods such as potato chips.

after studies showed that it smoothed wrinkles and lightened age-spots.

Although lipsticks had been used in the earliest civilizations, lipstick in easy-to-use push-up tubes was developed by 1915, the year in which cosmetics queens Helena Rubenstein and Elizabeth Arden began their 50 year rivalry. Rubenstein's innovations included the first waterproof mascara and medicated face creams, while Arden pioneered non-greasy skin creams and, also, lipstick shades to match skin tone and clothing. In 1916 Northam Warren, a preacher's son from Kansas, produced the first liquid nail polish, Cutex, and the first with a tint in 1917.

Smiles improved, too, after the Second World War with the gradual introduction of fluorides in water supplies, sometimes over the objections of people who believed fluoridation was a Communist plot to poison Americans. Dental researcher H. Trendley Dean had been the first to suggest that fluoride in the water could reduce cavities. Fluoride toothpastes followed in the 1950s; the first was Procter & Gamble's Crest.

1901 Patent filed for disposable razor blade

1906 An "everlasting wave" machine for hair styling

1911 Nivea face cream invented

1931 Electric razor marketed

1945 Fluoride added to water supply in Grand Rapids, Michigan

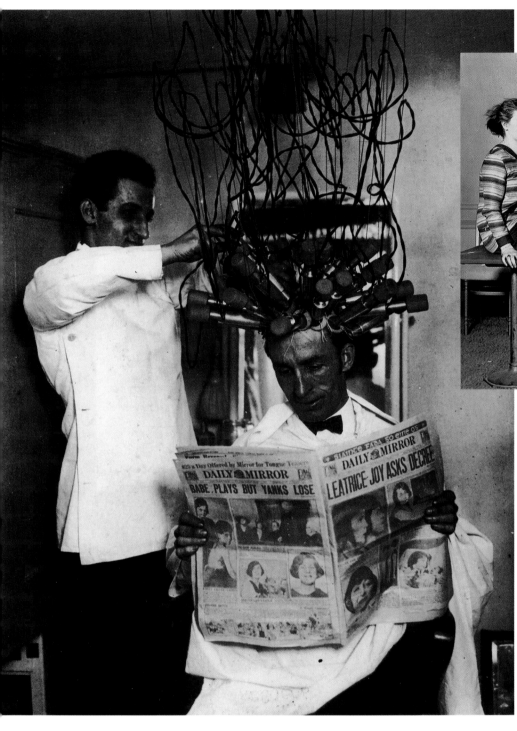

HAIR RAISERS An intrepid man (left) subjects himself to a permanent wave machine in New York in 1925. The equally intimidating hairdryer (above) also dates from the 1920s.

Rhinoplastic surgery—or nose reshaping —had first been attempted in the United States and Germany in the 1890s, and plastic surgery was already big business by the mid-1920s when Dr. Suzanne Noël was performing face-lift operations in the patient's home under local anesthetic.

A new body

Face-lifting techniques improved rapidly in response to American demand, with Rio de Janeiro in Brazil a mecca for affluent tourists in search of a younger look.

Plastic surgeons were implanting silicone from around 1960, using a silicone gel formulated in 1943 by a U.S.-based Scottish engineer, Gilbert Wright. Seeking a non-flammable substitute for rubber, Wright put a dash of boric acid into silicone oil in a test tube, and to his amazement, out popped a gooey blob that bounced right back when he dropped it on the laboratory floor. It snapped like an elastic band when tugged sharply, then slowly oozed back into shape when left alone.

At first, the bouncing blob seemed to be good for little but play—it was sold as Silly Putty—and for arthritis sufferers who squeezed it to improve their grip. Then, in 1960, it found a home in enlarging or reshaping breasts. Millions of women had received breast implants by 1992, when health concerns and a spate of lawsuits put the procedure under a cloud.

Liposuction was perfected by Dr. Yves-Gérard Illouz of France in 1977. The procedure called for a small incision in the thighs, hips or stomach, through which excess fat is suctioned out.

A new head of hair

From the early years of the century, France led the way in the chemistry of hair color. In 1909, Eugène Schueller, who later founded the company L'Oréal, successfully pioneered a chemical hair dye. Imédia, an organic dye invented in 1927, led to the development of a wide range of natural shades, and the first range of hair coloring for home application was introduced two years later.

The hair transplant made its debut in the 1960s, using a follicle-transfer technique developed in the United States by Dr. Norman Orentreich; and in 1985, a way to implant artificial hair was devised in Japan.

1950

1960 Plastic surgeons use silicone implants

1971 Twin-bladed safety razors developed

1977 Liposuction techniques perfected

1986 Lubricated razor blades launched

2000

THE RETAIL REVOLUTION

THE RISE OF THE SELF-SERVICE SUPERMARKET AND THE COMING OF THE CASHLESS SOCIETY

By 1900, the cash register (adapted from a machine that registered the turns of a ship's propeller) was already ringing merrily, and "consumer" was the new word that excited entrepreneurs. Chain-store pioneer F. W. Woolworth had 59 standardized gold-and-red outlets in the United States, and in Britain Jesse Boot had more than twice that number of shops plying pills and medicines.

Self-service supermarkets

By the First World War, Europe was peppered with heavily-staffed retail chains; England itself had 16 specialist retail businesses with more than 200 branches. In the

DO-IT-YOURSELF SHOPPING Customers check out of a Piggly Wiggly "self-serving store" in Tennessee. The concept led to the invention of the supermarket.

United States, however, Clarence Saunders was inventing the "self-serving store." He patented the concept and opened one in Memphis, Tennessee, in 1916, calling it Piggly Wiggly. Entrance and exit was by turnstiles, with baskets stacked at the starting point. The library-like shelves were stacked with everything from Quaker Oats to clothespins, each of the items carrying a printed price tag. "Women wait on themselves at Piggly Wiggly—one every 48 seconds," boasted Saunders.

Others expanded on his ideas. In 1930, the first King Kullen opened in the New York borough of Queens and is often considered to be the first true supermarket. The brainchild of retail executive Michael Cullen, it introduced promotional lures, parking for cars and the now-familiar ranks of "gondolas," or freestanding shelves. By 1948, there were nearly 12,000 such supermarkets in the United States alone.

In the post-war years, the population shift to the suburbs and the popularity of automobile travel encouraged the construction of large retail stores outside of urban areas.

This trend presaged the creation of malls, vast shopping centers with enormous parking facilities; by the end of the 1980s, there were 35,000 shopping centers across the nation. In August of 1992, the largest of these opened in Bloomington, Minnesota. The Mall of America, as it was called, boasted 400 stores, 44 restaurants, 7 amusement parks and 13,000 parking spaces.

Drive-in facilities of many kinds lined American highways from the 1930s, includ-

PLASTIC POWER Purveying prestige and convenience, Diners' Club expanded in 1953 by assuring: "Your credit is good wherever you go when you carry a Diners' Club card!"

1930 An early supermarket, King Kullen, opens in New York

1936 First shopping cart

ing drive-in banks from 1946. Most of these belonged to chains of enterprises whose success depended upon providing a familiar, predictable service. "Drive-through" was the logical extension of drive-in service, allowing customers never to leave their cars. The con-

SHOPPING ON WHEELS

Sylvan Goldman, owner of the Oklahoma-based Humpty-Dumpty grocery chain, noticed that women stopped shopping when their baskets got heavy. In 1936, he had handyman Fred Young attach wheels to a folding chair and install a basket on top. When habit-bound shoppers ignored the world's first shopping cart, Goldman hired a decoy to push it around heavily laden. Demand was such that he soon started a company to manufacture his invention.

cept achieved its ultimate expression in the 1990s, with drive-through divorce available in Las Vegas.

The full-service gas pump held out for some time. A few self-service "gaseterias" were an American novelty of the late-1940s, but it took cutthroat competition and inflation in the wake of the 1970s energy crisis to induce the big oil companies to follow suit.

Paying by card

The huge motoring market inspired the first form of credit card—for gasoline only—issued in 1938 by American oil companies as a means of encouraging brand loyalty. The concept was broadened by New York businessman Frank McNamara, after he ran out of cash and could not pay the bill for a dinner with some clients. McNamara and a lawyer friend, Ralph Schneider, launched the Diners' Club card in February 1950. Bills were charged monthly; soon the general-purpose credit card—where the credit-card company pays the retailer and charges the customer for the purchase—was born.

The first credit card offered by a bank was issued by the Bank of America in 1958: it would evolve into the Visa card, within 20 years processing more than $200 billion in purchases. In recent years, Americans have become dependent on credit cards, with thousands stumbling into consumer debt; in 1998, some 60 million households owed more than $7,000 to credit card companies.

Electronic-transfer systems and cards that functioned as electronic purses gave a late-century foretaste of the cashless society.

First came "swipe cards," with metallic strips or holographs encoded with a cash value that burnt away with use. These were followed by "smart cards" capable of storing and processing information, invented by French electrical engineer Roland Moreno. At century's end, more than a dozen countries were planning to introduce smart cards—electronic purses, rechargeable at banks, ATMs or by phone or over the Internet.

Computerized shopping

From the mid-1960s, "time-sharing" offered retailers access to the services of powerful computers. Managers were just beginning to look into this when computing reached the check-out in the form of the bar code.

As introduced in the early 1970s, a beam of light placed against a computer-coded label of black and white lines identifies each item in turn, registering its price automatically. Bar codes soon caught on in stores and supermarkets, and laser-scanners improved their speed and reliability. In 1980, IBM in

TALKING CART A shopping cart greets and trails customers in Japan's first fully automated store.

and NEC perfected the process simultaneously, using split-beam holographic lasers that could read a bar code from any angle, whatever its condition. Transactions are then recorded by a computer that automatically reorders goods purchased.

The proliferation of credit cards added a new dimension to retailing. TV shopping was born in 1985, when the first sales channel began broadcasting in the United States—a phone call was all it took to order on the Home Shopping Network.

Telemarketing—selling by phone—was a multi-billion dollar business by the 1990s. The technique brought retailing to rural areas where TSRs (telephone sales representatives) sold everything from life insurance to steaks.

"Cybershopping"—shopping from a home computer—also became a hot new prospect, as commercial operations set up shop with electronic addresses. The American Express Co. reported that Americans spent $4-6 billion purchasing goods online in 1998, and the figure only promises to climb in the next century.

ISBN 0-276-42165-5

BEAMING IT UP The venerable cash register was vaulted into the computer age by the advent of the laser-activated bar code reader.

1950

1950 First credit card

1958 Bank of America issues first general purpose credit card

1980 Bar code perfected

1985 First TV sales channel

1990s Smart cards
1990s "Cybershopping" by home computer

2000

FASTER FOOD

MASS-PRODUCTION METHODS MAKE EATING A MATTER FOR INSTANT GRATIFICATION

Convenience food, like the convenience kitchen, was an American invention dating from the early 1900s. Although the portable, preground hamburger had evolved from a sandwich popular with German immigrants, it was not until the invention of an electric meat grinder in 1900 that commercial production became a possibility. The new food was an instant success at the 1904 St. Louis Exposition, in the heart of

MEAL-IN-A-MINUTE The hamburger was born on the American prairies. By the 1990s—through the efforts of McDonald's and Burger King—it had conquered the world.

America's beef-raising country. To wash down the hamburger, there was cola, first bottled by the Coca-Cola company in 1899.

Fast-food favorites

The ice-cream cone was invented in 1903 by an Italian living in New Jersey, and the hot dog soon joined the hamburger in 1908, its name stemming from the whimsy of a cartoonist who depicted a dachshund trapped in a bun. The potato chip appeared in Britain around 1914, possibly invented by an immigrant from France named Cartier. It was commercialized in 1920 by Frank Smith, who set up his frying pans in a garage behind a pub.

By now, the "fast-food" menu was almost complete; all that was lacking was a factory-fast means of retailing it.

INSTANT SOUP An advertisement for canned tomato soup: fastidious as well as innovative, Heinz brought hygiene to industrial food processing.

The cafe, or cafeteria, evolved in the American Midwest from those restaurants that served quick meals to passengers at railway stations. The term was first used in 1902 by John Kruger, who adopted it from Spanish and adapted the Scandinavian open sandwich as a staple on the menu. But the first recognizably modern fast-food outlets were the White Castle hamburger-and-coffee restaurants, devised by Billy Ingram and Walter Anderson, which began to dot the American landscape in the 1920s. White Castle stands came in kit-form, their porcelain-covered steel panels designed for quick assembly.

Fast food at home

The preparation of home meals also speeded up, with the invention of pre-prepared baby foods in 1929. Spam (SPiced hAM), the world's most successful canned meat preparation, was devised by the Hormel company in 1936, and it soon achieved fame—or notoriety—by sustaining Allied forces through the Second World War.

HAMBURGER HONORS

Ray Kroc, owner of the McDonald's franchise, founded Hamburger University in 1960, offering degrees in "hamburgerology." Kroc standardized the hamburger patty at 1.6 oz. in weight and 3.875 inches in diameter; and he sponsored the invention of equipment—from a scoop that delivered precisely the right amount of french fries to an air-conditioning system that completely changed the air every three minutes. By 1995, McDonald's was the world's first global food chain, with 12,000 outlets arching from San Bernardino to Beijing.

After some 70 years of failure, the first successful instant coffee was formulated in Switzerland by the Nestlé company in 1937; they called it Nescafé. Frozen food was developed in 1924 by adventurer-inventor Clarence Birdseye, almost ten years after he had first had the idea from watching the Inuits of icy Labrador preserve fish and caribou meat. The first precooked frozen food went on sale in 1939, and frozen "fish sticks" appeared over a decade later in 1955.

Freeze-drying had been invented in Paris in 1906, but it was used only in medicine until the 1940s. The Second World War, however, involved the long-distance shipment of large quantities of food and, since dehydrated food has some 10 percent of the bulk of the original, it stimulated the development of a dehydration-freezing process, patented in 1949, which led to many new foods, including instant mashed potato, a fad of the late 1960s.

By the 1990s, science had begun to tinker with the essential substance of foods. Genetic engineering offered the prospect of foods to order: an ever-ripe tomato, for example, or perhaps non-stringy celery and a sweet carrot.

CURBSIDE CONVENIENCE Dating from 1908, the hot-dog stand is a familiar sight on the streets of New York and many other cities.

THE COLA WARS

The world's most popular soft drink was invented in 1886 in Atlanta, Georgia, by Dr. John Pemberton as he was seeking a means of making his cough medicines more palatable. When he added fizzy water to a sweet syrup, spiked with caffeine and flavored with coca leaves, he discovered that the concoction made a refreshing drink. A colleague gave it a name: Coca-Cola.

The recipe was never patented, but the proportion of ingredients was kept secret, the formula locked in an Atlanta bank vault. Bottled Coca-Cola had only been on sale for three years when a near-identical rival, Pepsi-Cola, was launched in 1903. The subsequent battle became one of the great marketing sagas of the century.

Coke's conquest of the world followed its introduction overseas by American forces in the Second World War. By 1977, Georgia-born President Jimmy Carter could note that Coca-Cola was represented in more countries than the U.S. State Department. Global politics were reflected in the fight for market share. Pepsi gained something of an advantage when it was first to penetrate the Iron Curtain, and because Coca-Cola was sold in Israel, Pepsi enjoyed a monopoly in much of the Arab world.

In April 1985, Coca-Cola flirted with disaster by deciding to change its secret formula. The sweeter "New Coke" was intended to reverse a decline in market share, but sales plummeted. In July, the decision was made to restore the original formula as "Classic Coke." By 1988, Coke had recovered much of the loss.

1955 Frozen
fish sticks
launched

1968 Instant
mashed potato

1990s Genetically
engineered foods

THE COMPLETE PACKAGE

INVENTORS ARE PRESSED TO SOLVE PROBLEMS CREATED BY MODERN FOOD PACKAGING

Until the early 20th century, everything was held together with paper, string and sealing wax, glass and unadorned tin-plate. When the revolution in packaging did begin, however, it was a staggered process, often lagging behind technological advances.

Although an economical means of smelting aluminum had been invented in the 1880s, and pure aluminum foil produced in France in 1903, its applications in the packaging industry were limited at first. In 1914, the Swedes began making milk-bottle tops of aluminum foil, but it became a global phenomenon only after the demands of the Second World War had established its superiority in light, impermeable packaging of all kinds.

Much the same was true in the canning industry, where it was the rising cost of tinplate that stimulated research behind the development in 1958 of the lighter, cheaper

PACK AND FREEZE Packaging frozen food was labor-intensive at first, as at this Californian farm where women pack beans for Birdseye in the 1940s.

WRAP UP The U.S. Government joined forces with Cellophane manufacturers to encourage wartime sales of wrapped sliced bread, with the slogan: "Keep it fresh . . . prevent waste."

aluminum can, by Kaiser Aluminum; Coors Beer was first to introduce it, in 1959. The invention of the pull-tab top in 1963 encouraged soft-drink manufacturers to follow the brewers' lead, with Coca-Cola and Pepsi switching to aluminum in 1967. Can walls were thinned, and by 1990 they had been reduced to less than 1/5000 of an inch, as thin as a magazine cover.

THE MAN WHO INVENTED SLICED BREAD

Jeweller Otto Rohwedder was obsessed with an idea that nobody else saw the point of: sliced bread. Devising a slicing machine was no problem, but holding the slices together and keeping them fresh was. Rohwedder began his quest in 1912, experimenting with a prototype that used hairpins but a near-fatal illness and losing everything in a factory fire diverted him. The invention of a bread-wrapping machine in 1925 spurred him to redouble his efforts, and in January 1928 he finally succeeded. Within a few years, 80 percent of bread sold in America was presliced, but fame and fortune eluded the man who had made it possible. He died in obscurity in 1960.

The idea behind aerosol cans (some of which are now made from aluminum) came from the Norwegian Erik Rotheim. In 1926 he established that a product could be sprayed from a container under gas pressure. However, until the development by Du Pont in the 1930s of inert chlorofluorocarbons (CFCs, or Freons), no such gas existed. And it was not until August 1939 that Julian Kahn in New York created a disposable spray can that could contain an aerosol. In 1941 a team working for the U.S. government designed the first working aerosol, which went to war as the "bug bomb," a Freon-propelled insecticide that saved innumerable lives in the Pacific fighting. Soon after the Second World War, Robert Abplanalp designed a plastic push-button valve in his New York machine shop, and it was this that propelled the cheap aerosol can into mass use from 1953 onward.

From paper to polymers

The first thin flexible plastic wrapping was invented around the same time as aluminum foil. On November 14, 1908, a thin cellulose film formed on the cotton that Swiss chemist

SULLIVAN'S TEA BAGS

In 1904, New York tea importer Thomas Sullivan sent out some samples in tiny silk sacks. He wanted to save money on the tin boxes he normally used, but he did not wish to appear cheap. His customers misunderstood. Instead of removing the tea, they put the sacks straight into the teapot. Unwittingly, Sullivan had just invented the tea bag.

THE THROWAWAY SOCIETY

Little or nothing was thrown away before 1900. The father of throwaway culture was William Painter, inventor of the disposable crown-shaped bottle-cap (and its opener), who advised one of his salesmen: "Why don't you invent something that can be used and thrown away. Then the customer will constantly be coming back for more?" That salesman's name was Gillette.

The throwaway razor blade was soon followed by the disposable paper cup, born in 1909 as the Healthy Kup, a hygienic alternative to the metal cups chained to public drinking fountains. Its inventor was Hugh Moore, an astute Kansan who warned against germs with the advertising slogan: "Influenza Sits on the Brim of the Common Drinking Cup." The disposable handkerchief, offering a similar sense of security, was invented in 1924 by the Kimberley Clark company of Wisconsin. Called Celluwipes at first, the name was later changed to Kleenex.

Throwaway diapers were introduced in Sweden shortly after the Second World War, but they leaked. Other attempts were equally unsuccessful, until Procter & Gamble researchers Robert Duncan and Norma Baker came up with the wholly disposable diaper, test-launched in 1966 as Pampers. The throwaway flashbulb also began to pop in 1966. The 1970s made throwaway chic, with disposable under-

PLASTIC PILE-UP Recycling had become a priority by the 1990s. PET, a plastic that could be compacted, shredded, and reprocessed, offered one solution.

pants, shirts, and even furniture enjoying fad success. The disposable toothbrush was an Italian contribution of 1979, and in France the BiC company took Gillette's innovation to its logical conclusion by inventing the disposable razor. Kodak followed suit ten years later with the Fling disposable camera. Disposable lighters and watches also flooded the market in the 1980s.

J.E. Brandenberger was treating for a color-printing experiment. It took time for him to realize that this film could be put to independent use, but by 1912 small quantities of "Cellophane" were being manufactured. Polythene was discovered in Britain in 1933 by Reginald Gibson and Eric Fawcett, who were experimenting with ethylene gas under immense pressure. They went home one weekend, and on Monday morning found that the gas had polymerized into a plastic, now called polyethylene.

The plastic bottle took longer to perfect than the polythene bag. PET (short for polyethyleneterephthalate), strong yet lightweight, was developed in 1942, but blow-molding it into bottles proved unsatisfactory. Production was limited until 1973, when Du Pont engineer Nathaniel Wyeth invented a stretching process that yielded a flexible bottle.

The Swedish carton manufacturer Ruben Rusing combined the latest in plastic, aluminum and paper technologies to create the tetrahedral—literally, "four-faced"—carton, or "Tetra Pak." Long-life milk was packaged in this way in 1961, followed by fruit juices, soups and wine, and many other products.

By the 1980s, however, the impact of the packaging revolution was so overwhelming and the new materials so indestructible that inventors were mainly concerned with containing its effect on the environment. Recycling technologies addressed the mounting problem of litter and garbage landfills, swollen with discarded material that was not biodegradable.

When CFCs used in aerosols and in styrofoam coffee cups and burger boxes were blamed for the depletion of the Earth's protective ozone layer, new propellants and containers were devised. Some manufacturers even began replacing plastic containers with paper ones. Would the day come when people would routinely take milk home in containers they brought with them to the store?

KEEPING US SAFE

BRINGING CRIMINALS TO JUSTICE: FORENSIC SCIENCE LAYS DOWN THE LAW

Intuitive deduction—of the kind favored by Sherlock Holmes—was the only method of criminal investigation in the early years of the century. After 1901, fingerprinting had increased the chances of success, but it was not until the 1950s that detectives could rely on further developments to help them "get their man." Since then scientific innovation became vital both in solving crimes and bringing the guilty to justice—ensuring the safety of the general public.

Promising inventions of the early years could not stand up in a court of law. The polygraph, or "lie detector," invented in

THE GREAT COVER-UP Slits in the eyepieces allowed the wearer some vision in this First World War body armor. Modern versions are made from special lightweight fabric.

1921, which measured a subject's blood pressure and pulse rate when asked pertinent questions, was not foolproof. Similarly, the "truth serum" sodium pentothal, formulated in 1936, induced a state in which the subject was too highly suggestible for any confessions to be considered legal. The 1940s produced a reinforced nylon bulletproof vest, but it was bulky and ineffective (and would not improve greatly until 1971 with the invention of super-tough Kevlar fiber).

Pointing the finger

The mid-1950s saw an improvement in fingerprint detection techniques, as well as the introduction of the Identikit—a method of building up an image of the suspect's face. But still, forensics remained an indifferent science until the emergence of the computer and the laser—tools that were unfortunately also to prove useful to criminals.

The computer demonstrated its sleuthing capacity in 1973, when it was used to match tiny glass slivers from a crime scene. It would shortly become invaluable for amassing data and computerizing fingerprint indexing. The laser became important from 1978, when Canadian investigators discovered that laser light could reveal otherwise invisible fingerprints up to ten years old. But, at the same time, cunning devices such as a computer-in-a-shoe were being used to cheat casinos in Las Vegas, and laser printers could forge almost perfect banknotes. Counter measures included micro-imprints, holograms and, in Australia, plastic bills.

By the 1980s, security cameras had become part of the defensive weaponry—as a deterrent, as a means of identification, and as a concrete record of a crime in progress. However, the greatest forensic advance began in 1985 with "genetic fingerprinting"—a means of identifying a suspect from a trace of blood, a single hair or a few cells of skin. The first conviction based on DNA evidence was made in Britain in 1987. At about the same time, strides in mass spectrometry enabled crime labs

CAUGHT IN THE ACT Video surveillance cameras provided evidence of carjackers in action at a traffic intersection in Glasgow, 1993.

to analyse paints, fibers and explosive residues. This was to become vital in the wake of terrorist bombings, such as the Lockerbie air disaster of 1988, which sparked efforts to contain such explosions. As early as 1973, the U.S. Federal Aviation Administration imposed strict security measures on all air carriers and airports, including mandatory baggage checks and electronic searches of the passengers themselves. These procedures were expedited by the design in the United States of a CAT-scanning military mine detector, capable of detecting plastic explosives through thick steel, which eluded ordinary airport X-ray scanners.

By the 1990s, technology had even entered the courtroom—with virtual reality and other computer animation techniques employed in the battle to sway juries. In 1992, a computer-generated re-creation of a

IN THE BAG Ordinary airport scanners use X-ray technology that clearly reveals any weapons in baggage—but currently they cannot detect plastic explosives.

murder helped to convict San Francisco pornographer Jim Mitchell. In the highly publicized double-murder trial of sports celebrity O.J. Simpson in 1995, the prosecution used video technology to dramatize the crime (as well as a damning array of DNA evidence). But, the jury, unimpressed, took three hours to return a verdict of not guilty.

1901 Sir Francis Galton's fingerprinting classification system introduced at Scotland Yard, London

1921 Canadian John Larson invents the polygraph

1971 Kevlar is used to make bulletproof vests

1985 Alex Jeffreys develops genetic fingerprinting in Britain

WORKING WONDERS

FROM THE CLICK OF TYPEWRITER KEYS TO THE HUM OF THE COMPUTER, AND FROM THE CONVEYOR BELT TO ROBOTS THAT ARE CAPABLE OF FUNCTIONING UNATTENDED, THE WORKPLACE HAS ALTERED BEYOND RECOGNITION OVER THE PAST HUNDRED YEARS. THE MATERIALS WITH WHICH WE WORK HAVE CHANGED TOO: FROM BASE METALS TO PLASTICS AND OTHER MAN-MADE COMPOSITES THAT SHARE THE MOST USEFUL QUALITIES OF THEIR CONSTITUENT MATERIALS.

CHANGES IN THE OFFICE

FROM CLICK-CLICK TO TAP-TAP: KEEPING PACE WITH THE DEMANDS OF BUSINESS

As the 20th century dawned, people could still remember the typical mid-Victorian office, where clerks perched on high stools and scratched at ledgers with quill pens. However, the typewriter (an early one from the 1870s was dubbed the "literary piano") had now become accepted to such an extent that *The Penman's Art Journal*—a periodical for scribes who were now losing their jobs to typists—resignedly observed how "the monotonous click" could be heard "in almost every well-regulated business establishment." The telephone, on the other hand, was still strictly for show—an impractical business tool until automatic exchanges became common in the 1920s.

The office at the turn of the century

Ink from spilt jars or dripping pens remained an office hazard, except for the proud owners of the first reliable fountain pens: after two centuries and hundreds of patented failures, a way to control the flow had been devised in 1884 by American insurance agent Lewis Waterman. Another American, George Parker, patented the "lever-fill" in 1904: you raise a lever which squeezes the air out of the rubber reservoir, creating a vacuum; then, when you release the lever, ink is sucked into the pen.

Copying was an awkward, messy procedure using ink-saturated carbon paper (invented early in the 19th century) until a Hungarian immigrant in London, David Gestetner, applied the typewriter's punch to a waxed fiber stencil sheet in 1888. The typewriter keys cut into and removed the ink-resistant wax coating of the stencil, thereby exposing the fiber below. The stencil is then covered with ink, which sticks only to the areas where the wax has been removed. When a roller is passed across the stencil, it transfers the ink onto the copy paper. Also in London, Prague-born A.D. Klaber improved the speed and ease of the whole process by replacing the roller with a drum roller; the result was the rotary duplicator, or Roneo machine, which was on sale by 1900.

Quick to anticipate the paper pile-up, a scramble of inventors came up with the paperclip in assorted forms; Johann Waaler, a Norwegian, is credited in 1900 with the version that took hold. The first desktop staplers appeared in 1914. The staples were loose and the machines often jammed—until the Boston Wire Stitcher Company designed

THE COPYING MACHINE

The American Chester Carlson was determined to find a faster way of copying documents than by hand. In 1938, he duplicated his first blurred image in the back of his mother-in-law's beauty shop in New York. With a grease pencil, he scrawled the date on a glass slide and, using a light bulb, projected this onto a photosensitive sulphur-coated zinc plate. He then dusted the plate with a powder made from moss spores, which stuck to those

FIRST PRINT Carlson's copy noted the date (October 22, 1938) and the area of New York.

areas where the dark image of the writing had preserved the original positive charge. The image was then transferred onto wax copy paper.

CLEAN COPY A French advertisement of 1904 (below left) promotes the rotary duplicator over the hand roller. Neither was a match for the duplicating machine (below), designed by French-born designer Raymond Loewy.

1900 Paperclip invented
1901 Electric typewriter invented
1902 Facsimile transmission (fax) invented

1914 First desktop staplers

1924 Spiral binding for notebooks and manuals

1938 First photocopy

1943 Ballpoint pen patented in Argentina

a simpler model in 1923; glued sticks of staples removed the labor of inserting one at a time. Spiral binding for notebooks and manuals was invented in 1924.

Thus equipped, the office became the central cog in a working environment that was to witness sweeping social change, starting with the mass-employment of women.

However much the grinding Roneo and similar stencilling machines contributed to the mounting paper tide, there was still no easy means of duplicating *existing* documents. This problem obsessed Chester Carlson, who spent the Depression years trying to devise a cheap, clean, dry method of photocopying—reproducing written or graphic material by photographing it. More than 20 major companies turned his invention down before a private research institute invested $3,000. In 1947, a small photographic paper-maker (later the Xerox Corporation) bought a manufacturing license from the institute for what it called "xerography"—from the Greek for "dry writing"—but early Xerox machines were complicated, big, and expensive. As a result, the photocopying revolution would not happen until 21 years after Carlson's original breakthrough, with the development of the Xerox 914—still a big and costly machine, but the first to use ordinary paper.

The ballpoint pen

The conquest of the ink blot was another act of dedication—this time by a Hungarian journalist named Laszlo Biro. Biro spent years seeking a way to use quick-drying printer's ink in a pen. In 1940, he moved to Argentina where he made the first ballpoint.

The ballpoint was launched commercially immediately after the war in Argentina and in the United States, where Biro had failed to take out a patent. Gimbel's department store in New York did the honors on October 29, 1945, selling out its stock within hours. In 1953, the French firm BiC developed a mass-production process that drastically cut the cost of ballpoints, which it was soon producing at the rate of 10 million a day. The felt-tipped pen was developed by the Japanese firm Pentel in 1963.

From typewriter to word processor

Electric typewriters met strong resistance at first, because they were expensive and people feared getting an electric shock from them. In 1935, after a decade of research, IBM (short for International Business Machines) launched the Electromatic, designed by R.G. Thomson and guaranteed safe. It was

LEAKPROOF WONDER
The ballpoint pen invented by Hungarian refugee Laszlo Biro first saw service with Allied bomber crews during the Second World War.

followed in 1944 by the Executive, which offered proportional spacing, in which the typewriter automatically adjusted the spaces between words so that each line was the same length. Nevertheless, 99 percent of office machines were still manual by the 1950s, and attitudes only changed as secretaries' salaries increased. The electric became a status symbol and a means of retaining able staff;

FIRST ELECTRIC

An electric typewriter was invented in 1901, but it cost ten times as much as an average home and it had bankrupted its creator, Dr. Thaddeus Cahill, by the time he had built 40 machines. More than 30 years were to pass before they became commercially viable.

advertisements claimed that a girl used 25 lb. of energy every time she pounded on a manual, but a mere $2^{1}/_{2}$ oz. per tap on an electric. The future was unveiled in 1961 when IBM launched the "golf ball" Selectric

THE ELECTRIFICATION OF THE WORLD AT WORK

During the 20th century, the workplace—in office and factory—was transformed by electrification. In 1900, in an address to the borough authorities of Chelmsford, Essex, Colonel R.E.B. Crompton, a pioneer of electric power throughout the British Empire, forecast how electricity would transform the way people lived and worked. His words seem even more prophetic a century later when much work can be performed at home on a computer and transmitted electronically:

"[The English countryside] in future, instead of being spoiled by densely populated industrial centers, might be covered with cottages extending for miles over the present almost uninhabited rural districts. The factory hands, instead of having to work under the shafting in factories, should be able by the electrical transmission of power to carry on industrial pursuits in their own cottage homes."

1961 Launch of "golf ball" typewriter
1963 Felt-tipped pen patented by Pentel

1980s Spread of desktop computers

typewriter which replaced the moving carriage and bar-set letters with a rotating ball printer that floated over the paper surface.

The electronic office

A magnetic tape was added in 1964 to create an "automatic" typewriter with a correcting capacity. By 1974, IBM's Memory model could store up to 50 pages of type and play it back automatically at 150 words a minute. The typewriter had evolved into the word processor. As more and more components could be crowded onto a single silicon chip

and as computing speeds increased, microelectronics took over, transforming every aspect of office life. The electronic calculator led the way, with 2.5 million sold in 1971, 80 percent of them made in Japan. That year, Texas Instruments introduced the Pocketronic, the first pocket calculator.

Although facsimile transmission (or "fax")—the technique of transmitting documents or images over radio links or telephone lines—had been invented in Germany as early as 1902, the technology took some time to take off. In 1974, the United Nations

CHANGING MESSAGE A German telegraph machine of 1925 (left) received messages typed on tape; the 1994 Hewlett-Packard Fax 700 transmits and receives exact copies.

established an international transmission standard that encouraged manufacturers to make their machines compatible. An upgraded standard, allowing for transmission at the rate of about a page a minute, was set

THE MISTAKE THAT MADE MILLIONS

Bette Nesmith Graham was a struggling bank secretary in Dallas, who took to correcting her typing errors with a dab of white paint.

It angered her boss, but other typists took to borrowing her paint pot. After five years of this, she began selling the paint in little bottles labelled "Paint Out." Eventually, she consulted her 12-year-old son's chemistry teacher and a paint specialist, and experimented in her kitchen with a quick-drying opaque fluid that could not be detected on white paper. She changed the name to Liquid Paper and offered it to IBM, but it was turned down.

By the end of 1957, she was selling 100 bottles a month, which her son, Michael, helped her fill. Sales improved when an office-supply magazine wrote about it, and by 1975, Liquid Paper was selling like the proverbial hotcakes in more than 30 countries. In 1979, it was bought by Gillette: the typist who had covered up her mistakes was worth $50 million, and when she died in 1980 she was collecting a royalty on every bottle sold around the world. Michael, meanwhile, had achieved fame as a member of the Monkees pop group.

1900

1950

1900 Paperclip invented
1901 Electric typewriter invented
1902 Facsimile transmission invented

1914 First desktop staplers

1924 Spiral binding for notebooks and manuals

1938 First photocopy   1943 Ballpoint pen patented in Argentina

FROM SANDPAPER TO SELLOTAPE

Pure serendipity led to the invention of office tape. The Minnesota Mining and Manufacturing Company (now 3M) had originally mined abrasive grit for machine tools, but it soon turned to making sandpaper instead. This led to dealings with the motor industry, which in 1926 was using newspaper as masking when spray-painting two-tone car bodies.

Dick Drew, a 3M lab assistant, devised an adhesive masking tape that ensured a clean paint finish and could be peeled off when the job was done; car plant workers called it Scotch tape. A narrower, transparent version was tried on the American office market in 1930, and marketed as Sellotape when introduced into Britain in 1937. The stick-without-sticking Post-it memo pad was another 3M invention. In 1970, researcher Spencer Sylver created a sticky resin that detached readily from surfaces. It was discarded as useless, but one Sunday, ten years later, researcher Art Fry remembered it when bits of paper marking pages in his hymn book kept falling out. "I don't know whether it was a dull sermon or divine inspiration," said Fry, who spent the next 18 months improving the formula to create a sticky paper that peeled off without leaving marks.

CLICKER **The Imperial Model B of 1914 was one of the first mass-produced typewriters.**

HUMMER **The IBM Selectric typewriter of 1961 revolutionized the offices of the 1960s.**

in 1980. Combined with advances in microchip technology and increases in transmission speed, this soon made the fax machine an essential business tool.

The desktop computer and the computer work station became the focus of office operations in the 1980s, vastly increasing the accounting, planning and communicating powers of even the smallest office; linked to computers in other offices by phone, via modems, it gave them access to previously unimagined sources of information. With the advent of notebook computers that slip into a briefcase, a portable "pocket photocopier" in 1986, and a sub-compact printer in 1992 (with color capability added by 1994), the office-in-a-suitcase became a reality. The office as we know it now ran the risk of rendering itself obsolete, at least in the accepted sense, as millions of workers stayed at home with equipment previously only available in a full-scale office.

TAPPER **The laptop computer of the 1990s liberated the office worker. Will the traditional office give way to the "virtual" office of individuals linked electronically?**

1961 Launch of "golf ball" typewriter
1963 Felt-tipped pen patented
by Pentel

1980s Spread of
desktop computers

CREATING THE COMPUTER AND PUTTING IT TO WORK

FROM COUNTING PIN HOLES TO EXECUTING TRILLIONS OF OPERATIONS A SECOND

Although the term computer was not used until the late 1940s, the marriage of electricity and mathematics which gave birth to the computer had been consummated in 1890 when statistician Herman Hollerith invented a machine to collate the United States Census.

Hollerith used cards with punched holes that allowed metal pin "feelers" to complete an electric circuit and, in that way, count and classify the data. In 1901, he designed a punch keyboard on which the operator typed in the numbers and, by 1910, hundreds of tabulating machines based on the same principle were on the market. In 1924 Hollerith's company became a founding element of International Business Machines—IBM.

Early machines were so enormous and their machine codes so difficult to master that access was limited to specialist research institutes such as the Massachusetts Institute of Technology, which in 1930 built the Differential Analyzer, a massive, cranky, electromechanical machine of shafts and gears that, was capable of resolving complex equations. From the late 1930s, the use of telephone relays instead of gears was pursued in the United States by Bell Labs and, in Germany, by Konrad Zuse. Eventually, Bell built a 10-ton machine with 9,000 relays, but its performance would not even have matched that of a schoolchild's pocket calculator today.

DREAM WORLD   A 1927 vision of the computer.

The first computers

A solution was found in wartime Britain. Under conditions so secret that its existence was not revealed for another 25 years, a team led by mathematician Alan Turing built Colossus, afterwards hailed as the first computer.

Colossus used banks of vacuum tubes, known as thermionic valves, to speed up calculations tremendously: with more than 2,000 valves, it could process 5,000 characters per second and, from 1943, it was decoding enemy messages.

The war effort also inspired ENIAC (Electronic Numerical Indicator and Calculator), a 30-ton, 18,000 valve monster occupying 1,800 square feet and capable

COMPUTER PRECURSOR   Herman Hollerith's tabulating machine incorporated metal pins that opened and closed an electric circuit in order to count and classify census data.

> ### COMPUTER PREDICTION
>
> The computer captured public imagination for the first time in 1952, when Remington Rand's Univac I accurately predicted Dwight Eisenhower's landslide victory in the Presidential election. The Univac team was so skeptical of the computer's conclusion that they reprogrammed it to reduce Eisenhower's margin—but the machine had it right the first time.

1900

1901 Hollerith's punch keyboard

1930 The Differential Analyzer

1945 ENIAC, the first all-electronic computer
1947 EDVAC uses binary n

1950

(when it did not overheat) of calculating the trajectory of a shell faster than it could be delivered. ENIAC, the first all-electronic computer, was built by a University of Pennsylvania team in 1945. It used so much power that it dimmed lights in the neighborhood when it was turned on.

These cumbersome early machines had to be rewired by hand for each new task, but in 1947 Princeton mathematician John von Neumann designed the EDVAC (Electronic Discrete Variable Automatic Computer), which received its instructions in binary code—sequences of zeros and ones registered at lightning speeds by the on-off pulse of an electric current. In 1950 the EDVAC team designed the world's first commercial computer, Univac I (for Universal Automatic Computer); it stored data on magnetic tape.

POWERING UP Technicians prepare the ENIAC machine (below) to tackle a problem; it was superseded in 1947 by the EDVAC (right).

The first computer to use transistors—elements that can detect, amplify and switch currents—in place of valves was built by Bell Systems in 1955.

The second generation

The first such "second generation" computer was launched commercially by Univac in 1956; and the first fully transistorized computer—the RCA 501—followed in 1959. Next year, Univac completed LARCH, the

THE QUEST FOR THINKING MACHINES

The computer is a phenomenal processor of information, but short on reasoning power. "It can do whatever we know how to order it to perform," wrote Lady Ada Lovelace, who had written instructions for a never-completed calculating machine devised by Charles Babbage in the 1830s. A century later, science began to address the Lovelace limitation. In 1938, an American engineer named Thomas Ross built a mechanical mouse that ran on toy railway tracks and, by never repeating a mistake, found its way through a maze of junctions; it was the first machine to "learn" from experience.

The quest for thinking machines began in earnest in the 1950s with the science of cybernetics and the founding of an Artificial Intelligence faculty at the Massachusetts Institute of Technology. Pioneers such as MIT's John McCarthy tried to teach computers to solve problems by devising logic programs such as LISP (List Processing) and GPS (General Problem Solver). The theory of "expert systems" was formulated in the 1960s and found practical use from the early 1970s in automated decision-making. One of the first, Mycin, prescribed antibiotics; in a test at Stanford Medical Center, it did better than doctors.

Efforts to make the computer understand spoken commands began with the research of Indian-born Raj Reddy, who in 1971 wrote the first voice-recognition software.

PREDICTING POLITICS By forecasting the 1952 Presidential election, Univac (below) alerted the public to the computer's potential.

COMPUTER LEARNING Students at Brown University use Apple Macintosh II microcomputers to follow a lecture in progress in management economics.

first large research computer with transistors: it used 60,000 of them.

Airlines were quick to exploit the commercial possibilities offered by the computer. By the mid-1950s, IBM had developed a system called SABRE (Semi-Automatic Business Related Environment), by which a network of a thousand or more teleprinters fed into a central managing computer (called a "data base") for constant, instant updating; American Airlines was first to computerize reservations in this way.

VIRTUAL WARFARE Virtual reality originated as a training tool for the military. As developed in the 1990s, it transported people into synthetic universes that looked and sounded—and even felt—real.

By the mid 1960s, fully fledged programming languages existed: FORTRAN for scientific and engineering applications, COBOL and ALGOL for business use and BASIC for novices. Time sharing, which enabled several operators to use a computer at once, was made possible by the invention of multiple-access computing by American John McCarthy in 1961; it was first applied in an aviation supply center in Philadelphia. By the 1970s, cargo-handling at most international airports was computerized, and the computer was also beginning to find more everyday applications, such as job-searching and in the "computer-dating" craze.

The third generation

IBM had retained its position in the market, when the second generation of computers appeared around 1960, and now embarked upon the creation of a family of fully compatible computers. This was its IBM 360 series, launched in 1964 to such success that its advent is seen as the beginning of modern data processing. The 360 also marked the transition to third-generation computers, in which integrated-circuit silicon "chips" replaced bulky transistors. Designers next used photo-reduction techniques to crowd hundreds, and eventually millions, of electronic components onto a slice of silicon, or microchip, smaller than a fingertip.

Advances in chip technology opened the way for the microprocessor, which would

THE TRANSISTOR AND THE CHIP

On December 23, 1947, three researchers at Bell Laboratories in New Jersey—John Bardeen, William Shockley and Walter Brattain—wired up a crystal of the element germanium and spoke into the circuit. Their voices were amplified, and the electronics age was born. In devising a smaller, low-power and cheap alternative to the fragile valve, they changed the future of human society. The crystal was a "semiconductor," which conduct-

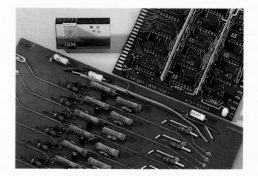

MAKING CONNECTIONS In the 1960s, computer circuit boards became smaller; the miniature version (top) dates from the 1970s.

ed electricity better than an insulator but less well than a metal, and was capable of operating as a switch as well as an amplifier, and of delivering signal-messages at a hundred-millionth of a second.

As transistors grew tinier and their application spread from miniature hearing aids for children (1952) to mass-produced transistor radios (1954), a barrier loomed: there was a limit to the number of soldered connections that could be made by workers peering through magnifying glasses. Out of American research efforts came the integrated circuit, co-invented by rivals Jack Kilby and Robert Noyce in 1958. Complete sets of electronic components could now be embedded, and connected, within a single wafer of silicon (which replaced germanium from 1960), to create a complex circuit. By a process of metallic coating and photoetching, this wafer could be mass-manufactured.

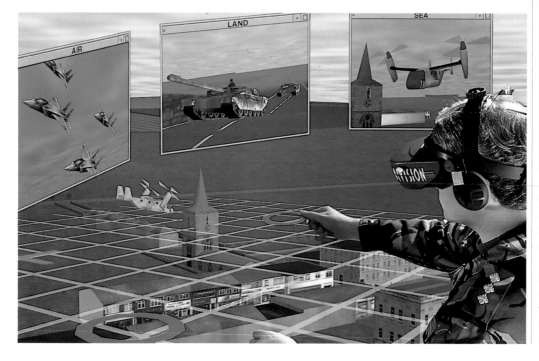

control a world of new equipment, from kitchen gadgetry to the Space Shuttle, and for ever-faster, smaller and cheaper computers. The microprocessor was invented in 1970 by American Gilbert Hyatt, and made its debut the following year as the Intel 4004. The design team, led by Ted Hoff, worked in a pleasant rural retreat south of San Francisco that would soon become renowned as Silicon Valley. It took them nine months to put together this chip that incorporated all the essential parts of a computer: memory, processor, input and output circuits. The result was a powerhouse on a silicon "trinket," 1/6 inch long and less than

COMPUTER BUGS

The dreaded computer "bug" is so-called because the first recorded bug was actually a real one —a moth which stopped the experimental Harvard Mark II computer in 1945. The moth's remains were extracted and then taped to the laboratory's logbook. Sorting out a malfunctioning computer became known thereafter as "debugging."

that in width; it could perform 60,000 operations per second and had the computing power of the 30 ton machines of 25 years before. The Intel 8080 of 1974 could execute 290,000 operations a second: this was the microprocessor chip that gave birth to the microcomputer and to mass-computing.

A prototype microcomputer, the ancestor of the PC, or personal computer, was created by David Ahal in 1974. About the size of a big television set, it featured a video screen, keyboard and central processor, but it was never developed. IBM designed one too, but saw no future in it at first, so microcomputers first went on sale as mail-order construction kits. In this way, the Apple computer was born, created in a California garage by electronics enthusiasts Steve Jobs and Stephen Wozniak in 1976; in 1977 they launched the Apple II, the first microcomputer available already assembled.

Personal computers

The development of mass-market microcomputers encouraged inventors to make them more "user-friendly." In 1975, Harvard student Bill Gates and classmate Paul Allen formed a company called Microsoft to adapt BASIC as a programming language for the new era. In 1980, they provided the operating program for IBM's new desktop

Personal Computer. When the IBM model was copied, or "cloned," by hundreds of other makers, the system became an industry standard for all but Apple, thus ensuring a global market for subsequent Microsoft products such as Windows, launched in 1985. By 1992, Microsoft was worth more than General Motors, and Gates—at age 36 —became the richest man in America, if not the world. In 1984, Apple launched the graphics-based Macintosh, which was manipulated by a screen-roving controller called a "mouse" (invented 18 years earlier by Douglas Engelbart).

The new supercomputers

At the other end of the scale, supercomputers had been doubling in power every two years from the 1950s to the 1980s—in response to the needs of aerospace engineers and astronomers, meteorologists and microbiologists, and so on. New words had to be coined to encompass the scale of their operations by 1985, when machines such as Cray 2 could perform a billion calculations

—one gigaflop—a second. By 1991, speeds were up to 16 gigaflops, but the supercomputer was superseded by a new "parallel processing" technology that employed strings of microprocessors. A system using 16,000 microprocessors was rated at two trillion operations a second in 1991.

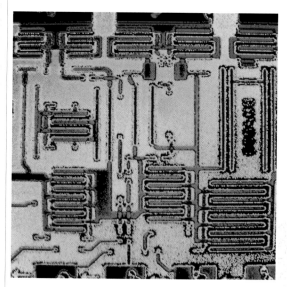

CHIP MAKING Gloved hands hold semiconductor wafers (below), the media for microcircuits such as the one on a silicon chip (above).

1950

1956 First second-generation computer launched commercially

1960s Coming of third-generation computers

1970 Microprocessor, the "computer on a chip," invented

1980 IBM's desktop Personal Computer

1984 Apple Mac
1985 Cray 2

2000

NEW INDUSTRIAL PROCESSES

FROM COAXING STEEL OUT OF COKE OVENS TO ENGINEERING LIFE ITSELF

Electricity was arcing through industry by 1900, making possible industrial processes beyond the capacity of coal, coke and steam. That year, the Norton company in Massachusetts built the first powerful precision grinding machines, using electric power that was cheap, clean and controllable; crankshafts were an early priority. The same year, a factory at Niagara Falls was

PAINT JOBS A car worker (top) spray-paints a Humber Saloon in the early 1930s without the benefit of protective clothing. Health procedures have improved continuously throughout the 20th century, culminating in the environmentally much safer conditions of some 60 years later (above).

making small quantities of nitrogen chemicals directly from the air, thanks to the cheap power of its pioneering hydroelectric plant. The plant's other products included a pure liquid oxygen, using a technique invented by the German scientist Karl von Linde, which involved compressing and cooling air until it liquefied, and then separating out its constituent gases. This important advance aided the development from 1904 of Frenchman Edmond Fouche's oxyacetylene welding torch (which uses oxygen).

By 1908, all the atmosphere's inert gases had been liquefied, and thereby separated from each other, for commercial use. Some found a home in light bulbs and others would serve inventions still unimagined; krypton, for instance, found eventual use in laser technology. A major breakthrough came in 1909, when Fritz Haber in Germany "fixed" and combined nitrogen and hydrogen.

The cutting edge

It was the development of precision machine tools (which cut, grind, hammer and press identical machine parts) that made the mass-production techniques of the 20th century possible. Many of these inventions, as well as that of spray painting in 1907, were driven by the motor industry.

Industry's cutting edge was improved early in the First World War, when Germany introduced tungsten-carbide tools. These were almost as hard as diamond, but brittle. When, in 1926, Krupp scientists incorporated gritty tungsten-carbide powder in cobalt, they created tools that cut four times faster than the keenest steel.

The first carbon-dioxide lasers were introduced in 1970, and from then on lasers brought new refinement to cutting and welding. The same year, an ex-Boeing scientist named Yi Hoh Pao invented a water-jet which sliced through concrete; his secret was an additive which prevented water from vaporizing when driven at force.

Heavy industry: steel and glass

By 1902, an electric furnace in France was being used to melt scrap iron for specialist, high-quality steels. Bulk steel, on the other hand, continued to be produced in a brick-lined steel vessel, known as a Bessemer converter after the English engineer who had patented the process in 1856. Molten

BULLET TEST Advances in glass production have involved rigorous testing procedures; here, a demonstrator in an English glass factory in 1938 points to the spot where a test bullet has hit a sheet of safety glass.

A MIXED BLESSING

Chemist-physicist Fritz Haber found a solution to world famine at the bottom of a tiny glass tube on July 2, 1909. This was synthetic ammonia, created from air (nitrogen) and water (hydrogen) by a revolutionary new process. Ammonia was desperately needed to make nitrates for fertilizers, because the main natural source—bird guano from islands off Peru—was running out.

Carl Bosch of the German firm BASF developed the laboratory experiment for large-scale production, but these fertilizers had to wait. Instead, Haber's life-force became a death-force, used to make explosives for the German war effort. Had it not been for Haber, Germany would have run out of ammunition and been forced to surrender by 1916. A few years later, Haber, a Jew, had to leave his beloved homeland. The Haber-Bosch process remains the source of vast quantities of ammonia for needs ranging from refrigeration to rocket fuel.

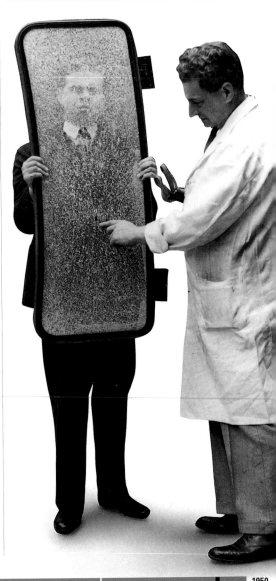

1900

1900 Precision grinding machine powered by electricity

1909 Synthetic ammonia produced

1926 Tungsten-carbide tools

1950

1948 Pure oxygen used in steel refining

pig iron was poured into the converter and then blasted with air to remove its impurities. A more efficient method of refining, using pure oxygen in place of air, was developed in 1948 by Austrian steelmakers and widely adopted by the 1960s. From the blast furnace, the molten steel is poured into a continuous casting machine—introduced in 1950—where it is cut up into slabs.

Glass production also took giant strides forward during the 20th century. In 1918, a means of manufacturing plate glass for windows was developed independently by Emile Fourcault in Belgium and Irving Colburn in the United States. And then, in 1959, the

English glass-maker Alastair Pilkington announced his "float glass" process. Pilkington had spent seven years perfecting a way of extruding, or floating, molten glass over a bath of molten tin so that it was completely flat, of uniform thickness and without flaws; the result was shiny-smooth—and yet cheaper—plate glass. An electro-float process followed in 1967. By infusing the surface with metallic particles, the light and heat sensitivity of a glass could be altered to any degree desired.

Life processes

The most audacious late-century developments were in biotechnology. The discovery at Cambridge University in 1953 of the molecular structure of deoxyribose nucleic acid (DNA)—the stuff of genes—enabled bioengineers to manipulate life itself. In 1973, American biologists Stanley Cohen and Herbert Boyer found a way to splice a piece of DNA and transfer it from one organism into the cell of another, marking the birth of genetic engineering.

ENGINEERING LIFE

The U.S. Supreme Court ruled in 1980 that "anything under the sun that is made by man" could be patented as an invention: a ruling specifically including genetically engineered life forms. The first patented creature was a microbe developed by the General Electric Company for cleaning-up oil spills.

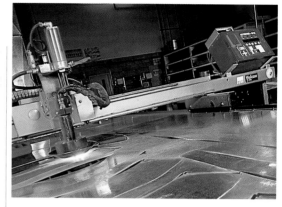

ROBOTIC SKILL An industrial robot cuts metal with "superhuman" speed and precision.

Commercial application began in 1976 with the launch of Genentech, a San Francisco company devoted to engineering life forms for industry and medicine. By the 1990s, the industry was producing disease-resistant crops, garbage-eating microbes, and strains of mice for cancer research.

WHITE HEAT At a steel mill in Ohio, blocks of steel from the blast furnace are passed between rollers that compress it into shape.

1959 Pilkington announces float-glass process

1970 Carbon-dioxide lasers

1990s Developments in biotechnology and genetics

THE AUTOMATED WORKPLACE

FROM THE ASSEMBLY LINE TO ROBOTS AND THE FULLY AUTOMATIC FACTORY

Although automation dated back to the 18th century, it was Henry Ford who boasted that he had invented the modern age – by installing a moving assembly line at his Detroit plant in 1913. For five years, Ford, like other car makers, had been building his Model T by assembling cars from piles of materials, with each frame put together on a sawhorse. But then he developed an idea first employed in a Yorkshire coal mine in 1905: this was the conveyor belt. It carried the cars at a speed slow enough for his line workers to carry out their sequenced tasks, but fast enough to cut the assembly time from half a day to 93 minutes.

FLOW LINE Assembly-line technology had reached the bakery by 1926. In an English factory, cookies in a continuous flow are being coated with sugar icing.

In 1919, André Citroën was the first European car maker to adopt Ford's methods. The British firm Morris Motors took these a stage further in 1924 by introducing a continuous-flow assembly line for engine parts, as well as whole cars: for example, a sequenced system of 53 machine tools turned out an engine block.

Electronic automation

By 1950, there were machines capable of performing more than 500 tooling operations. The first step toward computerization came in 1952, when engineers at the Massachusetts Institute of Technology developed a machine tool that was electronically programmed—or "numerically controlled," as it was termed—and worked from instructions stored on tape. By the mid-1950s, a few factories were so highly automated that they were able to lay off 90 percent of their workforce.

In 1965, British research engineer Theo Williamson anticipated the advance from automation to the fully automatic factory. The result, in 1969, was the Molins 24, the first computer-controlled flow-production system capable of running an entire manu-

THE PRICE OF AUTOMATION

Will Rogers predicted that it would take 100 years to tell whether Henry Ford "helped us or hurt us." Eighty years later, the debate continues. Although the moving assembly line increased productivity by 800 percent, many workers could not endure the boredom of such repetitive work and reacted to Ford's ban on talking by quitting.

More crafts died, as each advance in automation reduced the number of skilled jobs and increased the boredom factor. From 1972, instructions could even be automated: some assembly-line workers began to be fed computer-generated reminders over earphone relays. From 1950, Japanese industrialists experimented with ways to foster worker pride. In the 1980s they began to create work teams that were moved between tasks, stimulating interest and a competitive spirit.

facturing process unattended. The project was ahead of its time and fell victim to electronic advances, which enabled Cincinnati Melatron and other American companies to develop simpler, less costly systems.

From production control, the computer moved on to play an active role in product design. These techniques had first been

1913 Ford builds moving assembly line at Detroit plant

1919 Citroën adopts Ford's methods in France

1924 Morris Motors introduces continuous-flow assembly for engine parts

SUPERSONIC ANALYSIS   A Cray supercomputer was used to produce this graphics image of the airflow over an F-16 jet fighter.

developed by the U.S. military, and from the 1970s were adopted by the aviation and motor industries, then by industry in general. Computer Assisted Design (CAD) made it possible for any object to be visualized in three dimensions and tested under theoretical conditions, before building a prototype.

The first robots

By the late 1940s, remote-controlled manipulators called Waldos were developed to handle dangerous radioactive material. In 1956, inventor George Devol combined this technology with that of the numerically

controlled machine tool—in a mechanism he dubbed Programmed Article Transfer. Devol was joined by Joseph Engelberger, a young physicist with a love of science fiction, who adapted the system to create the first industrial robots. These were pick-and-place machines intended to replace humans in simple jobs that were dirty, boring or dangerous. They sold their first Unimate in 1962 to General Motors who used it to remove hot castings from molds. Unimate's twin became the first industrial robot in Europe, when it was put to work in a Swedish foundry in 1964.

Unimate's more dexterous offspring were able to spray-paint and spot-weld. Fifty robots replaced 200 welders at a Chrysler plant in Detroit in 1979, raising output by 20 per cent; and by 1980, Unimation was selling a robot called PUMA that was capable of carrying out basic assembly tasks, such as tightening nuts. The Japanese were quick to seize upon the potential and put thousands of robots on their assembly lines, while the rest of the world watched.

Computers, programmed with artificial intelligence, now gave sensor-equipped robots the "brains" to react to selected situations. The Hopkins Beast, an experimental robot built in Baltimore, had helped pave the way in

the 1960s. The Beast prowled corridors until it found a wall socket with which to charge its batteries; then it moved on.

"Seeing" robots were next. Equipped with visual sensors and a computer-coded recognition memory, they could select particular

HELPING HUMANKIND?

The term robot, derived from the Polish word for a drudge, dates from 1923. It was the name playwright Karel Capêk gave to the mechanical characters in his play *RUR* (which stood for Rossum's Universal Robots). In the play, the robots destroy humanity.

machine parts, or choose and pick items off a conveyor belt. WABOT-2, an experimental Japanese robot of the 1980s, could sight-read music and play it on an organ; another, called Melkong (Medical Electric King Kong), was programmed to wash invalids and even tuck them into bed. In 1990, Bell Labs created SAM (Speech Activated Manipulator), a seeing, talking, touching prototype capable of taking simple vocal instructions and reporting back to its human masters in the same way.

ROBOTS AT WORK
A Cybermotion SR2 robot (above) patrols a Los Angeles museum gallery, alert for smoke, fire or intruders. It is equipped with an electronic map, video "eyes" and ultrasonic detectors. A remote-controlled robot (right) is used by bomb-disposal teams for handling suspect packages.

RM 180

1952 MIT develops numerically controlled machine tool | 1956 Programmed Article Transfer | 1962 First Unimate sold—in the United States | 1969 Molins 24, the first computer-controlled flow-production system | 1980 PUMA robot carries out assembly tasks | 1990 SAM (Speech Activated Manipulator) robot

THE LASER

HOW THE DREADED DEATH RAY PROVED A BENIGN FORCE THAT TOUCHED ON EVERYONE'S LIFE

Although the German-born physicist Albert Einstein had, in 1917, described the process on which the laser depends, and the comic-strip hero Buck Rogers had been armed with a ray gun in 1929, it took another 30 years to turn theory

UNFULFILLED VISION Space scouts fire their deadly death ray guns in a 1934 comic. Billions of dollars would be spent in quest of the real thing.

and fantasy into reality; and to create a powerful beam of pure light that could cut through materials as hard as diamond.

Einstein had deduced that when atoms are hit by radiation—in the form of electromagnetic particles, called photons—they might be triggered into emitting radiation of their own—in the form of other photons, which travel as one, at the same wavelength and at the speed of light, with the first. The effect would be much the same as a human wave at a sports event, rippling larger to engulf the entire stadium. But the blinding speed of the process—less than a hundred-millionth of a second—made it impossible to check the validity of "the stimulated emission of radiation," as the theory was known.

In 1954, a Bell Labs team led by Charles Townes found a way to amplify microwaves —electromagnetic radiation—with short wavelengths that cannot be seen. They called their device the maser, short for Microwave Amplification by Stimulated Emission of Radiation; and their discovery would, in due course, make radio telescopes and satellite communication practical. The race was now on to achieve the same effect at frequencies within the visible spectrum.

Death ray or life force?

In 1958, Townes and Arthur Schawlow outlined proposals for a maser that produced visible light, or laser (Light Amplification by Stimulated Emission of Radiation), as it had already been dubbed. But their practical efforts failed. The breakthrough was achieved by a physicist named Theodore Maiman. For a fraction of a second on May 15, 1960, pulses of red light of incredible intensity illuminated his Malibu, California, laboratory. His contraption—a tiny mirrored ruby rod, lodged in a commercial flash-bulb—seemed so outlandish that it was mocked at first.

Maiman's invention was unveiled at a New York press conference and, the next day, a Los Angeles newspaper ran the banner headline: "L.A. MAN DISCOVERS SCI-

SELLING DOUBLE GLAZING

Glass manufacturer Andrew Pilkington demonstrated in 1968 how a laser could pick up conversations in a house by transmitting tiny vibrations from the windowpane. People fearful of eavesdropping could always install double glazing, he pointed out.

ENCE FICTION DEATH RAY." Instead of dealing death, however, the laser proved uniquely useful in communications, measurement, precise machining, and a range of

WONDER OF HOLOGRAPHY A boy is captivated by a hologram display at the Museum of La Villette in Paris.

benign applications that have touched on the lives of almost everyone.

Maiman's ruby laser emitted powerful pulses that could drill a hole in a diamond. Then, in December 1960, physicist Ali Javan at Bell Labs created the first gas laser, which emitted a continuous beam rather than a string of flashes. Many other types of pulse and constant-beam lasers were subsequently developed, often using exotic gases and crystals, to enable the power and precision of laser light to be fine-tuned for specific tasks:

HOW A LASER WORKS High-intensity light excites atoms in the mirrored rod that builds up to form a powerful laser beam.

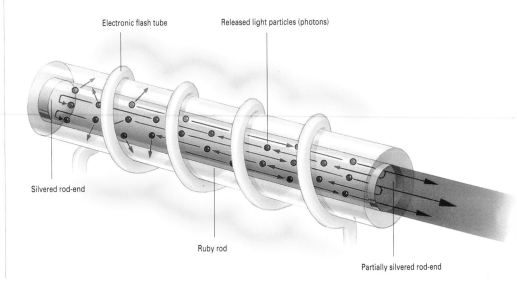

Electronic flash tube

Released light particles (photons)

Silvered rod-end

Ruby rod

Partially silvered rod-end

1917 Theory of "stimulated emission of radiation"

1947 Principle of holography devised

oceanographers wanted blue-green lasers for beaming through water, whereas biologists sought shorter (violet) wavelengths.

In December 1961, a retinal tumor was destroyed by a laser at Columbia-Presbyterian hospital in New York, and soon such operations became routine. In factories, lasers were used to process high-cost materials such as titanium, reducing waste and improving accuracy. Nor was the military entirely disappointed. Laser rangefinders of deadly accuracy were developed from the early 1960s, and infrared laser-guidance made "smart" bombs possible. In another advance, holography, devised by Dennis

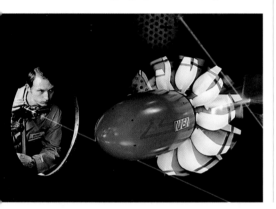

Gabor in Britain in 1947, was made practical by a split laser beam that created ghostly, apparently three-dimensional images. Testing began in 1963 and led to a wide range of uses, from bar-code scanners in supermarkets to guiding robots; embedded in Australian and British banknotes, they were used to confound counterfeiters.

Laser technology also joined the quest for controlled nuclear fusion (in which atoms are combined, rather than split, to create an explosive release of energy) and the search for a limitless supply of cheap, clean power. By 1981, Princeton University scientists had developed a laser that focused energy equal to all the power used by New York City in a single day. In California, the world's most powerful laser—Nova—hit a hydrogen fuel pellet with an astonishing 100 trillion watts of energy in 1986, to register the first laser-induced thermonuclear reaction (previously, nuclear fusion had generally been triggered by nuclear fission).

PRECISION BEAMS Laser light is used to measure tiny deflections in a whirling fan blade (left) and minute movements in a volcanic dome in California (below).

LASER WARS

The laser sparked a classic example of the patent wars that have attended 20th-century inventing. Charles Townes shared a Nobel prize with two Russians, since nobody could say who thought of what first. But Gordon Gould, a former student of Townes, was able to prove that he had conceived the laser before his mentor, and decades of court battles ensued. They were joined by Theodore Maiman, inventor of the first actual laser.

Gould scored a victory in 1987 and became very rich, even though he had sold most of his anticipated royalties to cover his $9 million in legal fees. Maiman was snubbed by the U.S. Patents Office and missed out on a fortune. Yet, he was nevertheless inducted into America's Inventors Hall of Fame.

The laser's medical applications were primarily in eye surgery, but in 1985 lasers were applied to clearing clogged arteries, and by the 1990s they were providing an alternative to traditional surgery in some heart bypass operations. Pioneered in San Francisco, a high-energy infrared laser beam literally shot tiny holes in the heart to create artificial veins; the procedure was bloodless because all moisture dissipated as steam.

1950

1954 Microwave Amplification by Stimulated Emission: maser

1960 Maiman's ruby laser
1961 Retinal tumor destroyed by laser

1986 First laser-induced thermonuclear reaction

2000

SEEING MORE . . .

MIGHTY MIRRORS AND RADIO ASTRONOMY REVEAL AN ASTOUNDING UNIVERSE

The visible universe has become both infinitely larger and infinitely smaller through spectacular advances in the telescope and the microscope. At the dawn of the 20th century, there was no way to see beneath the surface of things, and the heavens were fuzzy enough for people to cling to the belief that there were creatures on Mars intelligent enough to build canals.

Optical astronomy

The world's most powerful telescope in 1900 had a 50 inch lens. It had recently been built for the University of Chicago by George Ellery Hale, who in 1908 installed a 60 inch reflector mirror at Mount Wilson, California, and then in 1917 a 100 inch mirror, each of which was in turn the world's largest. Hale next tackled a project that was not completed until 1948. His 200 inch reflector on Mount Palomar, California, was eight times the size of anything that preceded it, and worked better even than a 236 inch Russian challenger, installed a quarter of a century later in the mountains of the Caucasus. Pollution drifting from Los Angeles gradually reached Palomar, obscuring the sky and driving astronomers and their array of new technologies to build in remoter places, such as peaks on the Canary Islands and Hawaii.

Meanwhile, the limitations of the human eye were overcome by increasingly keen cameras and by electron-detectors much more sensitive to light than photographic emulsions. The enhancement of images by computer and the capacity of computers to store and calibrate data revolutionized optical astronomy further. Previously invisible dimensions of the Universe were now revealed by rockets and satellites equipped with X-ray probes (from 1970), ultraviolet probes (from 1978) and infrared probes (1983). On April 25, 1990, the shuttle Atlantis placed the Hubble Space Telescope in orbit; it was designed to detect stars 50 times fainter than any visible from Earth.

In 1992, terrestrial optical telescopes took another leap forward with the completion on a Hawaiian peak of Keck-1, a 382 inch reflector composed of 36 hexagonal mirrors slotted together. An identical Keck-2 went on-line in May 1996. When electronically linked, these stretched the observable Universe to a range of about 14 billion light-years—80 trillion billion miles.

Radio astronomy

Radio telescopes, which detect radio waves emitted by the stars, peer farthest of all. In 1931, Czech-American engineer Karl Jansky traced interference on the transatlantic radio-phone link to the constellation Sagittarius. Although the first real radio telescope was built in the United States in 1937, it was the wartime development of radar that led to Britain pioneering radio astronomy. The first giant radio telescope—a steerable 250 foot dish antenna—was built at Jodrell Bank in England in 1957. Even greater detail was realized by British astronomer Martin Ryle, who linked receivers in series and compared their signals electronically. In 1977 the 27 dishes of an interferometer known as the Very Large Array, in New Mexico, formed the equivalent of a dish 16 ¾ miles in diameter; and in 1986, dishes in Australia and Japan were linked with one on a satellite to create a receiver more than 11,000 miles across. This device was capable of detecting celestial objects the rays of which had taken up to 20 billion years to reach Earth.

WHAT HALE COOKED UP

Crafting the 200 inch mirror of the Hale telescope has been described as the greatest single technological achievement of the first half of the 20th century. The glass was of the same type used to make heat-resistant cookware. Pouring it into the mold took 15 days, followed by prolonged, controlled cooling. This was done twice in 1934, and the second try was deemed satisfactory.

The 20 ton disc was transported very carefully across America, from Corning, New York, to Pasadena, California, by a freight train moving at a crawl. Grinding and polishing took a dozen more years, interrupted by the Second World War. After testing revealed a tiny deviation at one spot, more polishing rendered it flawless. The telescope was dedicated on June 3, 1948. Its performance was unmatched for 40 years.

STAR GAZER **The Hale telescope is rendered eerily transparent by rotating the dome and photographing it with a long time exposure. Stars' trails are seen in the background.**

1900 — 2000

1908 telescope at Mount Wilson, California

1937 First real radio telescope

1948 Giant telescope on Mount Palomar, California

1957 Jodrell Bank radio telescope

1990 Hubble Space Telescope placed in orbit
1992 Completion of Keck-1

... AND SEEING LESS

BREAKING THROUGH THE LIGHT BARRIER TO EXPLORE THE INNER UNIVERSE OF ATOMS

Microscopes had reached their natural limit by 1900, since an object much smaller than the wavelength of the light illuminating it cannot be imaged. To explore the depths of inner (as opposed to outer) space, therefore, a way had to be found past the light barrier, at about a hundred-millionth of an inch.

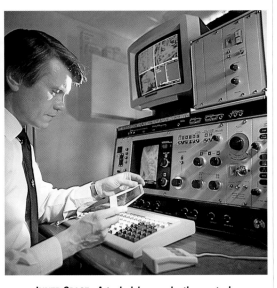

INNER SPACE A technician works the controls of a Hitachi scanning electron microscope.

In 1904, the German instrument makers Carl Zeiss took a lateral approach to the problem. Their Ultramicroscope illuminated particles from the side and, in this way, achieved better definition. Also in Germany, August Kohler proposed pushing back the barrier by using radiation of a shorter wavelength than visible light. The result in 1919 was an ultraviolet microscope that could magnify up to 2,500 times.

The electron microscope

By the 1920s, the Frenchman Louis de Broglie was arguing that a beam of electrons acted like light, but at a much shorter wavelength. This was confirmed experimentally in 1927, and the German physicist Hans Busch then devised a means of focusing the beam with a magnetic coil. The first electron microscope—with 12,000 powers of magnification—was built by Ernst Ruska in Berlin in 1931. Commercial manufacture of the first such microscopes began in Britain in 1935. These big machines, weighing as much as 7 tons, could be coaxed to magnify up to a million times, to distinguish individual molecules for the first time.

The object is introduced into a vacuum within the microscope, and then bombarded by a focused beam of high-energy electrons. As these electrons strike a fluorescent screen, the magnified image becomes visible —like a picture on television—or is recorded photographically. Some of these pictures are so perfect that they have a 3-D quality, capable of uncloaking the hidden universe to reveal a cancer cell skulking in its host, or the fiber-tangle in a nylon stocking.

Advances in the United States and Germany during the 1970s led to the first photograph of an individual atom. And then, in 1981, a major breakthrough opened the way for what had been previously been considered impossible: atom-by-atom exploration of matter. Invented in Zurich by Gerd Binnig and Heinrich Rohrer, the scanning tunnelling microscope (STM) was so sensitive that its fine-point probe registered, spaced, and measured each atom as a "bump" as it moved over the surface of a sample, amplifying it 100 million times.

The atomic force microscope, an STM refinement, was developed by Binnig in 1985. Viruses and DNA were among the first subjects of STM investigation. Research laboratories now launched an inner-space race in what was dubbed nanotechnology (from nanometer, a millionth of a meter).

THE ELECTROMAGNETIC SPECTRUM The human senses are oblivious to all but a tiny band in the mighty array of radiant energy. Radiation is classed according to its wavelength, or frequency.

MACHINES TOO TINY TO BE SEEN

Decades before microprocessors and super-microscopes had made the notion credible, an American physicist named Richard Feynman accurately envisioned the use of light—or electronics—to create circuits of atoms and infinitely tiny molecular devices.

His audience at the American Physical Society may have scoffed in 1959, but within 30 years most of his ideas had been realized. By 1990, a prototype microscopic electric motor—smaller than a human hair—had been developed, using the etching technique used in microchip manufacture. The following year, IBM researchers created a device, based on a single atom of xenon gas, which was theoretically capable of embedding the entire contents of the Library of Congress on one compact disc.

One long-term goal is to create robotic devices so small that they can enter the bloodstream to diagnose diseases and administer cures, or even to repair individual cells.

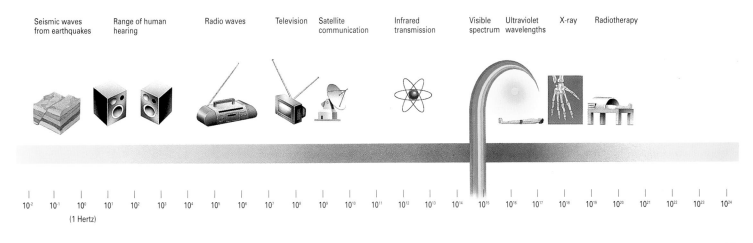

Seismic waves from earthquakes	Range of human hearing	Radio waves	Television	Satellite communication	Infrared transmission	Visible spectrum	Ultraviolet wavelengths	X-ray	Radiotherapy

10^{-2} 10^{-1} 10^{0} (1 Hertz) 10^{1} 10^{2} 10^{3} 10^{4} 10^{5} 10^{6} 10^{7} 10^{8} 10^{9} 10^{10} 10^{11} 10^{12} 10^{13} 10^{14} 10^{15} 10^{16} 10^{17} 10^{18} 10^{19} 10^{20} 10^{21} 10^{22} 10^{23} 10^{24}

1904 Ultramicroscope   1919 Ultraviolet microscope   1931 First electron microscope   1981 Scanning tunnelling microscope, or STM

MATERIAL CHANGE: METAL TO PLASTIC TO COMPOSITE

CLASSIFICATIONS BLUR AS MIXTURES WITH AMAZING PROPERTIES ARE CONJURED UP

The world of 1900 was robustly fashioned out of steel, wood, and stone. Aluminum was still a shiny novelty in search of applications; rubber was only beginning to find an industrial use, in the Dunlop tire; and the only significant plastic was brittle, inflammable Celluloid.

Working with metal

Turn-of-the-century metallurgists experimented with alloys to improve the temper, or hardness, of raw steel. In 1900, for example, American engineer Frederick Taylor added tungsten, chromium and vanadium to create a tool-steel that retained its hard cutting edge even when red hot.

In 1913, British manufacturer Harry Brearley found that rifle barrels made from steel that contained chromium did not rust. He encouraged a cutler to make knives from his alloy, and the stainless-steel industry was born. Aluminium, however, was naturally stainless and also light: ideal for the infant

"GEE WHIZ" — A MIRACLE

In April 1938, Du Pont researcher Roy Plunket was looking for a nontoxic cooling substance, or refrigerant, to use in air conditioners and refrigerators. He came up with a greasy white powder.

"Gee whiz, it's gone wrong!" he exclaimed, but brightened when the substance proved to be utterly inert – so stable that it was impervious to heat, electricity, or the most corrosive agents known. It was not until the 1960s that another of its amazing properties was exploited: it was the most slippery substance on Earth.

Plunket's powder was PTFE (polytetrafluoroethylene), better known by names such as Teflon. Popular fame came with the nonstick frying pan, while NASA used it to coat space suits, nose cones and heat shields. The electronics industry made it the perfect insulator for telephone and computer cables, and surgeons turned it to miraculous use in the form of thread and artificial veins and arteries.

aircraft industry if only it could be toughened. The solution came from Germany, where Alfred Wilm added pinches of copper and magnesium to create duraluminum, a high-strength alloy that would shape the future of aviation. Asbestos also found a major industrial use from 1916, when Italian pipe-makers found that a cement of the flaky mineral made a light, non-corrosive substitute for metal.

The plastics revolution

Although the first plastics (from the Greek word meaning "to shape") were derived from nature—in particular, cow's milk—plastic is more usually a man-made substance. What gives it its characteristic moldability is its composition of long chains of thousands of carbon atoms linked together. When scientists discovered this, they were able to duplicate the process and create scores of artificial plastics with properties beyond the limitations of nature. They were led by Leo Baekeland, son of a Belgian cobbler, who invented the first synthetic polymer—the forerunner of all modern plastics—in his home laboratory in Yonkers, New York. He wanted to call it oxybenzylmethyl-englycolanhydride, but opted for Bakelite. Moldable, durable, and resistant to heat and electricity, Bakelite was first produced in quantity in 1909.

In 1922, the German chemist Hermann Staudinger laid down a theoretical basis for the plastics industry by revealing how polymers, the giant molecules in the chains, could be created artificially by stringing together smaller molecules. This coincided with the realization that coal tars and petroleum were oozing with organic chemicals amenable to polymerization.

Synthetic substitutes for rubber—a natural polymer—were produced from 1927 onward. These included durable neoprene, which was created in 1931 by Wallace Carothers, the man who went on to invent nylon. New plastics now poured from the laboratories—polystyrene, polyvinylchloride

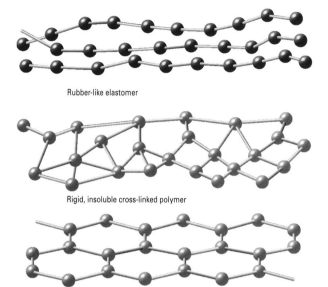

Rubber-like elastomer

Rigid, insoluble cross-linked polymer

Thermoplastic softens when heated

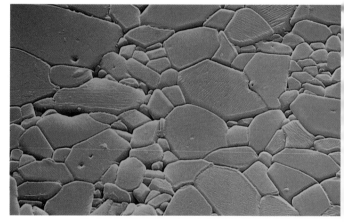

MATERIAL CREATION Plastic's secret lies in the way its molecules are bonded (top). Alumina seen in magnified cross-section (above) is hard and heat-resistant, yet moldable.

(PVC), acrylics such as Perspex and Plexiglass, polyesters, polyethylene, polyurethanes, epoxy resins, and silicones.

A composite world

Classifications blurred as metals, plastics and ceramics were combined to create composites, sharing the best qualities of their constituent materials. Spun or woven glass fiber was bonded with plastic resin to form Fiberglass. Carbon fibers were developed at Britain's Royal Aircraft Establishment in 1963; bonded in resins, they formed composites tougher than steel at a quarter the weight. Kevlar, a plastic fiber composite strong enough to stop a bullet, was developed by Du Pont researcher Stephanie Kwolek in 1965. And, from 1981, ceramic composites—silica fiber tiles—protected the Space Shuttle through fiery re-entry.

1900 ——————————————————————————————————————— 2000

1909 The first synthetic polymer
1913 Stainless steel developed
1931 Neoprene, a synthetic substitute for rubber
1938 Teflon discovered
1963 Carbon fiber developed
1965 Kevlar developed
1981 Silica fiber tiles

THE GLOBAL VILLAGE

THE INVENTIONS THAT FIRST CARRIED OUR VOICES ALONG WIRES OR TRANSMITTED THEM THROUGH THIN AIR HAVE CHANGED THE NATURE OF HUMAN COMMUNICATIONS—INDEED, OF THE WHOLE WAY WE CONDUCT OUR LIVES. BUT THEY WERE SIMPLY THE START OF A REVOLUTION BROUGHT ABOUT BY AN UNDERSTANDING OF ELECTROMAGNETIC RADIATION. BEAMED TO SATELLITES IN SPACE, DATA AND IDEAS CAN NOW BE RELAYED INSTANTLY AROUND THE WORLD.

RADIO RINGS THE WORLD

SETTING THE CENTURY ON COURSE WITH MUSIC AND VOICES CONJURED FROM THIN AIR

Over many years, many minds in many countries contributed to the invention of "wire-less telegraphy"—the harnessing of electromagnetic waves to radiate sound. But it was the untrained Guglielmo Marconi who put the finishing touches to their achievements. Pushed by his mother Annie, of the Jameson whiskey family, and encouraged (after his move from Italy to London) by the chief engineer at the British Post Office, Marconi proceeded by trial and error. At first, he used an electric spark generator, which was demonstrated by German physicist Heinrich Hertz in 1888, to transmit the radio waves and a "coherer," invented by Frenchman Edouard Branly, to detect the waves and turn them into an electric current. Marconi's refinements included a transmitter, which sent a sustained train of radio waves, all of the same wavelength, and a receiver tuned to this wavelength.

In 1901, a kite antenna hitched to a powerful generator was lofted over Cornwall in southwest England, and the first transatlantic signal

FAMILY FUN A 1920s advertisement stresses the warmth and intimacy to be had when listening to a "Radiola."

was sent by Morse code to an ecstatic Marconi in Newfoundland. But transmitting speech, rather than dots and dashes, was a different matter. A Canadian-born scientist, Reginald Fessenden, had achieved the first spoken words on the air in 1900, but the range was hardly a mile and more sophisticated equipment was obviously needed. Part of the solution was provided by one of Marconi's consultants, Dr. John Ambrose Fleming, who in 1904 invented the diode (a device with two electrodes) for picking up radio waves more clearly. On Christmas Eve of 1906, from a farm near Plymouth, Massachusetts, Fessenden made the first radio broadcast. Instead of using a sputtering electric spark machine for a transmitter, he used a whirring generator to produce radio waves that varied with the sound of his voice. As a demonstration, he sang, played the violin, recited from the Bible, and ended with a Christmas greeting to ships off the coast.

The Ambrose diode was superseded by the triode valve, patented in 1907 by American inventor Lee de Forest, whose addition of a third wire electrode created a precision amplifier sensitive to very subtle sonic vibrations. This was the key to future radar, television and computer development, and it led to an epic rights battle: in 1943, the U.S. Supreme Court would rule in favor of de Forest by declaring Fleming's American patent invalid. The enterprising de Forest made regular broadcasts from a studio in New

TUNING IN A demonstration from the inventor himself, Guglielmo Marconi, in a still from the first film about radio.

HIGH TECH This elegant receiver with complex antenna was designed to pick up short-wave transmissions from a distance. It was considered state of the art in 1925.

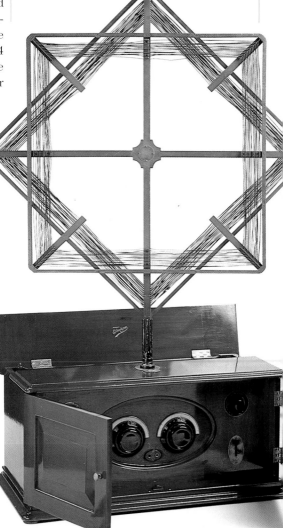

GUGLIELMO MARCONI: RADIO PIONEER

The pioneer of wireless telegraphy, Guglielmo Marconi, described to British radio how he received the first transatlantic radio transmission in St. John's, Newfoundland, on December 12, 1901: "Suddenly about half past twelve there sounded the sharp click of the tapper as it struck the coherer, showing me that something was coming and I listened intently. Unmistakably, the three sharp clicks corresponding to three dots sounded in my ear....The electric waves which had been sent out from Poldhu had travelled the Atlantic, serenely ignoring the curvature of the Earth which so many doubters considered would be a fatal obstacle, and they were now affecting my receiver in Newfoundland."

1900

1900 First words spoken on radio
1901 First transatlantic radio signal

1917 Armstrong's easily tuned
variable frequency receiver

1936 First commercial
use of VHF

1950

CRIME WAVES

The first criminal apprehended by radio? Dr. Crippen, the infamous wife-murderer. He and his mistress—disguised as a boy—fled from London in July 1910 aboard the liner *Montrose*. Suspicious, the captain wired a description to

Crippen and Leneve arrested wire later

his company, who alerted Scotland Yard. A chief inspector (his note shown above) was dispatched in pursuit aboard a faster ship, and Crippen was arrested when the *Montrose* docked, causing worldwide excitement and underlining the wonder of radio.

York in order to stimulate sales of his radio kits that amateurs (or "hams") could assemble themselves. In January 1910, he set up his equipment in the Metropolitan Opera House for the world's first outside broadcast: the great Caruso sang live to marvelling audiences gathered in the city's top hotels.

Family listening

The triode thermionic valve made receivers more sensitive and massively increased the range of radio communications. In 1924, for example, Marconi used a short-wave transmitter to make a spoken broadcast that was successfully picked up in Australia. The triode valve, incorporated into an easily tuned

POCKET SOUNDS The tubeless Regency TR-1, heralded the transistor revolution in 1954. The first "pocket" Sony radio followed within months.

receiver developed by American Edwin Armstrong, and the development of loudspeakers (which replaced earphones) facilitated the manufacture of radios for family listening. In the United States, the number of stations jumped from 60 to 600 between 1923 and 1925, and homes with radios soared to 60 percent in just ten years.

By the mid 1930s, Edwin Armstrong had perfected a technique called frequency modulation, which virtually eliminated 'static' interference from electric machinery and thundery weather. FM radio was born. VHF —Very High Frequency transmissions at shorter-than-short wavelengths—had been the subject of experiments by Marconi since the First World War; and a way of navigating by these beams was devised in Germany in 1934. VHF was put to commercial use with the first television transmissions in 1936.

Meanwhile, improvements in the microphone made broadcasters more mobile, but radios remained anchored by their bulk; even so-called portables were as big and as heavy as a packed suitcase. This changed spectacularly with the advent of transistor sets in the 1950s.

MATCH POINTS A sports commentator broadcasts from Frankfurt in 1931. Sports broadcasting evolved in tandem with the development of more mobile microphones.

1954 Launch of first transistor radio

1958 Experimental transmissions of stereophonic radio by BBC

THE WHOLE WORLD AT YOUR FINGERTIPS

THE NEW NETWORK THAT GIVES EVERYONE SOMETHING TO TALK ABOUT

In 1900, the telephone was a crude and insignificant instrument compared with the well-established telegraph. Lines strung between central exchange points and individual phones became as entangled as the switching process, and reception deteriorated over any distance. Calls were routed by operators plugging in the connections manually. Although a clumsy automatic switching method had been invented in 1889, it took a time for the system to become common.

In the United States, some 1.3 million phones were in use at the start of the century; by 1907 that number would increase fivefold. Bell System controlled most of the service—around 855,900 telephones in

PHONE HOME A "Railophone" call office, around 1910. The first British payphone was installed in a post office at the foot of Fleet Street, London, in 1906.

1900—but recognizing a golden opportunity, challengers sprouted up across the nation, and there were soon some 6,000 independent companies handling calls. It was not until the spread of trunk exchanges in the 1920s that dial phones became standard. Most phones were still of the "candlestick" type, with a separate receiver and mouthpiece, before the familiar cradle design took over in the 1930s.

The oceans continued to present a barrier, unsatisfactorily spanned by wireless radiophone links. A commercial transatlantic service was launched in 1928, but at $70 for a three-minute call—twice the average worker's weekly wage—it was a luxury that very few could afford. Any solution involving a transatlantic cable was impractical until the development of repeaters (to boost the electronic signals along the way) that were hardy enough to endure deep submersion. The first cable was laid in 1956 and it could carry only 36 calls at a time. By mid-century, a critical shortage of

MANUAL EXCHANGE Operators make the connections, top, in 1906. Even on this early cradle design from Berlin, above, callers had to wind a handle to speak to the operator.

1928 First commercial
transatlantic telephone
service

A SLOW START FOR THE TELEPHONE

It took many years for people to take the telephone seriously. This attitude dated from its conception, when Alexander Graham Bell beat rival inventor Elisha Gray to the patent office by two hours on March 7, 1876. Gray actually had the better device, but Bell's patent is generally regarded as the most profitable in the history of invention.

For many Americans, the telephone in its early years served more as a form of entertainment than as a means of communication. In rural areas, where kitchens housed makeshift switchboards and entire communities shared a single line, party-line calling was the norm. Said one farm-wife, when asked about her new phone: "Well, we liked it a lot at first... only spring work is coming on so heavy that we don't hardly have time to listen now."

operators was looming, particularly in North America where a quarter of a million operators were needed to put through long-distance calls. But communication technologies advanced even faster than phone use, with the result that by 1990 the number of operators was down by 93 percent, despite a 700 percent increase in phone traffic.

Europe lagged behind North America, where the Bell Telephone Company developed a faster, cheaper, and more reliable all-electronic exchange using computer circuitry. Bell began trials in 1960, and the world's first electronic exchange was operating in New Jersey by 1965. Twenty years later, the first steps were taken toward a digital system, with electronic touch phones gradually replacing dial phones. These developments prompted a plethora of new services, such as third-party "conference" calling, automatic call holding or transfer, and customized coding to eliminate the chore of dialling frequently-used numbers; it also enabled the simultaneous transmission of high-speed computer data.

Information technology

With the advent of microprocessors and integrated circuits, luxuries such as built-in answering machines and phones that can store numbers and dial them automatically (repertory dials) are now industry standard.

Perhaps the device with the broadest impact, however, has been the mobile cellular phone. Developed by Ericsson of Sweden and launched in 1979, the system uses palm-sized radiophones that transmit and receive calls to and from a local "cell"; the calls are then passed from cell to cell in a geographical network that covers a much wider area.

Between 1900 and 1997, the number of subscribers to cellular systems in the United States skyrocketed

from 5.2 million users to over 50 million. That number only promises to climb higher with the development of such technology as Motorola's Iridium system, which uses several dozen satellites to connect directly with the user's telephone, and promises service from anywhere on earth. So pervasive is this technology that now many theaters have rules banning people from bringing cell-phones to shows, so that their shrill, persistent ringing will not disrupt performances.

There remained the quest for visual contact between callers. Research has revolved around compressed-data digital transmission. In 1992, the Videophone 2500, which can transmit and receive a small picture over an ordinary phone line, went on sale.

DIRECT DIAL The cradle phone took over from the two-piece candlestick in the 1930s, and became the standard around which all models were designed for over 40 years.

TAKING THE MICKEY Touch-tone technology coincided with a new view on phone design in the 1980s. Mickey Mouse was just one of many characters to make a phone debut.

MOBILE MANIA The invention that became an obsession, the first cellular model was launched in 1979 by Ericsson in Sweden with the palm-sized radiophone.

1956 First transatlantic cable laid

1965 World's first electronic exchange

1979 Launch of first mobile cellular phone

EUREKA! THE PERILS OF INVENTING

YOU HAVE TO BE CREATIVE, YOU HAVE TO BE DETERMINED AND YOU HAVE TO GET THERE FIRST. THEN, STAND BACK—AND LET SOMEONE ELSE TAKE ALL THE GLORY

Inventors are popularly supposed to be crazy—and they have to be. They also have to be imbued with a sense of inquisitive wonder, doggedly persistent and optimistic, no matter how many disappointments they encounter. Few become rich or famous. Many more see their ideas exploited by others. According to one American estimate, around 25,000 ideas are stolen by unscrupulous marketing companies every year.

Often, inventors do not own their inventions. It is customary for employers to retain patenting rights over the achievements of their salaried researchers, who can hope only for a pat on the back and perhaps a bonus. The researcher responsible may not even get the credit, since this usually goes to the team leader. American Wallace Carothers is credited with the invention of nylon, but it was Dr. Julian Hill, a member of his team at the chemical company Du Pont, who achieved the breakthrough. Indeed, when Carothers came upon Hill with the peculiar, pliable material, he initially dismissed it as useless. But there is a twist in the tale. Carothers did not live to savor his success. He took his own life by drinking cyanide in April 1937, two days after his 41st birthday. Hill did not make his fortune, but he was treated well by Du Pont. "I was something better than a good scientist," Hill reflected before his death at the age of 91 in 1996. "I was lucky."

All successful inventors have to be lucky even to achieve any recognition. Eliot Sivovitch, an inventions specialist at the Smithsonian Institution in

PATENT PENDING One invention that never quite took off was the marine lifesaving apparatus, out of the water, left, and partly submerged, below.

Washington, operates by this golden rule: "Whenever you prove who was first, you will find someone else who was more first."

Every American knows that Thomas Edison invented the light bulb; the British counter that the honor belongs to Joseph Swan. In fact, more than two dozen inventors could claim to have had a hand. Only Edison had the drive and connections to develop complete lighting systems, so he seized most of the glory and the rewards.

Edison was unique in combining a fertile mind with business acumen. It was he who described genius as 1 percent inspiration and 99 percent perspiration. In Edison's case, though, the perspiration was not all his. He put scientists to work in virtually an inventions factory,

BACK TO THE FUTURE Eugene G. Higgins' outrageous plan for a skyscraper car park in the 1920s boasts some elements distinctly familiar to today's urban motorists.

and reaped the benefit of their labors. One of his scientists was the eccentric Croatian inventor, Nikola Tesla, who pioneered fluorescent lighting, AC power, and radio control. Ahead of Marconi, he had a grandiose scheme for a worldwide wireless system that was also to link the world's telephone exchanges and provide global navigation; he even conceived of a plan to transmit power by wireless. But he could not find backers and died penniless.

Tesla held hundreds of patents, but, as Edison pointed out, they often cost more to take out than they return in royalties. A patent is only a temporary monopoly granted by a country —there is no such thing as a world patent—which confers ownership of an invention for a maximum of 20 years. It can be bought, sold, licensed or hired, but it is not cast-iron protection. Inventors have to guard their rights with no government help. The situation is particularly fraught in the United States, where well over 100,000 patents are granted annually.

John Logie Baird, a loner-loser in the development of television, ruefully advised other inventors: "Sell for cash." Ronald Hickman, a successful British loner, found a more satisfying solution after accidentally sawing through a chair and becoming inspired to invent the Workmate folding workbench. He licensed it to Black & Decker, a major manufacturer with the assets and resolve to support the defense of his patent. Hickman's reward included a luxury Channel Islands home in which he set up a museum filled with illegal imitations of his creation, all successfully contested; they included one marketed by a major American retailer who had turned down the Workmate!

Many inventors invent for the sheer joy or compulsion of it, and some delight in devising the ridiculous. Kenji Kawakami is Japan's most celebrated mad inventor. His many creations include the shoe-umbrella and a twirling spaghetti fork with built-in cooling fan. Bizarre American patents range from the motorized bar stool to the musical condom, which, upon contact, breaks into a rousing rendition of the Hallelujah Chorus. There is even a professional hoax-inventor. Joey Skaggs has spent three

ON THE RIGHT TRACK One of the few inventors ever to make money from a creation was Percy Shaw, who designed cat's-eye road reflectors in 1934.

HEAD BANGERS In 1920, there were patent applications for a personal cover umbrella substitute and a helmet combined with gun/saucepan.

decades fooling Americans with such "inventions" as Dog Meat Soup, advanced as a nutritious solution to the stray-dog problem. In 1995, under the alias Dr. Joseph Bonusco, he duped scientific journals with Solomon, a computer program said to give infallible judgments in criminal cases. Skaggs makes his living by lecturing.

SATELLITES CIRCLE THE GLOBE

LINKING TOGETHER THE WHOLE OF MANKIND THROUGH COMMUNICATIONS IN SPACE

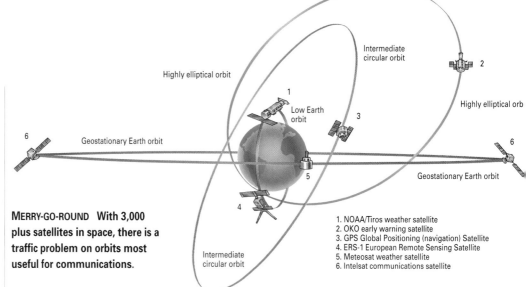

MERRY-GO-ROUND With 3,000 plus satellites in space, there is a traffic problem on orbits most useful for communications.

1. NOAA/Tiros weather satellite
2. OKO early warning satellite
3. GPS Global Positioning (navigation) Satellite
4. ERS-1 European Remote Sensing Satellite
5. Meteosat weather satellite
6. Intelsat communications satellite

In 1956, Britain's Astronomer Royal declared that "space travel is utter bilge." The following year, however, the beep, beep, beep of Sputnik 1 silenced the skeptics and startled the world into a realization of the potential of space communications.

Electronics evolved at the same time as rocket technology, resulting in rapid advances. By 1958, the tiny U.S. satellite Vanguard I

WHERE WERE YOU?

The first epoch-making event that drew the world together through satellite coverage was the assassination and then the funeral of President Kennedy, relayed by Telstar in November 1963.

was gathering and relaying data by means of a radio powered by solar cells; and that Christmas, the recorded voice of President Eisenhower transmitted greetings to control stations around the Earth from a satellite called SCORE (Signal Communication by Orbital Relay Equipment).

Communications satellites

Echo I, the first experimental communications satellite, was launched on August 12, 1960— a shiny balloon made of tough plastic coated with aluminum. In space, where it could be seen from the ground as a speeding spot of light, it inflated to a diameter of 100 feet and reflected back radio signals beamed from Earth. Focusing a beam on the balloon was a hit-and-miss affair, and the strength of the return signal was very weak. Nevertheless, Echo achieved its purpose by relaying sound and picture images from the United States to Europe.

Echo demonstrated the need for on-board amplification; and that October, the U.S. army lofted Courier 1B, a quarter-ton satellite loaded with more

than 19,000 solar cells to control the craft and boost signals. Courier fell silent after 18 days, but two more years of electronic and antenna development culminated on July 10, 1962, in the launch of Telstar, at 172 pounds and just 32 inches in diameter, a midget compared with Courier. Telstar was activated by the press of a red button in Andover, Maine, and for the first time the phrase "Live via satellite" flashed across television screens.

Telstar's capacity was limited to 60 simultaneous telephone calls or one television transmission, and its elliptical orbit allowed it to operate for only 20 minutes every $2\frac{1}{2}$ hours. But it so captured public imagination that it inspired a runaway pop music hit, "Telstar." Relay I, built by RCA, added color to the TV signal in 1963 but was similarly limited in capacity.

For more effective communications, a satellite had to be placed in an orbit so perfectly synchronized with the Earth's rotation that it became "geosta-

tionary," hovering permanently over one spot. The spinning synchronous satellite, invented by a Hughes Aircraft team led by Howard Rosen and launched experimentally in 1963, provided the solution. Syncom I exploded after launch, but Syncom II and III performed perfectly in relaying a continuous flow of signals from 22,300 miles in space.

The Syncom series was followed by Early Bird, which was launched into orbit over the coast of Brazil in April 1965 and became operational from June 28 as the world's first commercial communications satellite. It relayed 240 simultaneous phone calls or one color television channel, and established the first constant satellite link between North America and Europe. Early Bird's last task was to carry pictures of the first manned Moon landing in July 1969. By then it was known as Intelsat I, an already antiquated first link in an international communications

LIFT OFF Echo I, left, poised atop a rocket in 1960. Some 22 years later, communications satellites such as this Canadian Anik, below, were being dispatched by space shuttle.

POLE-TO-POLE The Landsat series of satellites undertook a detailed survey of the Earth. This view is of New York's Long Island and the Connecticut coast.

system. More advanced Intelsats, positioned in a globe-girdling arc over the Atlantic, Pacific, and Indian oceans, were succeeded by series after series of increasing capacity. By 1986, each Intelsat VI satellite carried 33,000 phone calls and up to 60 television channels, on beams that could be directed to individual Earth stations.

Direct broadcasting by satellite
The first step toward direct satellite transmission into people's homes, rather than via a ground station, was taken in 1974 with the launch from Cape Canaveral in Florida of ATS-6, a satellite carrying a powerful relay signal. First used to link remote communities in the United States, it was later moved to a position over East Africa to transmit to India.

In 1979 Canada's Anik B inaugurated the world's first television service beamed directly to home sets equipped with a small rooftop dish antenna. Europe soon embarked on its own satellite program. In the 1980s, the European Space Agency orbited a regional communications system. The Japanese, meanwhile, built JACSAT, which had the greatest capacity of any communications satellite outside the United States. Satellite technology was by now accessible enough for private enterprise to compete with governments; and by the 1990s, more than 200 satellites were orbiting the world.

THE NERVOUS SYSTEM OF MANKIND

The idea of the communications satellite was conceived in 1945 by science-fiction writer Arthur C. Clarke, author of *2001: A Space Odyssey*. Clarke described to readers of *Wireless World* how radio signals beamed into space might be bounced back to ground stations thousands of miles from the original transmitter. He also envisioned the geostationary satellite and accurately calculated the orbital height. Clarke called his concept "the nervous system of mankind . . . which will link together the whole human race, for better or worse, in a unity which no earlier age could have imagined."

PREDICTING THE WEATHER

Before the launch of the first experimental weather satellite, Tiros I, on April 1, 1960, high-altitude balloons and radioed reports from ships at sea had been the most hi-tech resources used by weather forecasters.

By the mid-1990s, because of refinements in technology, the unpredictable landfall of a hurricane could be anticipated within 100 miles, four times the accuracy of the 1970s. As a result, when the monster storm called Hurricane Andrew hit southern Florida in 1992, there was sufficient time to evacuate 1.5 million people, and only 13 lives were lost.

SPACE WATCH A satellite image of Hurricane Andrew travelling at 140 mph over the Gulf of Mexico on August 25, 1992, before it hit the coast of southern Florida.

1962 Launch of Telstar 1965 Launch of Early Bird, the first commercial communications satellite 1979 First direct broadcasting by satellite

THE INFORMATION SUPERHIGHWAY: FROM "SNAIL MAIL" TO E-MAIL

FAST-TRACKING THE MAIL—THEN ELIMINATING THE NEED FOR IT ALTOGETHER

Throughout the century, the mailman has remained a plodding island of continuity, somehow adrift from the century's technological swirl. Behind the scenes, however, as the mail sacks bulged bigger, the Post Office has been trying to contend with ever-increasing volumes of mail.

To expedite delivery, many countries turned to alternative transportation. In 1899, the first motorized mail collection took place in Cleveland, Ohio, using a Winton truck, covering 22

DELIVERY NOTES In the early years, mail was the prime form of communication in developed countries. Above, in France in 1914, and below, in Kent, England, in 1910.

miles of streets. In 1918, the U.S. Post Office began airmail service, at first using government planes and pilots, but soon contracting the work out to private operators. The job was not for the faint of heart. The planes had primitive navigational equipment, and the cockpits were cramped, cold, and noisy; 31 of the first 40 pilots on the New York to Chicago run died in crashes. But the pay was good—salaries reached $1000 a month—and flying had enough mystique to attract a steady stream of willing adventurers, including a young Charles Lindbergh, who flew the St. Louis-Chicago route.

A sense of mail order

By the 1960s, mechanized sorting seemed the only way

MAIL RAIL The underground train that sped mail under London streets to avoid the congestion above in 1926 is still in use today and making the same sort of time savings.

to solve what was now a worldwide problem. The invention of postal codes or zip codes created a sense of order and made automation possible. The first automated central post office opened in Rhode Island in 1960. It handled both letters and parcels; zip codes were read by an electronic eye and sorted into the appropriate bin.

AUTOMATIC SORTING Officials in Orléans, France, examine an early letter-processing system that reads addresses and consigns mail by region and district.

1918 U.S. Post Office begins Airmail service.

1926 Mail Rail underground system introduced in London

FORTUITOUS FALLOUT

The Internet is actually a lucky consequence of American fears of atomic war. Its genesis lies in the Advanced Research Project Agency Network or ARPANET, a computer network set up by the U.S. Defense Department that was specifically designed without fixed routes so that it could keep functioning after a nuclear attack.

With the threat diminished, the National Science Foundation was able to link its NSFnet network into ARPANET in the mid-1980s to give universities access to America's supercomputers. This released the genie and the Internet was born.

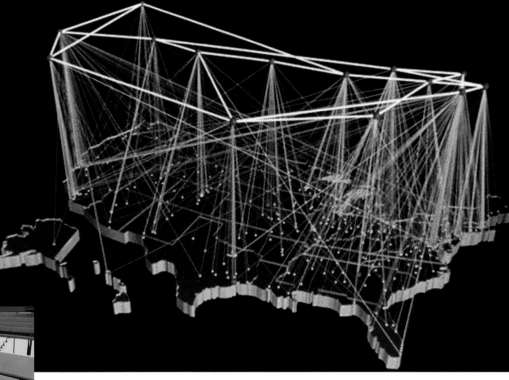

By the 1990s, optical character readers equipped with bar-coders could fast-track 11 envelopes per second in a fully automatic process 20 times faster than hand-sorting. In 1998, in fact, the Postal Service's 700,000 employees sorted through more than 190 billion pieces of mail, more than 41 percent of the world total.

Looking to the electronic future

The easier solution of abandoning addresses in favor of personalized codes was opposed for sociological reasons—people prized their sense of home. However, such a development was already taking place with the emergence of electronic mail, or e-mail.

Using a home computer, modem, and a coded address, millions of people were log-ging onto the Internet, a free global communications network. Instant correspondence could be anyone's for the cost of a local phone call—and yet this all happened by chance. In the mid-1980s, a group of San Franciscans interested in organic gardening and computer games found an easy way to make use of a computer network originally created for defence purposes. They set up a Bulletin Board System (BBS) by which they could exchange tips or chat over their computers. They called it WELL as a sort of acroynm for Whole Earth 'Lectronic Link.

BBSs blossomed across the world: CIX was one of the first in Britain and TWIX in Japan. The Internet's open structure made it impossible to track the expansion, but by 1994 there were an estimated 30,000 sub-networks interlaced within it, exchanging pictures and video clips, as well as text.

Along with electronic mail, innumerable specialized topics were the focus of comput-er linked "newsgroups." Other sub-networks, such as the World Wide Web (WWW),

DATA SURFING The Internet network in the United States, where it all started, top. The World Wide Web consists of over 10,000 host computers around the globe, left. Icons associated with sending e-mail, above.

included sophisticated information search and retrieval systems. By 1998, over 50 million individuals were using the Internet and the future was seen as one of information "superhighways" in which telephone, television, and computer merged in a world of limitless access and exchange.

AN OVERNIGHT SUCCESS

In 1973, the era of international 24 hour package delivery dawned through the enterprise of Yale graduate, Frederick Smith, son of the founder of a major bus company, Dixie Greyhound. Smith invested all he had and raised $72 million more to acquire 33 Dessault Falcon executive jets, each able to carry 7,500 pounds of mail. To win customers, he set a flat rate of $5 for as much as could be stuffed into a simple manila envelope. He called the mail service Federal Express.

THE PUBLISHING EXPLOSION

ELECTRONICS TAKE A LEADEN PROCESS FROM HOT METAL TO COMPUTER TERMINAL

A HOT ISSUE Linotype operators casting lines of type for a metal mold, below, have bowed out to editorial teams directly inputting their own copy on computer, right.

Technology had kept pace with the spread of literacy in the 19th century through the development of the rotary press, which speeded up the printing process. And by 1900, the labor of assembling type by hand was already giving way in favor of the keyboard-controlled casting process of machines such as the Linotype and Monotype, which partly automated newspaper and book production.

The reproduction of photographs using a screened etching process known as half-tone had been perfected by Americans Max and Louis Levy in the 1880s, and as early as 1873, the *New York Daily Graphic* had featured hazy news pic-

READ. . . AND SEE. . . ALL ABOUT IT! Lurid murder trials like that of Harry Thaw, convicted in 1906 of killing architect Stanford White for having an affair with his wife, showgirl Evelyn Nesbit, kept readers buying newspapers with photos of the principals.

tures on its pages. High quality picture reproduction finally became feasible when photogravure—the process of printing from a metal plate on which a photograph has been engraved—was adapted for rotary presses. The process was ideal for magazines but too slow for the daily press.

More significant was the invention of offset printing by Ira Rubel in New York in 1904. This advance on the century-old art of lithography came to Rubel by chance, when he noticed how a rubber pad could transfer the image from the inked printing plate onto paper—and produce a superior impression. A zinc printing plate, from which the image was transferred, or offset, onto an intermediate surface—a rubber-blanketed cylinder—and then rolled onto the paper, made the process even faster and cheaper. Color reproduction also

became more practical in the first decade of the century, through an adaptation of the halftone process which combined three tones—crimson, yellow and a greenish-blue—to create an effective full-color image. Books became brighter, and sales of picture-postcards boomed.

Typesetting transformed

While printing became ever speedier and cheaper, the making of the master impression remained a cumbersome craft, involving the manipulation of clumps of metal castings in page "forms." A means of improving this process had been conceived in the 1890s, but it took decades to become a reality.

The origins of photocomposition—typesetting by photography—can be traced to Hungary, but the first practical phototypesetter was developed in 1939 by American William Heubner who came up with a machine that projected characters onto film at the tap of a key. A pair of Frenchmen, Louis Moyroud and René Higonnet, took the process further with a method of projecting light through a spinning disc of type onto photosensitive material. They obtained financial backing in the United States, and the result in 1954 was the Photon series, capable of setting close to 1,000 characters a minute. A Penguin paperback, photoset in England in 1957, marked the first application of the process in book publishing.

Photocomposition systems proliferated rapidly, greatly speeding the printing process and stimulating the switch to offset. The introduction of fast web-fed offset presses, which print onto reels rather than individual sheets of paper, prompted newspapers to go offset from the 1960s. By this time, offset was firmly established as the most common form of printing.

Electronic publishing

Publishing next underwent an electronic transformation. In 1947 the Fairchild Corporation in the United States introduced the first electronic scanning device—a photoelectric beam scanned an illustration placed in a spinning drum, and sent signals to a cutter that engraved a copy of the image on the printing surface. Typesetting went electronic in the 1960s with the introduction of cathode-ray tubes and magnetic tape storage. The first computer-controlled system, Digiset, was a German invention. Its characters, stored in a computer's electronic memory, were displayed on a screen at the tap of a keyboard and projected onto photographic paper. Any number of video terminals could be linked to a single computer in this way.

By 1970, well over a thousand computerized composition systems were operating around the world. Then, the 1980s saw a further revolution, as computer technology

OFF THE PRESS Color reproduction with an electronic scanner, far right; a high-speed press, right; and a newspaper printing plant —the *Financial Times* in London, below.

rendered some traditional printing works redundant. The era of what was dubbed "desktop publishing"—fought for so long by the printing trade unions—dawned in 1982 with the launch of Postscript, the first software program specifically designed to manage an all-electronic printing process. Image-setters could now electronically integrate illustration with text.

In 1985, desktop publishing became a literal reality with the launch of PageMaker, the first software package developed for a personal computer. Even authors became a part of the integrated publishing process; by abandoning their typewriters for computers and presenting their text in disc form, they were in effect setting their own type. The

computerization of the gathering, transmission and assembly of words and pictures enabled newspapers to remain competitive in a communications race now functioning at the speed of light. Armed with a laptop, a digital camera, and a phone, reporters and photographers under fire in a war zone could, by the mid-1990s, transmit words and images around the world to newsdesks, with the subsequent editing and page layout performed electronically on computer screens.

In fact, until the presses roll, a newspaper's content need never exist on paper—but simply as a series of electronic impulses bounced between computer terminals. How long, people wondered, before the presses themselves became obsolete?

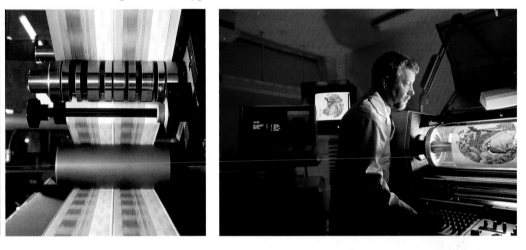

HIGHWAYS OF LIGHT

COMMUNICATION BY OPTIC FIBERS: BILLIONS OF BITS OF INFORMATION PER SECOND

Light was the earliest form of long-distance communication and by the late 20th century it was undoubtedly the best—pulsing billions of bits of information per second along tiny highways of glass.

The ancients had depended upon good weather for their bonfires and waved torches to signal messages. To be more useful, however, light had to be trapped and funnelled. The first breakthrough came in 1955, when Dr. Narinder Kapany, an Indian researcher

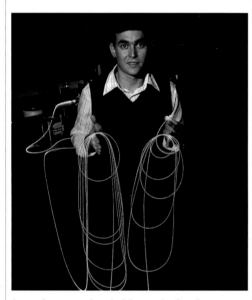

LIGHT SUPPORT A technician at the Corning Laboratories holds fiber-optic coils used in telecommunications applications.

at Imperial College in London, England, drew out filaments of optical glass until they were as thin as a human hair. When he shone a light down one end, it emerged intact from the other end, no matter how twisted or looped the strand.

Kapany's wispy light guides, or optic fibers, found their first use in medicine. Bundled together, they were, by 1958, being used by surgeons to examine the stomach. The breakthrough into telecommunications —made possible by the concurrent invention of the laser, the ideal signal carrier—began in 1966. That year, a pair of British scientists demonstrated that, by removing all impurities from the glass, existing electric cables could be replaced by interference-immune cables of optic fibers with infinitely greater carrying capacities.

Optical cables

Experimental optical cables were being laid in the United States and Britain by 1977. That year, the first TV signals were transmitted over optic cable by Bell Laboratories in the United States, and Bell Telephone installed its first commercial system in the heart of Chicago; the system carried video signals and computer data as well as telephone calls, all on pulses of light. Europe's first optic telephone link was established between two towns in southeast England, 8 miles apart. And in 1978, all homes in the little Canadian town of Elie, Manitoba, were fiber-webbed to integrate a full range of services, including multiple television channels, high-fidelity radio, the telephone and a computerized weather forecast. The first transatlantic optic cable was operating by 1988; it carried up to 40,000 telephone calls simultaneously on two fibers in either direction. The Pacific was fiber-cabled in 1989.

Nevertheless, the need for electronic boosting still limited the potential for optic communication suggested by Bell Lab experiments in 1985, which achieved the equivalent of 300,000 simultaneous telephone conversations over a single fiber. Bent upon an all-optical transmission system of limitless capacity, researchers studied the phenomenon that causes ocean waves to travel vast distances without losing their shape. Scientists at Bell created this effect in fiber cables and, using periodic laser "boost-pumps," they were optically transmitting signals more than 7,000 miles by the end of the 1980s. By 1991, experimental transmissions reached speeds of 32 billion bits of information per second—more than a dozen

ANOTHER FIRST FOR BELL

Alexander Graham Bell did not regard the telephone as his greatest invention, but was most proud, instead, of his "photophone," the first device to transmit voice by light. The caller spoke into a horn attached to a mirrored disc, which reflected light through a lens aimed at a receiving dish more than 200 yards away. As the voice caused the disc to vibrate, the intensity of the light beam fluctuated, altering the resistance of a photoconductive selenium cell at the center of the dish. The selenium was wired to a battery and a set of headphones, which vibrated in tune with the fluctuations, thereby reproducing the voice. Bell demonstrated the photophone on April 26, 1880, but for all his enthusiasm, the technology did not yet exist to make his invention more than a curiosity.

Almost 80 years later, the laboratory that carried Bell's name turned his vision into reality by participating in the development of the laser and fibre optics. By a curious coincidence, the core idea behind the laser had come to inventor Charles Townes on a spring morning in 1951, while he was sitting on a park bench directly facing Bell's former home.

times faster than existing telecommunications. Information "superhighways," accommodating the likes of interactive 2,000-channel high-definition television and cheap, clear, video phone calling, were, by 1999, all in the making.

MESSAGES OF LIGHT Optical fibers come in two types: single-mode conductors and multi-mode conductors. With a single-mode conductor, the narrow core enables the pulse of light to travel more directly at speed. This makes it suitable for long distances. With multi-mode conductors, a wider cable means that the pulse can travel along different paths—so slowing it down. It is less expensive to produce and is used over short distances.

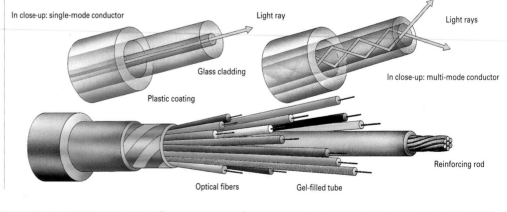

In close-up: single-mode conductor

Light ray

Light rays

Glass cladding

In close-up: multi-mode conductor

Plastic coating

Reinforcing rod

Optical fibers

Gel-filled tube

1955 First practical application of fiber optics

1966 Use of optical fibers for carrying telephone calls demonstrated

1977 A telephone system in Chicago uses fiber optics

1988 First transatlantic optic cable in operation

BREAKTHROUGHS IN MEDICINE

IN THE LATE 19TH CENTURY, MANY DOCTORS ADMITTED THAT NATURE, LEFT TO HER OWN DEVICES, WAS FAR MORE EFFECTIVE THAN MEDICINE. ONLY IN THE 20TH CENTURY, AS MEDICAL SCIENCE ENTERED AN AGE OF ACHIEVEMENT, DID RESEARCH INTO THE ROOT CAUSES OF DISEASE LEAD TO BETTER UNDERSTANDING; AND NEW MACHINES ALLOWED DOCTORS TO RECORD WHAT WAS HAPPENING INSIDE THE BODY.

AIDS TO DIAGNOSIS

THE CHANCE DISCOVERY OF X-RAYS AND THE WONDERS THAT FOLLOWED

For almost all of human history, accurate diagnosis of disease has been impossible. The ancient, rather rough-and-ready techniques of physical examination—feeling, listening, tapping, pressing—were first refined by measurement in the 17th century, when doctors began to use pendulums and thermometers to record the pulse rate and temperature. In 1896, they also acquired the familiar rubber cuff that measures blood pressure. Then, from the beginning of the 20th century, technology increasingly made possible a deeper level of understanding, at last allowing doctors to identify and quantify illnesses—or at least some of them.

X-ray vision

Some of the most influential diagnostic devices have come from a chance discovery made in Germany in 1895 by a professor of physics, Wilhelm Roentgen. Tinkering in a laboratory one evening with a cathode-ray

PICTURE THE SCENE One of Roentgen's first X-rays was of his wife's hand, 1896, below. An army surgeon takes a "Roentgen ray" photo of a soldier's thigh in 1916, right.

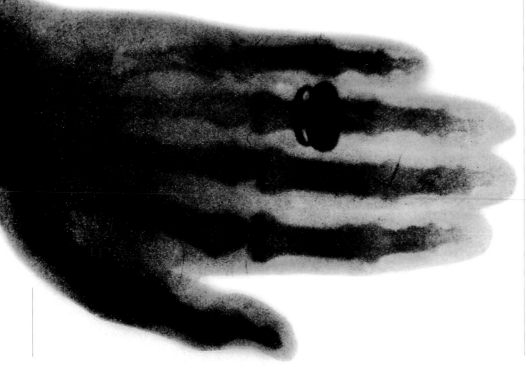

tube and a fluorescent screen, he discovered how to produce a new type of radiation. Once he realized that these X-rays, as he called them ("X" meaning unknown), could be used to view human bones, the discovery was to result in a medical revolution.

Over the next half a century, X-rays were routinely used to "photograph" just about anything in the human body. Even shoe shops boasted their own versions of the machines. It wasn't until the late 1950s that it became clear that X-rays—like other forms of radiation—could cause cancer, and that there needed to be more prudence in their use. At the same time, these negative effects of radiation were being put to positive use in treating cancers, in the new form of medicine known as radiotherapy.

Further refinements followed. In the late 1960s, G.N. Hounsfield at the electrical company EMI developed a technique for scanning the inside of the body. Known as computerized

axial tomography (CAT), the technique uses tightly focused X-rays taken in slices through the body—which are then integrated to form a three-dimensional image of a specific organ.

Electrical impulses

The heart, however, could not be monitored accurately by X-ray, because it consists of soft tissue only. To understand its workings, doctors harnessed another force, electricity.

The first major breakthrough came in 1903 when the Dutch physiologist Willem Einthoven invented a "string galvanometer" to record the electrical impulses produced by the heart. It worked by carrying the feeble electrical impulses in the arms and legs to a quartz fiber—the string—set in a magnetic

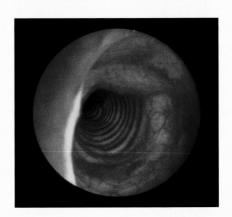

INTERIOR DESIGN An image of a human trachea or windpipe, the airway connecting the throat and lungs, is taken with a bronchoscope (a type of endoscope).

For some medical conditions, such as stomach ulcers, observation of the affected area was not without its problems. Endoscopes (tubes) inserted into the throat and anus had long been used for direct internal viewing, but the procedure was difficult and painful. The development of fiber optics—flexible glass tubes that carry light—made it possible to use endoscopes to see much farther inside the body, with far less difficulty for doctor or patient.

In 1965, Professor Harold Hopkins, of Reading University in England, used wafer-thin glass-fibre endoscopes as lenses, which both delivered light and relayed the scene back to the observer. Such fibers have made internal examination almost routine.

1901 Wilhelm Roentgen wins Nobel prize for physics with his discovery of X-rays

1924 Willem Einthoven wins Nobel prize with his electrocardiograph

1929 Hans Berger invents EEG

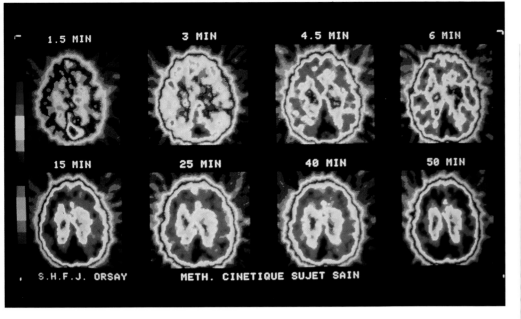

1.5 MIN   3 MIN   4.5 MIN   6 MIN

15 MIN   25 MIN   40 MIN   50 MIN

S.H.F.J. ORSAY   METH. CINETIQUE SUJET SAIN

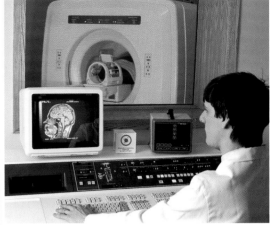

MIND AND MATTER A radiographer monitors the progress of a man undergoing an MRI scan, above. A series of eight PET scans of axial sections through a human brain, left.

field. The string vibrated in response to the impulses, and its movements were captured on a moving glass photographic plate.

Einthoven's 600 pound machine, the prototype of today's electrocardiograph, revealed that each heartbeat produces five main electrical pulses, which can provide an astonishingly detailed portrait of the heart, pinpointing any irregularity. He went on, with Horace Darwin, younger son of Charles, to produce a portable version, which could record the data on paper.

Electricity was also the basis for a new means of understanding the brain, pioneered by the German psychologist, Hans Berger, with his electroencephalograph (EEG) device in 1929. Tracing out the minute, shaky impulses produced by the brain and recorded by electrodes on the skull, the EEG revealed that the normal brain has several distinct states—excited, relaxed, drowsy, dreaming asleep, deeply asleep, in coma— and that the waves are produced by different areas of the brain. Moreover, different people have different patterns of brainwaves. Once these variations were understood, the EEG proved invaluable in diagnosis.

Scanning—the options

Massive investment in technological advances during the Second World War led to several breakthroughs in diagnostic equipment. One grew out of the new awareness of limiting X-rays, especially on pregnant women. Fortunately, a wartime device was ripe for medical use: asdic, the sound-echo machine used to detect submarines. In the late 1950s, it struck Ian Donald, Professor of Midwifery

at Glasgow University, that if sonar could tell the position and shape of a submarine, and show the image on a screen, it could also "see" a fetus. After showing that different tumors gave off different echoes, Donald turned his attention to pregnant women.

With computer enhancement that turned the echoes into visual images, the technique became a routine way to monitor all aspects of pregnancy. Innumerable women have now had the extraordinary experience of seeing a blurry image of their unborn child on an ultrasound scan.

Other diagnostic techniques evolved with fantastic speed in the postwar decades. The three-dimensional images produced by CAT scanning inspired a new technique which was particularly useful for examining the brain. Referred to as PET (positron emission tomography), it involves the patient swallowing doses of mildly radioactive glucose, which are absorbed in varying amounts by

different organs. The chemical's positive electrons react with the body's negative electrons, causing a release of gamma rays which are analyzed by computer. Glucose is vital to brain function, and is used up faster by more active areas of the brain. Monitoring its absorption reveals the brain at work, and identifies areas of disorder more accurately than the EEG.

The late 1970s also saw the emergence of nuclear magnetic resonance imaging (NMR or MRI), a highly sophisticated system that uses a powerful electromagnet to create temporary changes in the constituent atoms in the body. These changes are then analyzed and used to generate three-dimensional images of the internal organs. Unlike the CAT scanner, it does not depend on radiation. It is particularly good at recording biochemical processes, making it ideal for monitoring diseases such as muscular dystrophy and operations involving transplants.

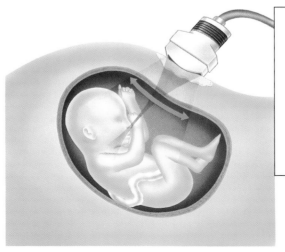

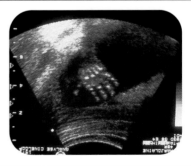

LIFE BEFORE BIRTH During prenatal ultrasound scanning, a transducer passed across the abdomen transmits images of the fetus to a monitor.

1952 Ultrasound first used on a human heart

1972 CAT scanner developed by Sir Godfrey Newbold Hounsfield in Britain

THE CUTTING EDGE

SURGERY ADVANCES FROM PATCH AND STITCH TO OPERATING DIRECTLY ON THE HUMAN HEART

In surgery, the First World War brought revolution. Out went traditional attitudes perpetrated by a hidebound, self-important surgical hierarchy. In came young, ambitious surgeons determined to heal fearful wounds, infection and pain, and do so as gently as possible. New attitudes were aided by rapid technological advances, which paralleled improvements in anesthetics and drugs. Soon after the Second World War, new inventions allowed surgeons to heal massive wounds—even rejoin severed limbs—and to operate directly on the human heart.

Heart surgery

Until the 20th century, the heart was as much a symbol as an object—the seat of anguish and joy, but not an organ that could be examined, treated or surgically repaired.

All that changed quite suddenly in 1940, with the development of cardiac catheterization—the insertion of a tube, via a needle, directly into the heart along a vein. This technique developed from an experiment conducted by a dedicated young German doctor, Werner Forssmann, in 1929. His work was taken up by two Americans, Andre Cournand and Dickinson Richards, who started by experimenting on animals. Their first heart catheterization on a human patient took place in 1940, in what proved to be a safe and painless operation.

Heart surgery took a great leap forward as a result. Surgeons could now measure how much blood the heart pumped, and the amount of pressure used. This meant they could compare normal hearts with diseased ones—those with narrowed passages and abnormal links between the chambers—and consider how to set about repairing them.

But repair meant operating on the exposed heart. How to isolate it? Would the heart stop beating? If so, would it restart? In 1931, American Doctor John Gibbon had devised a solution. It should be possible, he thought, to divert the bloodstream through a machine that would pump it around the body and replace the lung, extracting carbon dioxide and injecting oxygen. The quiescent heart could then be operated on.

However, it was not until after another 22 years of lonely experimenting that Gibbon finally had his machine. In 1953, after several successful operations on dogs, the doctor and his team were ready for their first human patient. On May 6, in Jefferson

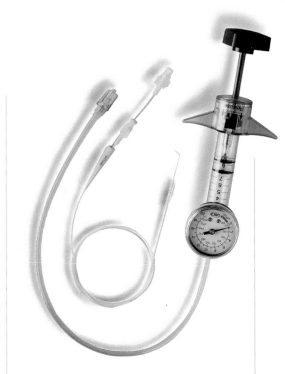

HEART SICK A mini profile balloon dilation cardiac catheter is used to gently inflate constricted arteries.

College Hospital, Philadelphia, they operated on an 18-year-old girl with a hole in her heart. For 26 minutes, she was kept alive with her blood circulating through Gibbon's machine, while he sewed up the hole. She

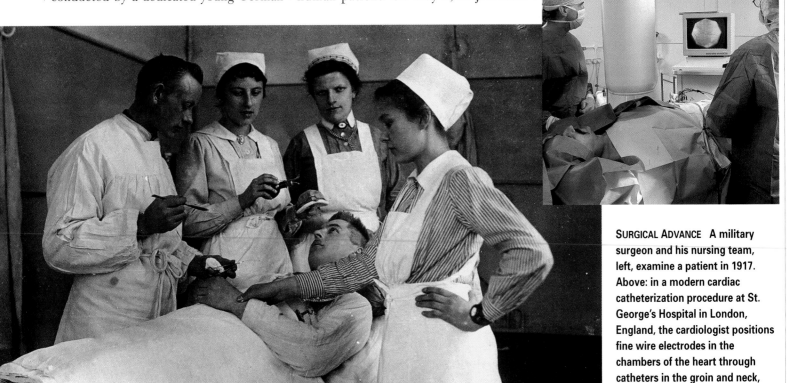

SURGICAL ADVANCE A military surgeon and his nursing team, left, examine a patient in 1917. Above: in a modern cardiac catheterization procedure at St. George's Hospital in London, England, the cardiologist positions fine wire electrodes in the chambers of the heart through catheters in the groin and neck, guided by the monitor.

1921 Microscope used in ear operation

1929 Werner Forssmann invents the cardiac catheter in Germany

1940 First heart catheterisation on a patient in U.S.

recovered perfectly. Later, three other patients died, and Gibbon could not stand the emotional strain. He stopped operating.

Over the next few years, the principles first established by Gibbon were applied by other doctors, with refinements such as the use of hypothermia to bring the heart to a halt. After 1960, surgery on stopped hearts became commonplace.

One vital innovation was the artificial heart valve. The first—a self-contained ball valve in an artery leading away from the heart—was implanted in 1952 by the American surgeon Charles Hufnagel. But it was cumbersome, and clicked at each beat. Ten years later, however, there were a dozen different designs, which gave thousands of people with diseased hearts new hope of life.

Repairing damaged limbs

One long-standing dream, to re-attach severed limbs, became a theoretical reality in 1908, when Alexis Carrel devised a method of stitching together blood vessels. But the dream took decades to realize, for it also demanded microsurgery of a high order, with sophisticated surgical microscopes, thread

CHANGE OF HEART An X-ray image of the human heart, right, showing a mechanical valve in place. It is regulating the flow of blood from the left ventricle into the aorta, the body's main artery, for distribution around the body. A prosthetic aortic heart valve is about the size of a coin, below.

finer than a human hair and the ability to join nerves. A microscope was used in an ear operation in 1921, but true microsurgery, with multiple microscopes to allow the cooperation of several surgeons, did not emerge until the

1960s. In 1962, a 12-year-old boy in Boston lost his right arm in an accident. He was rushed to Massachusetts General Hospital, where the arm was packed in ice and salt, then re-grafted into place by Ronald Malt and Charles McKhann. Two years later, the boy had regained the use of his arm.

The extraordinary possibilities of microsurgery were revealed in a dramatic case at the end of 1986. In New York on Christmas Eve, Beatrice Ramos threw herself and her

FORSSMANN: A MAN AFTER HIS OWN HEART

In 1929, Werner Forssmann, the inventor of the cardiac catheter, was a 25-year-old surgical intern in the Berlin City Hospital. A colleague described him as a "queer, peculiar person, lonely and desolate," which perhaps explains why he took such risks with his own life.

He was inspired by an illustration in a veterinary journal of a vet taking blood from a horse with a catheter—a long, slim rubber tube—inserted into a vein. It struck him that it should be possible for a catheter to be inserted so far along a vein that it would reach the heart. This would allow drugs to be placed there directly during an operation, with instantaneous effects, rather than having to be injected slowly via a vein. He tried it on a corpse. It seemed to work. Now all he needed was a living body. There was one immediately at hand: his own.

Persuading a colleague to help, he used a wide-bore needle to insert a catheter into a vein at his elbow, and pushed it in 16 inches. At this point, his colleague backed off. Undeterred, a week later Forssmann dragooned a nurse into helping him. He cut his vein open, inserted the needle with its catheter attached, and began to push the catheter in. With the nurse holding a mirror, he watched his progress on an X–ray screen. With 2 feet of the tube inserted, he felt a burning sensation, and saw that the end of the catheter had entered the right atrium of his heart. He stood there for a moment, wondering how to record evidence of what he had done. Then he knew. With the catheter in place, he left the horrified nurse, walked up two flights of stairs and into an X–ray room, where he demanded that a colleague take pictures. He then went back downstairs and lay as if in a stupor, while the whole hospital buzzed with the rumor that he had committed suicide.

When Forssmann published his results, he became a celebrity – more so when in 1931 he repeated the experiment, this time injecting a radio-opaque substance into his heart to produce the first angiogram. He went on to have a respectable career as a surgeon, but true recognition did not come to him until 1956 when he shared the Nobel prize for medicine with those who had built on his work throughout the 1940s. He died in 1979.

BACK TO THE FUTURE

One surprising result of microsurgery was the reintroduction of leeches to medicine. After veins and arteries are reattached, the veins sometimes cannot be used at once – but the limb must still be supplied with oxygenated blood. Left to themselves, the arteries would do the job – but the blood has nowhere to go. The limb would rapidly become filled with blood. A leech attached to a severed finger, for example, drains off the blood and injects anticoagulant (which prevents the blood clotting). This allows the skin to bleed for a further 12 hours, time enough for the veins to recover.

13-month-old son, Vladimir, under a subway train. The train ran over the boy's legs. His right foot and left leg could not be saved. At first glance it seemed he would have to have two false limbs, but the surgeons saw a radical way forward. They attached his left foot to his right leg.

1952 Charles Hufnagel implants artificial heart valve
1953 First heart operation using John Gibbon's lung-heart machine

LIFESAVING MACHINES

KIDNEY AND HEART FAILURE ARE NO LONGER DEATH SENTENCES FOR THE AFFLICTED

Some patients with long-lasting, life-threatening debilities need machines that offer permanent help, rather than one-time surgical intervention. The two devices that have proved most beneficial counteract failure of the kidneys and the heart.

Kidney machines

Human kidneys are remarkable. In a process known as dialysis, the two kidneys filter impurities from the blood – expelling them in urine. Each kidney contains a million tubes—nephrons—that process liquid through two types of sieve, separating a wide range of impurities and regulating the balance between salt and water. Between them, they process 40 gallons of liquid per day.

Humans can function with just half of one kidney. However, if both fail, the impurities build up rapidly—with lethal consequences

TREATMENT AT HOME   No more intrusive than a television set, the home kidney dialysis machine had been thoroughly domesticated by 1966.

within days. In fact, renal (kidney) disease is almost always partial, with insidious effects over many years. In 1914, soon after the renal functions were analyzed, scientists in America devised a machine to take over from the kidney. The key to the process, known as "vividiffusion," was to create a semipermeable membrane that would allow impurities through when blood ran over it. It worked, but their only patient was a dog.

Almost 30 years later, one man remembered their work. Willem Kolff, working in a hospital in the Netherlands during the Nazi occupation, improvised a new kind of dialysis machine, using sausage skins as a membrane and a beer barrel. Rather than let the Nazis know of his invention, he persuaded some escapees to smuggle it to England. He followed when the war had ended.

After the war, his device was incorporated into other designs with various alterations to the membrane. These machines proved vital for people with severe kidney failure in cases —such as poisoning—in which the kidney could be returned to normal. But they could not be used for long-term treatment because the tube carrying the blood back into a vein would clog. Every operation needed a new point of entry, and the body has only a limited number of suitable points. The solution came in a spin-off from the U.S. space

program. With tubes made of inert, non-stick Teflon, clogging was much reduced. In the early 1960s, Belding Scribner at the University of Washington in Seattle began treating people with chronic kidney failure. But it was a costly, time-consuming process, in which patients had to come into the hospital twice a week for 16 hours each time. That, coupled with the expense and rarity of the machines, meant that medical teams were faced with terrible ethical decisions about who should have dialysis. Rejection was, in effect, a death sentence.

Scribner worked on simplifying his machines, and reducing their size. In 1964, the first patients were treated in their homes. Since then, dialysis machines have been used in thousands of chronic kidney cases, saving and extending countless lives.

The pacemaker

The second major advance in the treatment of chronic disease was the pacemaker, which regulates the beating of the heart. Since the heart beats in response to its own electrical impulses, it can be activated by a shock. On the basis of research with electrocardiographs and resuscitation, Paul Zoll, at Beth Israel Hospital in Boston, invented an external shock-maker—a needle to be inserted through the skin at the apex of the heart,

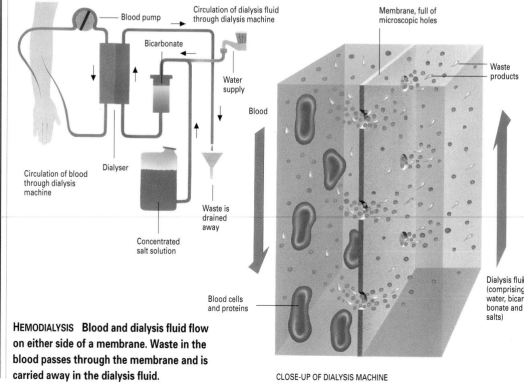

HEMODIALYSIS   Blood and dialysis fluid flow on either side of a membrane. Waste in the blood passes through the membrane and is carried away in the dialysis fluid.

CLOSE-UP OF DIALYSIS MACHINE

1914 Basic experiments in renal dialysis in Boston

1943 Willem Kolff in the Netherlands invents a dialysis machine with another electrode on the skin surface on the rib cage. The first clinical test, on October 7, 1952, was on a 65-year-old man with congestive heart failure, a block caused by an electrical fault in his heart. Despite injections of drugs, he suffered from heart irregularities. Zoll wired him up, and, when the electrocardiogram showed that the heart had stopped, he delivered brief electrical shocks. For 52 hours, the man's heart was driven only by Zoll's device. On October 9, it began to beat again on its own. Shortly after, the man was able to leave hospital.

Improvements soon followed. At the University of Minnesota in Minneapolis, Clarence Lillehei became convinced that electrodes could be attached directly to the heart, but the power source had to be small and rigidly controlled. He contacted a former TV repair man, Earl Bakken, who had proved adept at repairing medical

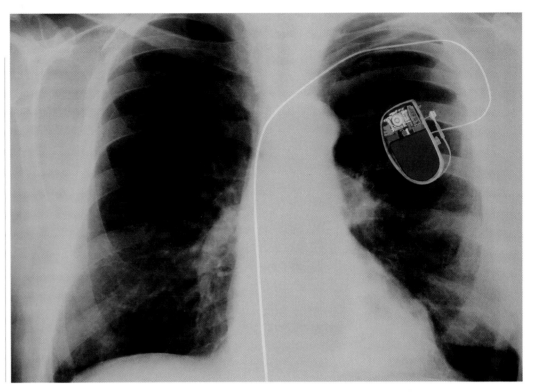

HEARTBEATER An X-ray shot of a battery-operated pacemaker, implanted above the ribcage of a patient. A yellow lead connects it to the heart, at lower right.

THE ARTIFICIAL HEART: REALIZING A DREAM

If a heart valve can be replaced, why not a whole heart? That idea inspired the man who devised the kidney dialysis machine, Willem Kolff. In 1957, he implanted an artificial heart into a dog, which sur-

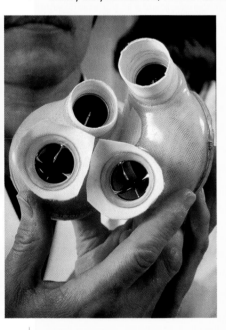

THE JARVIK-7 The aluminum and plastic artificial heart used in the first human implant, December 1, 1982. It was externally powered by compressed air and electricity.

vived for 90 minutes. It was an experiment that seemed to have little significance. Then, in the early 1960s, Christiaan Barnard began experimenting with transplanted hearts in South Africa. His first transplant patient survived for 18 days, and died not from tissue rejection—a common problem with organ transplantation—but from a lung infection. A month later he performed his second transplant; the recipient lived for 563 days after the operation. However, because the majority of patients who received heart transplants soon died, the number of them performed worldwide dropped from 100 in 1968 to only 18 in 1970.

Experimenters kept the idea of an artificial heart alive. In 1970, Robert Jarvik at the University of Utah devised a model that ran on compressed air which, when implanted in calves, kept them alive for about two months until their bodies outgrew it. Then, in December 1982, Barney Clark, a 61-year-old dentist, became the first human being to receive an artificial heart, implanted by William de Vries at Salt Lake City. Clark survived for 112 days. Some 90 artificial hearts were implanted in the 1980s, but amid great controversy.

In the 1990s, the American company Thermo Cardio Systems developed an electric heart, powered by an external battery, which sat alongside and supported the patient's own heart. Originally viewed as a bridge for patients waiting for a transplant, the artificial heart is now seen as an alternative. Since the first implant in Texas in January 1991, there have been more than 65 performed worldwide.

equipment; he came up with a power source the size of a cigarette pack. The problem was that the small opening in the chest for the wires was subject to infection. In Lillehei's words: "The next step was to make it a little smaller, coat it with plastic, and put it inside the body. So there you had it. The first implantable pacemaker!"

In 1957, Earl Bakken set up a business, Medtronics, to make pacemakers. Twenty years later, its sales were $180 million a year. In Europe, parallel research allowed the Swedish doctor Ake Senning to implant an internal pacemaker in 1960.

Despite the immediate success of pacemakers, there was a longer-term problem. Many patients died after a few months or so. Research showed that, at one particular moment in the heartbeat—represented by the so-called T-wave in an electrocardiograph—the heart could fibrillate (or flutter) if stimulated. In the long run, a pacemaker could kill as well as save.

The solution was an "on demand" pacemaker, providing current only when the heart needed it. Invented in the late 1960s by Barouh Berkovits, at the American Optical Company, this pacemaker has since extended hundreds of thousands of lives.

1954 First successful kidney transplant, Boston

1964 Kidney dialysis performed in the home
1967 First human heart transplant by Christiaan Barnard in South Africa

1988 A man is fitted with a plutonium power sourced pacemaker with a life of 20 years

WONDER DRUGS

PENICILLIN AND POLIO VACCINES HEAD A HEFTY ARMORY IN THE FIGHT AGAINST DISEASE

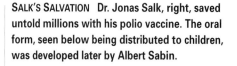

SALK'S SALVATION Dr. Jonas Salk, right, saved untold millions with his polio vaccine. The oral form, seen below being distributed to children, was developed later by Albert Sabin.

The 20th century was the age of the "magic bullet"—a phrase coined by chemotherapy's founder Paul Ehrlich—of drugs that could be designed precisely to cure a disease. Gradually, it became clear that many created side effects or stimulated new, virulent forms of some organisms, but that did not detract from the nature of the new science, with untold benefits for millions.

Penicillin and antibiotics

The story of how Scottish bacteriologist Alexander Fleming discovered the antibiotic penicillin in his untidy little laboratory has assumed the status of modern myth—with its mixture of chance, hard work, frustration and,

GREEN GODSEND The original culture plate on which Fleming observed the growth of penicillin.

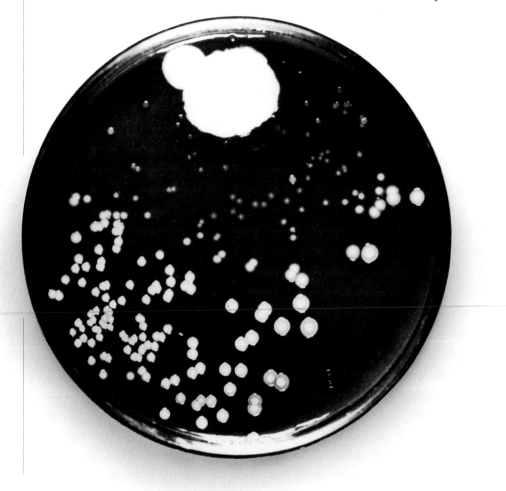

finally, success. Certainly the medical profession took little notice when he revealed his findings publicly in 1929. The world had to wait until 1941, when Oxford research team Howard Florey and Ernst Chain appealed to America's Department of Agriculture to help the drug into production in time to treat Allied troops at the front dying of infections.

As work on penicillin progressed, scientists were also researching other antibiotics —natural and artificial. The first group, sulphonamides, drastically reduced meningitis deaths from 65 percent to 20 percent. In 1948, streptomycin, derived from a type of bacteria, marked the beginning of the end of tuberculosis.

Research into viruses

Another area of research focused on viruses, a class of disease-causing organisms implicated in everything from yellow fever to the common cold. Perhaps the most significant anti-viral invention of them all was the one that conquered poliomyelitis (polio).

Polio, which can lead to paralysis, was much feared, and epidemics were common. In 1950, there were 33,000 cases in the United States alone. By that time, the search for a vaccine was already well advanced.

In 1939, President Roosevelt, himself a polio victim, established the National Foundation for Infantile Paralysis (NFIP) to fund research. By 1954, the NFIP was testing the vaccine on 1.8 million children—the largest clinical trial in history. The results were miraculous—not one child went on to contract the disease.

There were still some problems that needed to be ironed out, however. The NFIP's vaccine—developed by Jonas Salk— was not completely effective against all three forms of polio. Also, treatment was in the form of injections (with up to eight boosters). All of this was resolved by Russian-born virologist Albert Sabin, whose more effective, faster-acting "live" vaccine could be taken orally. The result was the vaccine on a cube of sugar familiar to literally millions of children over the last 30 years.

1910 German medical pioneer Paul Ehrlich discovers cure for syphilis

1945 Alexander Fleming, Ernst Chain and Howard Florey share Nobel prize for their work on penicillin

1954 Mass trials of Jonas Salk's polio vaccination

CONTRACEPTION AND CONCEPTION

CONTROVERSIAL TECHNIQUES TO MANAGE THE CREATION OF HUMAN LIFE

No invention has been quite so controversial as the Pill, no issue so bitterly argued as contraception. Major religions, governments, pharmaceutical companies, pressure groups and individuals by the million—all have had their cases to argue. Yet despite the authority of those bitterly opposed to contraception at all, the marketplace has welcomed more and more sophisticated products —from condoms (male and female) to intrauterine devices (IUDs) and the contraceptive pill itself. Millions of women, though, found themselves the victims of side effects, and of a new problem: having chosen to control conception, how, when the time comes, can a woman control fertility?

The invention of the Pill

Throughout history, in cultures throughout the world, there have always been potions that claimed to prevent conception. Some were based on myth or folklore, others were herbal remedies.

When the American Gregory Pincus developed the first contraceptive pill in the 1950s, his work was a progression from earlier findings that wild yams in Mexico yield a substance that can be transformed into the female sex hormone, progesterone. Once Pincus had established that a modified form of progesterone inhibited ovulation, the stage was set. A campaign by the feminist and birth-control crusader Margaret Sanger brought Pincus a $115,000 research grant. The end product, norethynodrel, went on sale in 1960.

Since that time, the Pill has been refined to reduce the risk of side effects such as an increased risk of thrombosis leading to heart attacks and strokes. Overall, the risks were small, but enough to introduce various modifications (particularly in the 1970s) as well as other alternatives.

The 1980s saw the introduction of injectable hormonal contraceptives, for example, as well as the PC4 post-coital pill. Often known as the "morning after" pill, the

PC4 is actually effective three days after unprotected sex. In 1986, the RU486 or abortive pill became available as an alternative to surgical termination in France (where it was invented). In 1999, the Danco Group,

PILL TALK The chance of an unwanted pregnancy while taking oral contraceptives ranges from 0.1 to 7 percent.

a small pharmaceutical company, announced plans to manufacture the drug and market it in the United States by the end of the year. The latest research is concentrated on the much-awaited male contraceptive pill, which is being tested in the United States and France. What effect it will have on society can only be guessed.

Treating infertility

Thanks to the Pill, women acquired near-total control over their own fertility. But what a growing minority of women – and men — wanted was medical help in controlling their lack of fertility. Certainly the techniques were there: during the late 1960s and 1970s, the combination of microsurgery, ultrasound, endoscopy and new drugs allowed doctors to examine, stimulate, remove and replace as never before.

Among the best known developments in this area was *in vitro*—in glass—fertilization (IVF). Developed in England by Dr. Patrick Steptoe and Dr. Robert Edwards, this method involves a number of interrelated techniques culminating in scientific fertilization of one or more embryos outside the body, then replacement back into the womb. Since then, tens of thousands of women have given birth through IVF.

IVF opened up more high-tech possibilities, including Gamete Intrafallopian Transfer (GIFT), in which gametes—eggs and sperm—are placed into the Fallopian tube; egg donation; embryo donation; and surrogate motherhood.

IVF CONCEPTION A microneedle (right) drives a sperm into a human egg. A pipette (left) holds the egg steady.

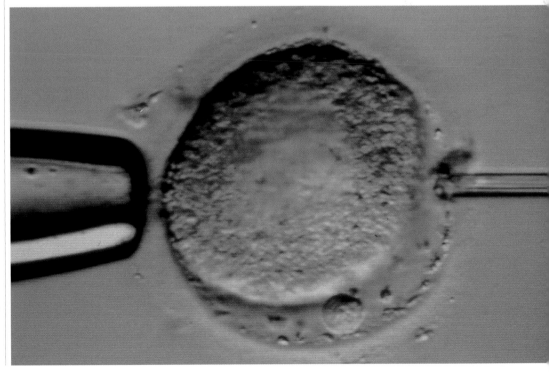

1960 First oral contraceptive went on sale in the U.S.

1978 Birth of Louise Brown, the first "test-tube baby," in Britain
1984 First baby born by egg donation, in Australia

REGAINING NORMALITY

REPLACING DAMAGED AND LOST HUMAN PARTS IMPROVES THE LIVES OF MILLIONS

People have always dreamed of restoring the damaged body to its original condition, whether replacing the lost parts or using an artificial aid to compensate for any physical impairment. The invention of the electrical hearing aid in 1902 and the plastic contact lens in 1938 have made immeasurable contributions to the improvement of hearing and sight.

Advances in technology have resulted in inventions that have changed the lives of millions of people—in areas where evolution has never seen fit to lend a hand. Decaying joints, for example, have always plagued animals with backbones. There were Neanderthal men, 40,000 years ago, who would have benefited from hip replacement. The first major survey of bone-related illness in 1938 estimated that 6.5 million Americans endured a form of rheumatic disease, with the loss of 97 million days' work a year. In every Western country, the economic and emotional cost is beyond reckoning.

Hip joints are particularly vulnerable. The hip's ball and socket, the key joint in locomotion, moves in three dimensions and can carry up to five times the body's weight. But when it seizes or collapses, life becomes a bed-bound misery.

This century, pain and inflammation have been tackled to some extent by drugs, but the only lasting remedy is a new joint. In the

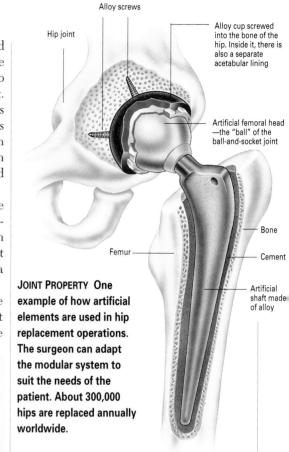

Labels: Alloy screws · Hip joint · Alloy cup screwed into the bone of the hip. Inside it, there is also a separate acetabular lining · Artificial femoral head —the "ball" of the ball-and-socket joint · Bone · Femur · Cement · Artificial shaft made of alloy

JOINT PROPERTY One example of how artificial elements are used in hip replacement operations. The surgeon can adapt the modular system to suit the needs of the patient. About 300,000 hips are replaced annually worldwide.

THE COMING OF THE CONTACT LENS

For almost 700 years, ever since eyeglasses were first used in the 13th century, the principles of aiding eyesight hardly changed at all. This century, however, glass has been replaced by plastic, and in a rapid series of developments external lenses have become an extension of the eye itself.

The first contact lenses were made in 1887 from glass. It wasn't until 1938, with new technological developments, that they started to be made from plastic. Whether glass or plastic, the lens was made by taking an impression of the eye and forming the lens on this mold or to dimensions specified by the practitioner. By contrast with what followed, these first "scleral" plastic lenses were very large, covering the whole eye. At first, this meant that the eye could not "breathe," and they became uncomfortable after an hour or two. Then it was realized that they were equally effective with a small hole drilled through them, so that some people were able to wear them for much longer periods. These proved suitable for people playing sports, such as near-sighted football players.

In 1948, contact lenses shrank to cover only the cornea, as part of the search for a longer wearing time. This had advantages: the fitting of corneal lenses demands less time than sceral lenses, making them cheaper to supply. However, there were disadvantages, too. They were still hard lenses, which had to be cut from solid Perspex. Like the sclerals they did not breathe, so the cornea tended to swell and lose its natural sensitivity.

In 1960, a Czech polymer chemist, Otto Wichterle, described a new principle for lens-making. In the science journal *Nature*, he proposed a soft lens made of a jelly-like, water-absorbing "hydrogel" plastic. The plastic would be poured into molds of prescribed shape, allowed to set, then removed and the edges polished. He pointed out that the technique could easily be used in making contact lenses. The idea was bought by the American optical company, Bausch and Lomb, which prepared to market them. Suddenly, though, they found their plans thwarted by a declaration from the U.S. Food and Drug Administration that the soft lens was deemed a drug. That entailed a whole new battery of tests, delaying the launch until 1972. Today, soft contact lenses are used by tens of millions of people, who take for granted the fact that they can buy them without fuss, fit them easily and then forget all about them.

SECOND SIGHT A hard contact lens ready for positioning on the eye.

last years of the 19th century, a French surgeon, Louis Ollier, performed 270 elbow replacements. But the hip joint was another matter. For decades, no material could cope with the load, or match the bone's natural slipperiness. In the 1940s, an American surgeon, Marcus Smith-Petersen, attempted to address the problem. He reduced the size of the ball of the femur, or thighbone, and at the same time enlarged the socket. He then inserted a loose-fitting, polished metal cup to hold the femur. But in the course of time the joint seized up.

Another approach, by two French surgeons, the Judet brothers, tried replacing the top of the femur with something the shape of a giant plastic thumb-tack driven down into the thighbone. It worked better, but the plastic tended to seize against the bone and emitted a disconcerting squeak when the patient walked. The result was a steady loosening of the joint, and its eventual collapse.

The father of hip replacement

The breakthrough came in January 1960, as the result of work by John Charnley at the Manchester Royal Infirmary in England. It was an operation that owed as much to engineering as to medicine. Charnley had made

WALKING WOUNDED Horrendously injured victims of antipersonnel mines learn to use artificial limbs at a special center in Phnom Penh, Cambodia, in 1985.

a particular study of joint lubrication. "An animal joint," he pointed out in an article in *The Lancet*, "is rather more slippery than ice." The question was, how to match it? The solution lay in making the ball hard, and the socket soft and smooth. He found his answer in Teflon, the non-stick plastic polytetrafluoroethylene (PTFE), which he formed into a serrated bowl that was hammered into the hipbone. He then replaced the femur's ball-shaped head with a smaller stainless steel one, less than an inch across, which fitted exactly into the plastic bowl. Both bowl and the shaft were bonded to the bone beneath with an acrylic cement.

The new hip worked well. Between the first operation and his report in *The Lancet* on May 27, 1961, Charnley performed 97 operations. He found that the patients could walk after just five weeks. After two months, they could go home, pain-free.

One other great challenge for surgeons in such operations is infection, a common cause of failure in early hip replacements. Antibiotics largely cured the problem, but Charnley made a further major contribution. He devised a "clean-air theater" in which purified air flows in one way only over the patient's exposed body during surgery.

Since then, hip replacements have become routine—over 200,000 operations are performed in the United States and Europe every year. And age has proved no barrier. Hundreds of octogenarians have had

their hips replaced. On November 16, 1995, Britain's Queen Mother, at 95, was given a new hip. Though one of the oldest people ever to have the operation, she took her first steps within two days.

New hope for those without limbs

One of the most appalling weapons of the late 20th century has been the antipersonnel mine. In Afghanistan, Myanmar (Burma), Mozambique, Somalia, Ethiopia and numerous other countries, wars have left millions of these brutal little devices—which weigh about 1 pound—concealed in forests and

HIGH-TECH ADVANCES An artificial leg with sensing capacity is fitted to a patient in New York in 1990; while, right, a young girl is at ease with her computer-designed arm.

fields. In Cambodia alone, 30,000 people—a random cross-section of men, women and children—have had one or both legs blown off. Proportionate to total population, this is 87 times the percentage of amputees in the West.

The artificial legs they received until the early 1990s had not changed in principle from the metal and wooden ones known for generations. One response in Cambodia and other poverty-stricken countries was to simplify and cheapen designs, but then came the possibility of progress—in the form of computer-aided design and computer-aided manufacture (CAD/CAM).

One of the most advanced systems is the Seattle Shapemaker, so called because it was pioneered at the Prosthetics Research Foundation in Seattle. It involves making a plaster cast of the shattered limb, from which a computerized scanner surveys its shape. The machine then tailor-makes a design, and stores the digital equivalent of a plaster cast for future use. Thanks to this system—already at work in Vietnam in 1995 —a once-complex and lengthy process has now been made much simpler and faster.

1960 First plastic hip replacement, by John Charnley in Britain

1987 Disposable soft contact lenses become available

1995 Computer-aided design and manufacture of artificial limbs in service in Vietnam

MAKING UP FOR LOST ABILITIES

TECHNOLOGY AND SPORTS ARE UNLIKELY PARTNERS IN BRINGING HOPE TO THE DISABLED

Until the latter part of the century, it was accepted that the disabled either lived in an institution or were housebound. There was little impetus to increase mobility or communication for such a silent minority. Over the last 20 years, however, with the growing voice of the disabled movement, technology has been a liberating force. Whether special racing chairs for the sports-oriented, "The Mekong" flat-pack for victims of antipersonnel mines in Cambodia, or highly sophisticated Patient Operated Selector Mechanisms for the totally paralyzed, new inventions are helping to achieve maximum independence for millions.

Between the wars, wheelchairs were armchairs on wheels. Then in 1932, American

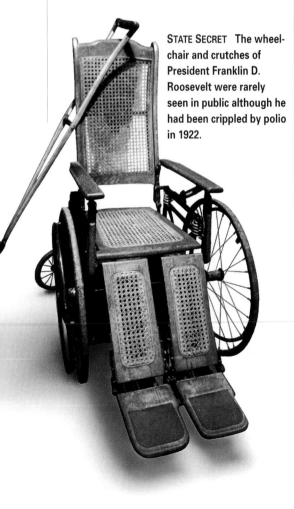

STATE SECRET The wheelchair and crutches of President Franklin D. Roosevelt were rarely seen in public although he had been crippled by polio in 1922.

engineer Harry Jennings designed a folding wheelchair for his friend, Herbert Everest, who had become a paraplegic. The result cut the weight from 90 pounds to 50 pounds, and their partnership, Everest and Jennings, went on to dominate wheelchair design for the next 50 years.

In the last two decades, the improvement in the design of equipment for the disabled has been vast—and much of the impetus has come from sports. There is a new belief that innovation in equipment should push the barriers forward in terms of what can be achieved, rather than aim for the bare minimum in mobility. Every top-class marathon has its wheelchair entries, and these tough, spidery machines outclass their forebears as much as modern racing bicycles outpace early velocipedes.

This change in attitude is rooted in the work of Sir Ludwig Guttmann, a German refugee neurologist, who set up the spinal injuries center in Stoke Mandeville Hospital, England, in 1944. His aim was to improve the rehabilitation of patients paralyzed by spinal-cord injuries. In 1948, he organized an archery contest for 16 paralyzed ex-servicemen, and dreamed of a time when the disabled would have their own Olympics. By the 1990s, the Special Olympics had become a respected international event in the sporting calendar.

Racing chairs

A turning point in design came after an American sportswoman, Marilyn Hamilton, crashed her hang-glider into a mountain in 1978, damaging her spine and losing the use of her legs. Dismissing the wheelchair ordered by her physiotherapist as a "stainless-steel dinosaur," she contacted two friends who designed hang-gliders, Don Helman and Jim Okamoto. The result was the Quickie, a low-slung, sporty model weighing only 26 pounds, made from the aluminum tubing used in hang-gliders.

Hamilton, Helman and Okamoto went into partnership. In 1980, sales took off among the 1.5 million Americans who needed wheelchairs. A folding "Quickie" followed in 1983. Suddenly, thousands of disabled people were finding new freedom at home, driving, in sports, and at work.

By 1985, Hamilton's company had sales of $15 million. Bought by Sunrise Medical, a large equipment company, it went international, and spawned competitors. Quickies

ON THE SPOT Motivation's chair, flatpacked (right), half-assembled (left) and complete (background). It can be made and repaired locally, in countries such as Cambodia.

diversified, like cars and bicycles. Toddlers had their own versions. People could order them in energetic colors, such as bright pink. In 1993, a powered version came out.

America and Europe, with their combined market of 3.5 million, were not the only areas to benefit from the development of the Quickie. It also inspired a British quadraplegic, David Constantine, to apply the conceptual and technical revolution to the disabled in the Third World—where 18 million people stood to benefit.

In developing nations, where the high-tech $3,000 wheelchair is not affordable, Constantine's charity, Motivation, has

REVEALING THE VOICE THAT WAS HIDDEN WITHIN

Physicist and best-selling author of *A Brief History of Time*, Stephen Hawking, disabled by motor-neuron disease, lost his voice when he had a tracheotomy. Here he describes the voice synthesizer developed by California computer expert Walt Woltosz: "His mother-in-law had the same condition as me, so he had developed a computer program to help her communicate. A cursor moves across a screen. When it is on the option you want, you operate a switch by head or eye movement or, in my case, by hand. In this way, one can select words that are printed out on the lower half of the screen. When one has built up what one wants to say, one can send it to a speech synthesizer or save it on a disc. It is slow, roughly one-tenth the speed of normal speech. But the speech synthesizer is so much clearer than I was previously . . . my youngest son, who was only six at the time of my tracheotomy, never could make me out before. Now he has no difficulty. That means a great deal to me."

1932 The folding wheelchair is designed by American Harry Jennings

1944 Sir Ludwig Guttmann sets up a spinal injuries center in Britain

worked (in Romania, Indonesia, Bangladesh and several other countries) to devise wheelchairs that can be made and repaired on the spot, with local materials. In Cambodia, where thousands are disabled by mines every year, Motivation devised a wooden three-wheeled chair that could be built for under $50. It comes packed flat and takes just an hour to assemble.

By the mid-1990s the Quickie was no longer considered a sporting chair. Practically anyone unable to walk could benefit, while disabled athletes devised wheelchairs to their own specialized needs.

Computers give control to the helpless

Some disabilities deprive victims of far more than the use of their limbs. With progressive nervous and muscular disorders, such as multiple sclerosis, sufferers lose the ability to perform routine tasks, and may even lose the power of speech. Until the late 1960s, the most that the totally paralyzed could do was attract attention by blowing a whistle suspended above their beds.

The first major advance in this area came in 1969, when engineers at the spinal injuries hospital in Stoke Mandeville in Britain realized that if patients could blow a whistle, they could also operate microswitches to control electrical apparatus. This gave patients a degree of control over their environment, operating devices—curtains, TV, intercom—through cables. This environmental control unit was called a Patient Operated Selector Mechanism (or POSM). It seemed appropriate that patients should refer to it as a *possum* (Latin for "I am able"), and so the name was adopted for both the machine and the company that developed it. By the mid-1980s, Possums had acquired microcomputers, and could run data networks by remote control. In 1993 came a portable unit, which could be re-programmed for individual needs.

In parallel, Possum developed computerized voice synthesizers, operated by small movements—"puff-and-suck" or even the twitch of an eyelid. Using these minute reactions, patients could select options, such as a letter, a word or a phrase, which could be built into sentences, then spoken by the machine, printed out or stored on disc.

The combined effect of these inventions has been to increase control, freedom and self-esteem in the severely disabled.

CONQUERING SPIRITS Skier Raynald Riu competes in the giant slalom event at the 1994 Winter Special Olympics in Norway, right, while wheelchair racer Tanni Grey shows her paces, below.

1969 Invention of the Patient Operated Selector Mechanism (Possum)

1978 Development of the Quickie wheelchair

GENETIC ENGINEERING

CRACKING THE CODE OF LIFE RAISES AWESOME POSSIBILITIES . . . AND RESPONSIBILITIES

Some 4,000 human diseases are caused by defects in genes. It has been estimated that one in every 20 babies born has some sort of genetic disorder. After the discovery in 1953 of how the genetic code works, scientists dreamed of tackling genetic faults at the source—by tinkering with the genes themselves. But the task was formidable, and it had two components: first to identify the genes, then to replace them. Only toward the end of the century did it seem that one day it might be possible.

It had long been known that some diseases were due to a genetic fault. In 1803, an American physician noted that hemophilia was suffered by men and carried by women. But it wasn't until James Watson and Francis Crick cracked the genetic code in 1953, with the help of previous findings by Maurice Wilkins and Rosalind Franklin, that doctors could understand why.

Crick and Watson discovered how information governing heredity is carried in the chromosomes of human cells in the form of DNA (deoxyribonucleic acid). This DNA determines individual physical development and is present in every human cell.

With further research, it became clear that genetic disorders were not all of a kind. Sickle-cell anemia, borne by up to 40 percent of West Africans, is caused by a single wrong element in one gene—a single-letter fault in DNA's alphabet. In Down's syndrome, the victim has three copies, instead of the normal two, of one particular chromosome, with its thousands of genes. Other syndromes are caused by having one chromosome less than normal. And tuberculosis is more likely to affect those with a genetic predisposition to catch it. In each case, what specific role is played by genes? To answer this, scientists embarked on a massive international project in the mid-1980s to map the chromosomes carried within human cells.

Rewriting history

Some of the results have already marked a turning point in medicine. By the mid-1990s, researchers had identified 2,000 genes, including those that are responsible in part or in whole for a number of genetic diseases. Among them: cystic fibrosis, Alzheimer's disease and cancer of the colon. The next stage was to alter the genes—in effect, rewrite the recipe for genetic information. This technique, genetic engineering, is done by using enzymes and viruses as tools to snip a sequence of DNA and to insert the new information into a cell, modifying its activity and that of its descendants. In the 1970s, scientists removed the section of DNA responsible for making insulin and re-inserted it into a bacterium to make human insulin. In 1982, insulin produced by genetic engineering was first used to treat diabetics.

Finally came the first direct treatment of humans. In 1990, scientists in Maryland took defective white blood cells from a four-year-old girl who lacked an enzyme vital to her immune system, modified them, and reinserted them. The cells, with their replacement genes, triggered production of the missing chemical—though the cure did not prove permanent.

The future for this line of research promises to be truly astonishing, a new era in which human beings will have the power to determine their own environment—by controlling the genetic content of plants and animals—and their own evolution. In theory, genetic disease could become a thing of the past – assuming the practical and ethical considerations can be reconciled.

THE CODE-BREAKERS Maurice Wilkins (left), Francis Crick (third from left) and James Watson (right) accept the Nobel prize, 1962.

DNA: CRACKING THE GENETIC CODE

Hereditary information that is passed on from one generation to the next is carried in a kind of chemical code in the nucleus of living cells. In a human cell, each nucleus contains 46 chromosomes (in 23 pairs) and they, in turn, carry the genes. These genes are made up of giant, complex, chain-like molecules of nucleic acids known as DNA—deoxyribonucleic acid.

In 1953, building on the research of many others, James Watson and Francis Crick realized that DNA consists of four chemical bases—adenine, guanine, thymine and cytosine—which in varying sequences store the genetic code. The chemicals are linked in pairs—adenine-thymine and guanine-cytosine—and form two strands twisting round like a spiral staircase. This is what is known as the "double helix." When a cell divides, the genetic code is reproduced by the DNA unwinding down the middle and each individual strand then building up an identical match. By solving the mystery of human heredity, Watson and Crick paved the way for a whole new science—genetic engineering.

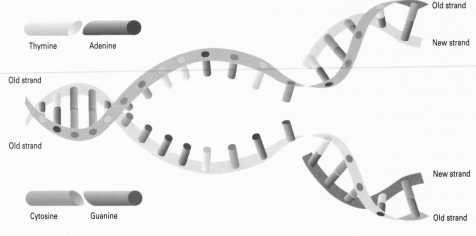

Thymine · Adenine
Old strand
Old strand
Cytosine · Guanine

Old strand
New strand
New strand
Old strand

1900   2000

1953 James Watson and Francis Crick announce their discovery of how the genetic code works (Britain)

1982 Insulin produced by genetic engineering used to treat diabetes

1990 First direct treatment of humans using genetic engineering, in U.S.

THE ENERGY EXPLOSION

AS THE POPULATION HAS GROWN, WE HAVE DEVELOPED EVER-HIGHER LEVELS OF TECHNOLOGY TO UNLOCK THE EARTH'S NATURAL RESOURCES. COAL IS HARDER TO EXPLOIT THAN WOOD, BUT OFFERS GREATER RETURNS OF POWER—AN EQUATION REPEATED IN TURN WITH PETROLEUM AND NUCLEAR ENERGY. MUCH THE SAME HAS BEEN TRUE OF THE DEVELOPMENT OF AGRICULTURE, AS FERTILIZERS AND MACHINERY HAVE RELEASED UNDREAMED-OF HARVESTS.

UNLOCKING THE RICHES OF THE EARTH

OIL SEEMED A RARE RESOURCE UNTIL NEED SPURRED EXPLORATION AND INGENUITY

Every day, more than 2,000 million gallons of oil pour from the Earth's interior. Whole industries depend on it, few could exist without it. Wars are fought for it, and control is assured for those who win.

The ancient world knew about oil. It was skimmed off where it was found seeping from the ground, and used in lamps, for cleaning and for caulking ships. By the end of the 19th century, its main use was as paraffin to burn in lamps. Then came another

THERE SHE BLOWS On March 15, 1910, the Lakeview No. 1 gusher blew under Maricopa in Arizona, spewing out a record-breaking nine million barrels over 18 months.

market, the automobile. Suddenly there was demand for natural gasoline, the one by-product of crude oil that had previously been deemed useless or dangerous.

By 1911, the oil industry was already a massive international business. But despite improvements in the drilling equipment to get the oil out, the yield of gas from the crude was poor. With the distillation methods in use, it was 20 percent at most—and that was dependent on the highly variable qualities of the original crude.

The solution came in 1913, thanks to a new refining process patented by William Burton—at that time, head of manufacturing at Standard Oil of Indiana. Known as "thermal cracking," it used heat and pressure to split oil's larger molecules into smaller, more volatile ones that could be used in engines. Not only did this double the yield to 45 percent, but it freed the motor industry from the arbitrary quality of crude oil.

A new tool—and a new fuel

Demand inspired production, and both inspired exploration. One of the problems in the early days was the impossibility of determining from the surface rock whether there was likely to be oil beneath. One way of finding out was to use echo sounding.

Using seismographs, the technique involved setting off explosions then picking up the vibrations with sensors scattered across the surface. By recording the varying vibrations reflected by different types of rock, geologists could map the sub-surface features—and so accurately predict the presence of oil. In 1918, the deepest wells

In 1891, when Patillo Higgins found springs with gas bubbling through them on Spindletop Hill in Texas, he was convinced there was oil. He formed a company, did some exploration, but found nothing. He brought in a driller, Captain Anthony Lucas, but still with no success.

Desperate, and short of cash, Lucas found two freelance prospectors to back him, cutting poor Higgins out. Drilling resumed. On January 10, 1901, in a fantastic release of pressure, 6 tons of drill rig exploded upward from the oil well—heralding the arrival of the first gusher.

With oil spewing out at 75,000 barrels a day—about half of America's total production—the roar could be heard miles away. Some people thought it was the end of the world. Far from it: it was the birth of a new one, the Texas oil boom.

reached 6,000 feet. By 1930, using seismography, it became worth drilling down to 10,000 feet.

By the late 1930s, aircraft started to make new demands on the oil industry. Aircraft engines needed superior quality, highly refined—or "high octane"—fuel, but current refining methods meant that it was expensive and in short supply. The answer lay in "catalytic cracking," a new process developed by a Frenchman, Eugène Houdry. This differed from thermal cracking in that it relied on catalysts—chemicals that increase

FIRST OIL FIELD Baku on the Caspian Sea—part of the former Soviet Union—was a major leader in the world oil market from the turn of the century onward (below).

1900
1913 Thermal cracking is developed, in the U.S.
1922 Turbo-drilling developed in the former Soviet Union, reducing wear on machinery
1940 Catalytic cracking is developed by Frenchman Eugène Houdry
1947 First offshore platform strikes oil, in the Gulf of Mexico
1950

NORTHERN GAS The flame that is often seen at the top of an oil rig is natural gas that accompanies the oil. Above, natural gas is burned off at an oil well in northern Alaska.

the rate of chemical change without themselves being permanently changed. As well as increasing the yield from crude oil, it resulted in superior products. In 1944, the Allies backed an undertaking to raise production of high octane fuel. Within a year, the U.S. was making half a million barrels a day—enough to hasten an Allied victory.

The arrival of offshore oil

By 1945, the industry's technology was recognizably modern. But demand, particularly in the United States, was insatiable, and some sources—such as the Middle East—not always reliable. Soon, the Cold War demanded that new sources should be found, and they were—offshore, in the Gulf of Mexico.

Floating platforms were used to drill into the ocean floor and, by 1947, oil had been struck 10 miles off the Louisiana coast.

This, in effect, gave birth to a whole new industry—and was ultimately to alter the economic face of Europe. Not much oil had been produced in Europe, but on June 18, 1975, the first oil flowed from the North Sea rigs onto British shores. It was the start of an economic bonanza that would prove vital for Britain's economy for more than 20 years.

The various successes of the oil industry in recent times were tarnished, however, by the events of March 24, 1989, when the oil tanker *Exxon Valdez* ran aground in Alaska's Prince William Sound, spilling over 20 million gallons of oil over the course of two days. The spill was one of the worst environmental disasters in recent times; more than 1,100 miles of Alaskan coastline was coated in oil, killing tens of thousands of shore-nesting birds and sea mammals, and severely threatening many of Alaska's important salmon fisheries.

THE BIRTH OF A GIANT

Constructed in the mid-1970s, Ninian Central was not only the biggest platform in the North Sea but, at the time it was built, it was also the largest man-made object ever to be moved.

The platform was designed to perform several functions: to drill for oil, extract it, re-inject sea water into the evacuated seabed, gather gas, and pump the oil ashore. Built in Scotland, it took 2,000 people three years to make a platform 445 feet across at its base. The bottom section was towed into open water and partly submerged, acting as a base for the top deck—to bring it to its total height of 776 feet. When completed it weighed almost 600,000 tons.

In May 1978, eight tugs took it on a 516 mile journey northeast of Britain to the Ninian field. The field, which has two other platforms, has produced steadily ever since, with a peak of 300,000 barrels a day.

BIG RIG More than four times the height of the Statue of Liberty, Ninian Central is the largest of three platforms in the Ninian oil field.

Drilling rig

Helideck

Flare boom

Living accommodation

Breakwater well

Water storage

Diesel storage

1969 Oil is discovered in the North Sea

1975 Oil from North Sea starts to flow into Britain

1995 World's deepest offshore oil platform built in the Gulf of Mexico

UNLEASHING THE ATOM

THE SQUEAKY CLEAN DREAM OF A NUCLEAR AGE FADES IN THE DARK, DIM REALITY

Once upon a time, all fuels – wood, coal, petroleum—were based on dead plants. To burn them, to release their energy, was generally a dirty business. This century has seen the emergence of the first non-plant fuel, one that produces energy with no visible dirt. But nuclear energy, seen initially as the fuel with a bright, clean future, turned out to be dirtier than most could ever have imagined.

On December 2, 1942, an emigré Italian physicist, Enrico Fermi, was about to complete a crucial experiment. In a squash court in Chicago, he had improvised the world's first atomic pile, aiming to test an idea that would define a new era: the nuclear age.

It was an idea that had not been around for very long. In 1919, Briton Ernest Rutherford had shown that the nucleus of an atom could be broken by bombarding it with particles. It took a great deal of energy and he doubted his discovery had much practical use, but he hadn't counted on uranium.

In 1934, in Italy, Fermi had noted that uranium was highly unstable. If bombarded with sub-atomic particles, neutrons, it broke down into lighter elements. In 1938, these early experiments by Fermi were repeated by Otto Hahn and Lise Meitner in Germany, who went on to discover nuclear fission: the splitting of the atom. In the same year,

CHAIN REACTION Bombard uranium with neutrons and the uranium atom will split— releasing vast amounts of energy.

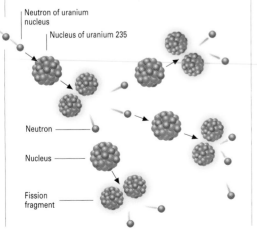

Neutron of uranium nucleus

Nucleus of uranium 235

Neutron

Nucleus

Fission fragment

Fermi fled fascist Italy for the United States to teach physics at the University of Chicago. At the same time, realization of the implication of Hahn's findings in the hands of Nazi Germany galvanized the American government into funding the Manhattan Project—a plan to produce the first atomic bomb.

One vital strand in this research was Fermi's work on the controlled release of nuclear energy. In theory, since some sorts of uranium nuclei have a tendency to split spontaneously —in the process releasing neutrons— sufficient amounts of the right type of uranium (uranium 235) can create a chain reaction and so produce energy.

This can occur in two ways. Placing two large lumps of uranium together creates a critical mass that destroys itself. But if the amount of uranium is small and controlled (by the addition

COOLING THE HOT ZONE The cooling of the "hot" elements of a nuclear power plant is a simple process, but the hydraulics (above) are tested to the limit.

of rods of boron or cadmium that soak up the neutrons), the effect is an explosion in slow-motion and the steady production of nuclear energy.

To see what would happen in practice, the squash court experiment centered on Fermi's atomic "pile"—lumps of uranium surrounded by blocks of graphite. The graphite was designed to act as a "moderator," slowing the neutrons and making it more likely that they would cause fission. Additionally, there were spaces into which cadmium rods could be fitted to control the

reaction. Fermi allowed the nuclear reaction to go on for 28 minutes. The coded news of his success declared: "The Italian navigator has entered the New World."

The first commercial pile

After the Second World War, the British, French, and Soviet governments all started their own nuclear programs. Primarily, they each wanted their own atomic bomb, but, secondarily, they wanted nuclear energy to replace depleted coal reserves and to act as an alternative source to oil.

Britain took the lead, embarking on a nuclear energy program to make nuclear reactors that could perform two tasks. First, they would "breed" plutonium for bombs. Second, they could supply electricity.

In essence, the principle is simple. Nuclear energy (radiation) heats a coolant— usually water, gas or sodium—which in turn boils water. (Two heating systems are used to avoid the risk of radioactive contamination.) The steam is used to drive turbines, which feed current into the National Power Grid.

By 1952, a reactor had been designed, and, just four years later, it was ready: Calder Hall in Northwest England. Although a

1919 First observed nuclear reaction, Ernest Rutherford, England

1938 Otto Hahn discovers nuclear fission

1942 Italian physicist Enrico Fermi achieves a controlled nuclear reaction

(where the fuel rods literally melt, possibly leading to radiation escaping).

Most disastrously, in 1986, a poorly designed and run reactor in Chernobyl in the Ukraine blew up, releasing a vast cloud of radioactive debris. The national and international ramifications were immense: 220 villages abandoned, 3,861 square miles too dangerous for habitation, 150,000 people evacuated. Four years later, sheep in northwest England and Wales were still too radioactive to be eaten.

Disasters combined with longer-term concerns about the nature of radioactive pollution: that there is no "safe dose" of radioactivity, and that there is no foolproof method of disposing of the 100,000 tons of radioactive waste generated by reactors each year. Some of that waste will remain radioactive for 100,000 years!

In the mid-1990s, nations became wary of an industry that provoked such controversy. None, however, showed any wish to abandon programs that were comparatively safe and efficient. Fermi's squash-court experiment may not have marked the beginning of a golden age, but it was certainly the beginning of something new and lasting.

BRAVE NEW WORLD Operations continued at Chernobyl after 1986, below, despite "Dead Zone" warning posters; top left, Cruas-Meysse is one of France's nuclear power plants.

non-commercial nuclear power station had opened in Obninsk, 70 miles southwest of Moscow, in June 1954, Calder Hall was the world's first industrial-scale station.

By the mid-1990s, nuclear energy had taken its place as a major contributor to world energy generation. Twenty-five countries had a nuclear energy program, almost half of them producing a third of their electricity in this way. The United States had 111 nuclear plants in 1990, as compared with only 18 in 1970. However, this number was significantly lower than originally projected; improvements in efficiency—plants ran at an impressive 76 percent of capacity in 1996—have increased the generation of electricity at each plant without requiring the construction of additional generators themselves.

The tarnishing of a dream

Meanwhile, however, disaster and growing concerns had dampened the initial enthusiasm. In 1957, the core of one of the Windscale military reactors, which adjoin Calder Hall, caught fire, releasing radioactivity across much of Britain. The same year, an explosion in a nuclear waste dump in Kyshytym in the Soviet Union contaminated 150 square miles, forcing the evacuation of 270,000 people. An estimated 10,000 died. In 1979, a reactor at Three Mile Island, Pennsylvania, suffered a partial meltdown

THE POWER OF THE SUN

SUSTAINABLE ENERGY WITH AN ANCIENT PAST STARTS TO REALIZE ITS POTENTIAL FOR THE FUTURE

Human beings spend much of their lives gathering and using energy—burning wood, coal, peat and nuclear fuel. Yet the amount of energy reaching the earth, free, from the sun is 30,000 times all that currently used by humans. The sun is the primary source of energy on which all life depends, and humankind has long dreamed of harnessing its power directly—with some success. Solar-energy devices have an

IN HOT WATER

In 1929, the French government built an ocean thermal-electric conversion (OTEC) plant—to collect solar heat from the sea—off Cuba. They later built others but they proved uneconomic.

ancient pedigree, in sea-water evaporation pans for producing salt and fresh water; solar furnaces; and solar-steam generators. All these make effective use of solar energy, but until recently they could not match the reliability, power and cheapness of systems that burn fuel. Nor could they turn solar energy directly into electricity. Only in the last few decades has the technology started to match the potential—an advance that will see further huge strides in the future.

In 1954, scientists at Bell Telephone's laboratories in Murray Hill, New Jersey, noticed something odd about the devices they were working on: a new type of rectifier that used silicon (which is a nonmetallic element) to convert alternating to direct current. The new rectifiers seemed to put out more electricity when they were standing in

STAR CAR
Sunraycer, winner of the first international solar-powered car race, held in Australia in 1987. It averaged 42 mph over the 1,950 mile route.

sunlight and the team leader, Morton Prince, realized why: silicon had the ability to convert sunlight into electricity.

It was not the first time such discoveries had been made. In 1839, the French electrochemist Antoine Becquerel had noticed that if he shone light on a battery its output increased. Later, other metals, including copper and selenium, were shown to be photosensitive. In fact, the first device to produce electricity from sunlight—a photovoltaic cell—had been made in 1893.

Silicon, however, was much better at capturing and converting solar energy; and it was this that gave Prince an idea. Bell had rural telephone systems that were beyond the reach of electricity and needed batteries to power them. For years, Bell had been losing money on them because the batteries did not last long and they had to be changed. What if silicon could be used to build solar-power batteries?

In answer, Bell developed a solar cell consisting of thin wafers of silicon, with traces of arsenic and boron. The result was impressive: the cells were ten times as efficient as any previous device. The only problem was that they were too expensive to develop, and too unreliable in practice—the cells needed direct sunlight because ordinary light was not good enough. Bell had to stop all the development work.

Inspiration from space

The findings inspired support from a rather different source, however. When the United States sent up a second satellite on March 17, 1958, as part of its space program, it carried a silicon solar panel made of 108 cells to recharge its batteries. What's more, it worked superbly—much to everyone's surprise. No one had expected it to last, and it had not been given an on-off switch. As a result, it went on producing signals, cluttering up the airways for five years. After that, all satel-

SOLAR FLIGHT The sun-powered Solar Challenger conquered the English Channel in July 1981. Solar cells on the wings and tail provided power to two tiny batteries.

lites were powered by photovoltaics, with deep-space vehicles carrying as many as 40,000 cells.

In space, of course, there is unlimited direct sunlight. On Earth, given the night-and-day cycle and bad weather, the cells were unreliable and expensive. In 1970, each watt of power cost up to $200. The terrestrial future for solar cells seemed less than

SUN POWER STATION Solar One in California uses 1,818 sun-tracking mirrors to generate electricity.

promising—at least until Arab nations quadrupled the price of their oil in 1973. So came the impetus for a massive research program implemented and funded by the U.S. government under Richard Nixon.

A new generation

Results came quickly. New materials boosted efficiency by more than 20 percent, and improved some basic practical qualities. For example, the panels—which consisted of cells sitting in rubberized bedding, all contained in aluminum trays—mysteriously seemed to fall apart after a month or so. It

1929 The French build a plant to collect solar heat from the sea, off the coast of Cuba

transpired that termites had discovered that the rubber bedding was ideal for building nests. New panels were covered with glass—and now have a life span measured in decades, even in the Amazon rain forest.

In recent years, solar cells have become well established, even in temperate regions, and power anything from electronic calculators to buildings. A solar-powered plane flew the English Channel in 1981; and solar-powered cars raced across Australia for the World Solar Challenge in 1987. Perhaps inevitably, Australia boasts some of the most extensive uses of solar power. In the Northern Territory, more than 80 percent of households use it to heat their hot water.

In the future, it is likely that fewer gains in efficiency will be possible. But costs continue to drop steadily—opening the door on a revolution that is still to happen.

HOME TRUTHS Solar energy can be adapted for northern climates. This self-sufficient solar house is in Freiberg, Germany.

THE POWER OF REFLECTION

Solar cells are not the only way to harness the sun's energy. According to legend, the ancient Greeks constructed a barrage of mirrors that concentrated the sun's rays on the approaching Roman fleet and set their sails alight during the siege of Syracuse in 212 B.C. Exactly the same principle underlay the building of industrial-sized solar furnaces such as the "sun oven" in the French Pyrenees (below). Other solar furnaces include the huge Solar 1 in Mexico, but such devices have their limitations. They have to be large, and they need many hours of direct sunlight—so are best suited to desert areas. However, in hot, dry conditions, the highly polished, delicate mirrors become covered in dust. They have to be washed frequently, a labor-intensive activity that requires a lot of water—a scarce commodity in desert regions.

1954 Bell Telephone scientists notice silicon's ability to convert sunlight into electricity

1958 U.S. satellite is launched with silicon solar panels

1974 President Richard Nixon gives green light to funding for solar power research

1987 First World Solar Challenge for solar-powered cars, Australia

WIND AND WAVES

GOING FOR GREEN WITH CLEAN, FREE AND ENDLESS SOURCES OF ENERGY

For centuries, civilizations have exploited natural resources such as wind and water. The water wheel was the first hydraulic engine ever invented, and was used as far back as the 1st century B.C. to turn grindstones in mills. These days, environmental concerns focusing on the depletion of resources such as coal, as well as fears about the safety of nuclear fuel, are bringing attention back to these basic sources of power. They are clean, they are free and—in the case of wind, at least—they are available almost anywhere in the world.

The winds of change

The idea of using windmills to generate electricity was obvious enough—the first one was built in Denmark in 1890. Small devices became common in the 1940s, but only in the 1970s did research start seriously into wind power as a national resource.

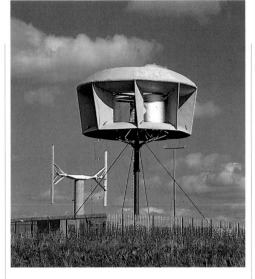

WINDJAMMERS Two experimental vertical axis wind turbines in wind-swept South Wales. Balancing cost and return for these systems tested the mettle of designers.

CURRENT AIR Whirling "egg-beater" turbines (above) and the more familiar triple-bladed rotors (below) were both installed on windy Altamont Pass, California, in 1985.

RIVER RETURNS The Zambezi powers much of central Africa, dammed first at Kariba then here at Cabora Bassa, Mozambique.

Developments evolved on two tracks—single, large-scale machines, and smaller ones operating en masse as wind "farms."

No one has ever doubted the potential of wind power. A recent European Union study has estimated that if all the most suitable sites were developed, Europe could have 400,000 wind machines supplying the Continent's electrical needs three times over.

Until recently, however, there was a big gap between theory and practice, as scientists experimented to produce the best balance between conflicting criteria. The crucial decision involved the size and design of the machine (old-fashioned windmills, for example, could never be strong enough to operate at speeds efficient for the generation of electricity). One way to exploit the wind was to build very large machines—double the blade length and you quadruple the amount of energy that can be produced. At first sight, then, it seemed the bigger the machine the better.

That was the route chosen by early wind-energy designers such as Palmer Putnam, an American engineer, who in 1941 headed the team that designed a wind turbine for the S. Morgan Smith Co. Their creation, a monster 100 feet high, with two blades 174 feet across, towered over the Green Mountains in Vermont. But the machine lost one of its blades in 1945 and was subsequently dismantled.

There have been a number of successors to the Smith-Putnam turbine, notably the American MOD 5-B in Hawaii; and a British one on Burgar Hill in the Orkney Islands north of Scotland. This giant, with its two blades, each 100 feet long, had cost some $30 million by the time it was commissioned in 1988. It was well on its way to pro-

1941 Palmer Putnam's monster wind device installed in Green Mountains, Vermont

ducing at full capacity—providing enough electricity for 2,000 people—when cracks appeared in the hub section of the blades. In 1993, the government announced plans to have it demolished, but private investors stepped in to save it.

Another route was to develop small-scale generators, like those that had already proved useful to farmers in the American Midwest and the Australian outback. This smaller-scale approach, backed by the U.S. government, lay behind a massive growth of wind turbines in California in the 1980s. Several of these wind farms are able to generate as much power as a nuclear plant. Today, with over 17,000 turbines, California generates half the world's wind energy.

As wind farms continue to prove themselves, the two original approaches have started to merge. Wind turbines have increased in size—to about 80 feet in diameter—and are now built in large numbers. The only problems they pose are that they are not noise-free and must stand on extensive, exposed sites.

Currently, wind energy supplies the needs of 1.25 million people and, in 1993, sales exceeded $1 billion. From 1985 to 1990, performance improved 50 percent, while generating costs almost halved.

On the crest of a wave

Meanwhile, technology has also tried to make use of water power with techniques that have been

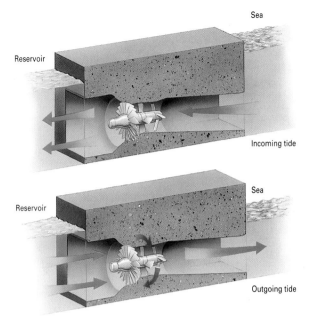

MOON RIVER At the experimental Annapolis tidal power station in Nova Scotia, Canada, high tidal waters are sluiced into a reservoir. Electricity is generated as the water is sluiced back to the sea on the ebbing tide.

around a lot longer. Hydroelectricity, a major power source, is well over 100 years old—all of the inventions that made it possible were developed during the 19th century. By the 1990s, however, its potential had been severely reduced, mainly because most favorable sites in the industrialized world had already been exhausted.

Using similar principles, another pollution-free alternative seemed to lie in tidal energy, with—in theory—great potential for nations surrounded by coastline. France led the way in 1967 but, as with hydroelectric power stations, the initial development costs are extremely high and there are thorny environmental implications. Canada has the only other commercial-sized development.

One way forward in terms of cheap, renewable sources of energy may lie in wave power. Wave-power devices require little initial investment and can be set up offshore or on coastal rocks. The first, a single module in Scotland, is capable of producing enough power to supply a small town. In the future, it is anticipated that they will be grouped (as in wind farms) to increase capacity, the main initial potential lying in island communities worldwide.

1950　　　2000
1967 First tidal barrage constructed, Rance River, Brittany, France
1981 First wind farms, in Altamont and Tehachapi, California
1988 First wave-power device, Scotland

FROM FAMILY FARM TO AGRIBUSINESS

THE ANCIENT SCOURGE OF FAMINE GIVES WAY TO MODERN PROBLEMS OF OVERABUNDANCE

In the early years of the century, farming in Europe still bore signs of its medieval roots: labor-intensive, varied, and based on horse power. In the vast expanses of the American prairies, however, change was under way. There, the first tractors, combine harvesters and other machinery enabled ever fewer hands to farm ever more acres. After 1945, as the new techniques spread, the steady climb in efficiency brought extraordinary changes—to the Western world at least. In the 1860s, it took 50 man-hours to handle an acre of grain. In the 1960s, it took just three. An ancient scourge—famine—gave way to a modern one—food mountains.

What the First World War and farming had in common was that they both needed vehicles to carry loads through mud. To do this effectively, the weight of the vehicles—cumbersome steam-driven machines that bogged down easily—had to be distributed as widely as possible. Farming led the way to a solution, thanks to a caterpillar-type device for tracked vehicles patented in England as far back as 1825.

In 1904, this idea was taken up by Benjamin Holt in California, who incorporated it into a steam-driven tracked vehicle, and, two years later, a gasoline-driven one. But instead of going into service as workhorses for farmers, they were utilized by the Allied forces in the First World War. They, along with similar inventions such as the Bullock Creeping Grip and the Killen-Strait (also from the United States), became warhorses on the western front.

The wartime production of tanks led to new, better-tracked tractors. In 1925, Holt merged with another manufacturer, Best, to form Caterpillar, and the best-known name in tracked vehicles was born.

Speed, comfort and silence

By 1920, tractors of all kinds—tracked and wheeled—were common in America, and no longer rarities in Europe. This was, in large measure, the result of Henry Ford's involvement. Following the success of his

HARVESTING REWARDS

During the Second World War, under the lend–lease agreement with the United States and the Ministry of Agriculture's Goods and Services Scheme, American equipment became available to British farmers. In *Seventy Summers*, farmer Tony Harman describes what happened at that time:

"Like many other people, I took on as much as I could afford—an American-made crawler tractor and a British-made plough to go with it, a combine harvester and a drier and a pick–up baler to go with that, and, later on, an American wheeled tractor which was much faster and more advanced than any tractor I had had previously. The crawler tractor, a Caterpillar diesel, cost just £784 [about $200] . . . I remember thinking at the time it was terribly expensive . . . The Caterpillar had a very big output and, unlike horses, never got tired, so we could have two people working it in shifts, and so plough three or four times as much as we had previously. . . .

"When the combine arrived from America, it came in two or three huge packing cases and was of a new type . . . It arrived with a book of instructions, and the next day, two agents from the manufacturers, the International Harvester Company, were to come and put it together. Will Barnett and I had a good look at it and I did not understand it at all. The next day, Will Barnett worked with the two fitters to put the machine together and at the end of the day the man in charge said to me: 'This machine will work well and you won't have any trouble at all, not like in some places.' I asked why he thought this, and he replied: 'Your man must have read the book through from start to finish because he understands it as well as we do.' 'Well, that's very strange,' I said, 'because the man cannot read.'"

THE ALLIS-CHELMERS MODEL U tractor was available with either iron wheels or pneumatic tires.

FRUIT MACHINES In the 1990s, giant mist-blowers treat apple trees in France.

model T car, Ford produced a wheeled tractor on the same lines: sturdy, simple, reliable and cheap. He formed a new corporation, Henry Ford and Son, to manufacture it, and it was so popular that the new Bolshevik government in Russia bought 25,000 models.

By modern standards, Fordsons—as they were known – like all wheeled tractors, were basic: they had iron wheels with lugs that bit into the ground to provide traction, metal seats and no cabs. Although they could plough well enough in dry weather, they tore up roads and slipped when ploughing wet soil. Rubber-rimmed wheels, like those on traction engines, allowed road travel, but were no good for field work.

These problems inspired a new development in 1929, when an American company, Allis-Chalmers, first built a tractor with a set of oversized rubber tires. It went into production in 1932 as the Model U, but, although it performed well, farmers were concerned about punctures. The company decided to use an extraordinary marketing strategy. It hired a local racing driver to take a specially adapted model round a track at 35 mph at the Milwaukee State Fair—causing a sensation. The next step was a whole team of specially adapted tractors, which went on tour staging races at state fairs. Finally, a racing driver, Ab Jenkins, managed to clock 67 mph in a Model U on a course on the Utah salt flats. The record still holds.

The publicity worked. A million people saw the tractors; millions more saw the press coverage. The tractor sold well, rubber tires were accepted, and every other manufacturer followed Allis-Chalmers' lead. By 1937, almost half of America's tractors had tires.

Bringing in the harvest

Horse-drawn reapers had been around since the early 19th century, and tractor-drawn ones were common enough in the early decades of the 20th. In Australia, in 1938, a reaper towed by a tractor harvested 3,300 bushels of wheat (100 tons) in a day, a record that stood for 33 years.

However, as America emerged from the Depression, it became clear that there would be a market for a self-propelled reaper-thresher, and not only in the U.S. Australia, Argentina, and Europe were all significant markets and, in late 1937, agricultural machine manufacturers Massey-Harris saw the potential. They tested the first self-propelled reaper-thresher, a machine 16 feet wide, which they termed a "combine harvester" or combine. A smaller, lighter version, the No. 21 SP (for "self-propelled") went into production in 1941.

The timing was perfect. World war had brought to a sudden end the design of new farm machinery—steel was needed for ships—and had created an unprecedented demand for home-grown food. The 1942 North American cereal crop was the largest ever—wheat alone topped 75 million tons. And yet demand continued to rise. Joe Tucker, the Massey-Harris vice-president, sought permission to build an extra 500 combines as a special contribution to the war effort, arguing that each one would harvest half a million extra tons of grain, and release 1,000 tractors for other work.

Tucker won his case. When the machines were finished in time for the 1944 harvest, they became the "Harvest Brigade." They swept into the prairies with military precision, working north as the grain ripened. By September, when they reached the Canadian border, they had harvested 750,000 tons per million acres, saving 300,000 man-hours and 500,000 gallons of fuel. The combine had proved itself at home, and went on to do so in Europe after the war.

HARVEST HOME In the U.S., the great march of combines has been a familiar sight for 50 years.

1955 Tractors on American farms exceed the number of horses and mules

FIGHTING PESTS WITH CHEMICAL POWER

THE NEVER-ENDING RACE TO OUTFLANK FAST-EVOLVING PARASITES

Boosting harvests with new machinery was one way of improving agricultural efficiency. Another was to apply chemical fertilizer, which has increased yields many times over. Yet a third method was to kill the pests that destroy crops, the catastrophic losses inspiring a sequence of new chemical inventions. But since the pests themselves evolve defenses against every new invention, each chemical battle is part of a never-ending war.

Locusts plagued Egypt in Biblical times, and they have plagued much of Africa since. On the ground, a swarm can cover 500 square miles—50,000 tons of hungry insects, consuming their own weight every day. So when, in 1939, Swiss chemist Paul Muller patented a powerful insecticide that was sta-

WHAT'S YOUR POISON? The century has seen intensive use of pesticides, above and below, but we are starting to pay the price.

ble and did not seem to affect other animals, its arrival was greeted euphorically. From 1945, the poison, DDT (dichlorodiphenyltrichloroethane), was used almost indiscriminately.

Briefly, it seemed that mankind was winning the war against all kinds of destructive and disease-bearing pests. Millions of lives were saved, but the euphoria was short-lived. In 1947, a DDT-resistant strain of insects emerged—a pattern that would be repeated with many other pests and poisons.

The war now became a frantic race to outflank evolution. New poisons bred resistance that in turn inspired increased dosages and more new poisons. Each new development had its impact on the environment, with growing concern from consumers and ecologists.

DDT: the magic fades

One of DDT's apparent advantages was that it was long-lasting—a quality that was to prove double-edged in the early 1960s when biologist Rachel Carson revealed the extent to which it had entered the food chain. The public furor caused DDT to be banned or severely restricted across the industrialized world.

Still, new pesticides appeared every year, designed to be ever more specific, always with less impact on the environment and on other species. In the United States in the

A SEX-TRAP TO SAVE COTTON

Every year, the pink bollworm moth ravages cotton crops worldwide, occasionally resulting in 90 percent losses. Pesticides have proved ineffective because the bollworm caterpillars eat their way inside the cotton bolls, where they are protected. Until recently, the only controls were traditional ones that also destroyed other beneficial insects.

In the 1970s, Derek Campion at the Natural Resources Institute, started work on a program in Egypt, where the pink bollworm is the major pest. His idea was to attract male moths on a false trail away from the females, so that they could not mate. All farmers had to do was dab artificial female pheromones on plants in the cotton fields at the right time to attract the males, who would end their lives disappointed and confused. It was cheap, it was safe and it worked. Crop quality improved, environmental impact diminished, costs

dropped. In one village, El Manzala, farmers had also made wonderful honey, until boll-worm pesticides killed the bees. Once the local farmers used pheromone, the bees returned and so did the honey—24,250 pounds in the first year.

1970s, more than 300 companies marketed 8,000 pesticides, with the market growing at 10-15 percent annually. Chlorinated hydrocarbons multiplied, and still there were problems. When Scottish grasslands were sprayed with dieldrin, a chlorinated hydrocarbon, golden eagles and many other creatures at the top of the food chain perished.

Locusts exemplify, in extreme form, some of the problems faced by governments and chemical companies. The lands they devastate are economic borderlands, which in financial terms do not repay the immense effort and expense of an all-out assault. In any event, experts agree that a generalized assault would be bound to fail, for no attack could hope to touch more than 10 percent of the locust population.

Recently, the emphasis has shifted away from widespread assaults to localized ones, and from chemicals to other means of attacking pests, using natural products—fungi, bacteria, viruses. Though there are success stories, experts doubt that any one invention will prove a universal panacea. Pests—especially locusts—are here to stay.

CONQUERING DISTANCE

THE INTERNAL COMBUSTION ENGINE, INVENTED IN THE MID 19TH CENTURY, ACCELERATED THE PACE OF LIFE IN THE 20TH. HITCHED TO A SET OF WHEELS, IT BECAME THE AUTOMOBILE AND, WITH A PROPELLER ATTACHED, THE AIRPLANE. THE INVENTION OF THE JET ENGINE SHRANK THE WORLD FURTHER; THE ROCK-ET BROUGHT RELEASE FROM THE EARTH ITSELF. HUMANKIND WOULD LAND ON THE MOON WITHIN 70 YEARS OF THE FIRST POWERED FLIGHT.

THE AUTOMOBILE: FROM HORSELESS CARRIAGE TO DREAM MACHINE

THE AUTOMOBILE INDUSTRY SET THE PACE FOR THE INDUSTRIAL DEVELOPMENT OF THE 20TH CENTURY

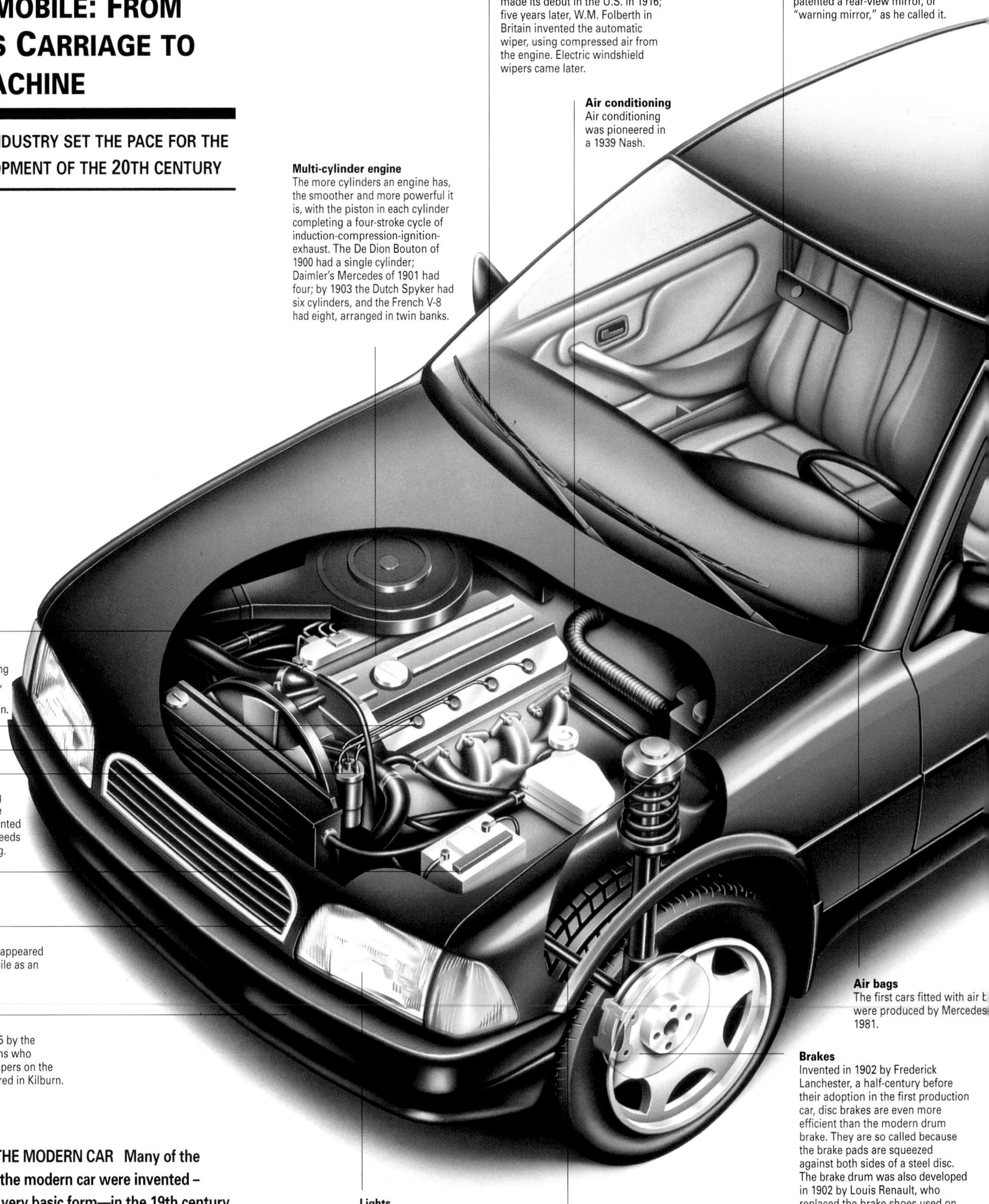

Windshield wiper
A mechanical windshield wiper made its debut in the U.S. in 1916; five years later, W.M. Folberth in Britain invented the automatic wiper, using compressed air from the engine. Electric windshield wipers came later.

Rear-view mirror
In 1906, Frenchman Alfred Faucher patented a rear-view mirror, or "warning mirror," as he called it.

Air conditioning
Air conditioning was pioneered in a 1939 Nash.

Multi-cylinder engine
The more cylinders an engine has, the smoother and more powerful it is, with the piston in each cylinder completing a four-stroke cycle of induction-compression-ignition-exhaust. The De Dion Bouton of 1900 had a single cylinder; Daimler's Mercedes of 1901 had four; by 1903 the Dutch Spyker had six cylinders, and the French V-8 had eight, arranged in twin banks.

Fuel injection
In 1906, a system of vaporizing and spraying fuel into the cylinders, without a carburetor, was developed in Britain.

Spark plugs

Cooling fan

Distributor
A device for applying electric current to the spark plugs was invented in 1908 by Edward Deeds and Charles Kettering.

Battery

Chrome
Chromium plate first appeared on the 1925 Oldsmobile as an advance on nickel.

Bumper
First patented in 1905 by the London firm of Simms who installed rubber bumpers on the cars they manufactured in Kilburn.

Air bags
The first cars fitted with air b were produced by Mercedes 1981.

Brakes
Invented in 1902 by Frederick Lanchester, a half-century before their adoption in the first production car, disc brakes are even more efficient than the modern drum brake. They are so called because the brake pads are squeezed against both sides of a steel disc. The brake drum was also developed in 1902 by Louis Renault, who replaced the brake shoes used on carts with curved shoes which pressed outward onto the inside of a drum turning with the wheel. Anti-lock braking was perfected by Bosch in Germany in 1972, and systems were being installed in production cars from 1978.

ASSEMBLING THE MODERN CAR Many of the components of the modern car were invented – sometimes in a very basic form—in the 19th century, long before their development and adoption. This illustration of a composite, modern car focuses on those components that were developed during the 20th century.

Lights
An electric system, including headlights, sidelights and taillights working on an 8 volt "accumulator" (or storage battery), was offered by the Pockley Automobile Electric Lighting Syndicate of England in 1908.

Front-wheel drive
The first front-wheel drive appeared on a 1934 Citroen 7.

1900							1950
1901 Daimler's Mercedes	1904 Michelin tires with a raised flat tread give a better grip	1908 Debut of Model T Ford	1912 The electric self-starter makes driving easier 1913 Assembly-line production by Ford	1922 The "Baby" Austin 7		1934 Volkswagen "Beetle" designed	

Safety glass
Shatterproof glass was invented in 1909 by French chemist Edouard Benedictus, who sandwiched a thin sheet of Celluloid between two sheets of glass. From 1920, these windshields were sold as Triplex (with non-yellowing plastic replacing Celluloid from 1936).

Muffler

Catalytic converter
The first modern catalytic converter was developed in 1974 by General Motors.

Tires
Tires were made at first of iron or solid rubber, but inflated tires soon demonstrated their superiority when, in 1904, Michelin devised a raised flat tread to give a better grip. The tubeless self-sealing tire appeared in 1947; and radial-ply in 1953.

Seat belts
Although patented in 1903, seat belts were first fitted on a mass-produced car in 1963, by Volvo.

Speedometer
Introduced in 1902 by the British firm of Thorpe and Salter.

Gear selection
By 1929, Detroit's General Motors was offering a smooth-changing synchromesh gearbox on its Cadillacs; and in 1934, Chrysler introduced overdrive with a fifth gear that automatically engaged to improve performance and slash fuel consumption at high speed.

Self-starter
The first practical electric self-starter was devised by American engineer Charles Kettering in 1912 —with urgent encouragement from Cadillac manufacturer Henry Leland, who was nursing an injury from a kicking crank handle.

ecades before the development of the automobile, a crafty American lawyer named George Selden applied for a patent for a "road locomotive" with "nonanimal" traction. Dated 1879, this application anticipated—in extremely vague ways—the shape of things to come. Actual inventors would go on to patent bits and pieces, such as a combustion system, a steering mechanism, or brakes, but Selden's claim was for the whole thing. Therefore, when cars took to the road, Selden received royalties on American-built vehicles—until the car manufacturer Henry Ford declared the Selden patent worthless and eventually won the ensuing court case. It is a story that illustrates both the complexities involved in the granting of patents and the way in which the invention of component parts is critical – particularly with products such as the car— to the development of the whole.

By 1900, the automobile—which was to transform everday life in the 20th century as

ROYAL WARRANT **Daimler supplied cars for the British royal family from 1900; this Daimler Kimberley was built in 1901.**

much as any other single invention—was already in development. In hundreds of hand-crafted experiments that fed upon each other, German engineering was being complemented by French flair, and both of these would shortly be seized upon by American enterprise. The French partnership of De Dion and Bouton was producing more than 50 makes of car with a single-cylinder gas engine, which developed 4.5 horsepower at 1,500 rpm and snorted merrily.

Although none of its individual features was new, the first visibly modern car took to the road in 1901. It was designed by the Germans Wilhelm Maybach and Paul Daimler for financier Emile Jellinek, and

1950   2000

1953 Citroen's new suspension system   1959 Bombardier's snowmobile   1974 Modern catalytic converter developed   1981 Air bags fitted to some Mercedes

named after his daughter, Mercedes. The car had a handsome, low, pressed-steel chassis and a long hood with a cellular, or honeycombed, radiator for cooling the engine. The wonders beneath the hood were equally state-of-the-art: there was a four-cylinder 35 horsepower engine, and a gear lever, worked by a patented gate, that made selection possible for the first time.

For the first decade of the century, motoring was for the hardy, with the windshield a dangerous, easily shattered extra. In 1909, however, French chemist Edouard Benedictus invented non-shatter safety glass by sandwiching Celluloid between sheets of glass.

Night driving was also precarious, as drivers relied upon oil lamps until the introduction in 1901 of the acetylene gas lamp, which generated so bright a beam that slats had to be placed over the glass. The first completely electrical system, including headlights, sidelights, and taillights, was offered in 1908 by a British company.

During the automobile's early years, governments did their best to curb headstrong drivers, giddy with the possibility of a speedy new toy. A 1902 Vermont law required that cars be preceded by an attendant waving a red flag, and that same year,

FUN FOR ALL An advertisement from a 1932 issue of *Vogue* promotes the electric self-starter (invented in 1912), which made driving so much easier.

CARS FOR THE MASSES

It was not until Henry Ford was 40 that he had the vision that would make him the world's first billionaire. "The way to make automobiles is to make one automobile like another automobile," he told prospective investors in 1903, "just as one match is like another match." His supreme creation, the Model T, was born in 1908 and the man his workers called "the speed-up king" did not discontinue production until 15 million of them had rolled off the line by 1927. In his autobiography, he described the principles of the assembly line and the type of person best suited to work on one:

"A Ford car contains about five thousand parts. Some of the parts are fairly bulky and others are almost the size of watch parts. In our first assembling we simply started to put a car together at a spot on the floor and the workmen brought to it the parts as they were needed in exactly the same way that one builds a house. The first step forward in assembly came when we began taking the work to the men instead of the men to the work. Along about April 1, 1913, we first tried the experiment of an assembly line. We tried it on assembling the fly-wheel magneto. We try everything in a little way first. I believe that this was the first moving line ever installed. The idea came in a general way from the overhead trolley that the Chicago packers use in dressing beef. That line established the efficiency of the method and we now use it everywhere. Now the line assembles the whole car. The speed of the moving work had to be carefully tried out. The idea is that a man must not be hurried in his work – he must have every second necessary but not a single unnecessary second. The chassis assembly line, for instance, goes at a pace of six feet per minute. In the chassis assembling are forty-five separate operations or stations. The first men fasten four mud-guard brackets to the chassis frame; the motor arrives on the tenth operation and so on in detail. The man who places a part does not fasten it.

MOTOR MAN Henry Ford at the seat of his first (1896) car. "A great many things are going to change," he predicted, and he made sure they did.

The man who puts in a bolt does not put on the nut; the man who puts on the nut does not tighten it. On operation number thirty-four the budding motor gets its gasoline; it has previously received lubrication; on operation number forty-four the radiator is filled with water, and on operation number forty-five the car drives out . . . Repetitive labor is a terrifying prospect to a certain kind of mind. It is terrifying to me. I could not possibly do the same thing day in and day out, but to other minds, perhaps I might say the majority of minds, repetitive operations hold no terrors. In fact to some kinds thought is absolutely appalling. To them the ideal job is one where the creative instinct need not be expressed . . .The average worker wants a job in which he does not have to think."

Minneapolis gave out its first speeding ticket—a $10 fine for reckless driving at the speed of 10 miles per hour. In Britain, anti-motoring magistrates kept cars to a crawl; the speed limit was only 12 mph in 1900. This did not deter pioneers such as the British firm of Thorpe and Salter, which introduced the speedometer in 1902. It was scaled from zero to 35 mph—an audacious gesture, given that the speed limit had only just been raised to 20 mph.

Toward mass production

The auto industry in America got off to a slow start, compounded at the turn of the century by a stiff tax on imports. The high-society tone of the opening of the first automobile show, in New York in 1900, reminded one commentator "of the Horse Show at its best." Vehicles powered by steam or electricity predominated, but a single-cylinder gas runabout, with tiller steering, caught people's eye. This was Charles Old's Curved Dash. In 1901, he was turning out ten of these Oldsmobiles every week, and 100 a week by 1904, foreshadowing the revolution to be brought about by mass production.

Scorning the hand-crafting traditions of Europe, Cadillac in 1903 began selling cars with fully interchangeable parts, and 1908 saw the debut of the Model T Ford, a car revolutionary in its utilitarian durability and rapid assembly. In 1913 Henry Ford installed a moving conveyor belt to perfect his assembly-line system, producing his millionth car two years later. The Model T "Tin Lizzie" created—and filled—the first mass market for automobiles. It sold for as little as $290, was rugged enough to negotiate the roads of the day, and was so simple that rural

1900   1950

1901 Daimler's Mercedes

1904 Michelin tires with a raised flat tread give a better grip

1908 Debut of Model T Ford

1912 The electric self-starter makes driving easier
1913 Assembly-line production by Ford

1922 The "Baby" Austin 7

1934 Volkswagen "Beetle" designed

folk could fix it. "I did nothing," Ford insisted. "I merely assembled into a car the discoveries of other men." But his organizational genius had a social impact that went far beyond the creation of America's major industry. The success of the Model T led him to introduce in 1914 the eight-hour workday—at the unheard-of daily rate of $5. In 1923 the big manufacturers capped the mass-production revolution by inventing design obsolescence; each year thereafter,

MICHELIN MAN The roly-poly figure helped to create worldwide brand loyalty for the pioneering French tire company, Michelin.

new models were introduced to stimulate sales and to squeeze out smaller rivals.

Ease, safety and style were now what concerned inventors most. Dipping headlights, antifreeze for radiators, interior heating and the electronic fuel gauge had all appeared by the late 1920s. Ford had stipulated black as his sole color option, but the advent in 1924 of a spray-on cellulose lacquer unleashed the rainbow.

The postwar world

The pace of innovation accelerated soon after the Second World War. Air conditioning, pioneered in a 1939 Nash, was well received in America, as were power-steering and automatic gear-changing. Refinery advances in 1949 produced more efficient fuels with higher octane levels, and in the 1950s aluminum alloys made engines lighter and more durable. In 1953 Citroen perfected a revolutionary suspension system combining a gas and an oil-based liquid, which compensated for the bumpiest road and the most lopsided car-load. This was fitted to some models from 1955 onward, along with power-assisted brakes, transmission and steering, but the cost limited sales.

CENTURY OF PROGRESS Over the past 80 years, production lines have evolved from Henry Ford's conveyor-belt concept (top) to the automated line (above), where robots assemble Peugeot cars in a French factory.

Environmental concerns in America spurred a spate of creativity to curb pollution. General Motors was first to devise a catalytic converter that chemically treated the most noxious emissions. By 1988, when Ford introduced a cheaper converter, Toyota of Japan had pioneered a low-pollution engine that conformed to exacting emission standards without a converter. Seat belts, first installed by Volvo in 1963, became stan-

1953 Citroen's new suspension system

1959 Bombardier's snowmobile

1974 Modern catalytic converter developed

1981 Air bags fitted to some Mercedes

INVENTING THE SNOWMOBILE

The death of a baby in the winter of 1926 inspired the invention that has given mobility to people in snowbound lands throughout the world. Canadian mechanic Joseph-Armand Bombardier had no means of rushing his sick young son to the nearest hospital, 20 miles away; and so when the boy died of a simple case of appendicitis, the grieving father resolved to invent a snow vehicle to match the automobile.

By 1935, Bombardier had devised a system of traction using a drive sprocket and rubber track, but it was not until March 1956 that he perfected and patented his design for "a small vehicle with a light motor and with a single track as wide as the vehicle itself." He had invented the snowmobile. Bombardier's machine made its debut in 1959 as the Ski-dog; by 1960 it had become the Ski-doo, evidently through the inspired mistake of a shipper who had wrongly stencilled some crates. The name stuck and the response was immediate. "Santa's sold his reindeer," a publicist declared, as thousands of dog teams across the Arctic were hastened into retirement.

dard in American cars during the 1960s and eventually obligatory, as they did in Europe, by the 1980s. Air bags to cushion collisions were perfected by Mercedes in the 1970s and installed in many models from 1981.

Active protection dates from the late 1970s, when a few steering columns were designed to collapse on impact, and it went on to become a priority with designers in the early 1990s. Whiplash was countered by Audi with a head-securing seat belt that

locked during collision, while some cars had a steering wheel that jerked forward to avert chest-impact.

Many cars now carried more computing power than had been required to take men to the Moon. A prototype of 1985, the twin-turbocharged Nissan CUE-X, incorporated a performance-optimizing "drive-by-wire" electronic control system, equivalent to the most advanced avionic design; four-wheel power steering; and a laser, which monitored the range and motion of the vehicle ahead and instructed the on-board microcomputer to slow down when it registered imminent danger. The dashboard featured a route-guidance screen and a display that showed servicing information.

Four-wheel steering became an option on some car models, increasing comfort as well as safety. The combination of sensors, sophisticated electronics, and computers prompted a wave of inventions: from sensor-responsive suspension systems that made allowances for road conditions and driving style, to Japanese wipers that adjusted their speed to rain-intensity, and a British anti-glare rear-view mirror. Volkswagen developed a laser-guided self-parking system and Audi toyed with a car with twin engines. New materials came into use, often adapted from aviation, such

ELECTRIC MOTORS The Auto Red Bug was one of many failed attempts to popularize electric cars. Pollution forced a reappraisal by the end of the century.

as headlight-glass adapted from the cockpit canopies of advanced jet fighters.

Toward the end of the century, the industry turned full circle with a race to develop a practical, pollution-free electric car. This quest had been abandoned almost a century before because batteries of the time had limited range and power.

CAR RENTALS
In 1918, a 22-year-old Chicago car salesman named Walter Jacob thought people might like to rent cars rather than use taxis. He started with a fleet of 12 Model T Fords. In 1923, he sold out to a man named Hertz.

TEARAWAY TEARDROP Streamlining, popular in the 1930s, reasserted itself in the 1990s—as in this 1993 Jaguar XJ220.

TAKING OFF ON TWO WHEELS

FROM LUMBERING MACHINES TO STREAMLINED SYMBOLS OF PERSONAL POWER AND SPEED

The motorcycle and the car evolved together around the turn of the century; in 1901 the familiar low-slung engine which responds to a twist-grip throttle was devised in Paris by Michel and Eugene Werner. The idea of hitching a sidecar to the bike occurred well before there were machines powerful enough to take one. This had been achieved by 1910, and in 1916 an articulated assembly which allowed the bike and sidecar to "lean" into curves was designed in the United States. Sidecars became hugely popular in Britain, where as many motorbikes as cars were in use until the mid-1920s, when the economies of mass production brought down car prices.

Motorcycle milestones

America's most famous designer and manufacturer of motorcycles, Harley-Davidson, Inc., originated in 1903 when William Harley and brothers William, Walter, and Arthur Davidson set up shop in Milwaukee. Their bikes, which by 1909 could exceed 60 mph, became so popular that four years later, more than 150 competitors had entered the market. But Harley-Davidson maintained their supremacy by supplying motorcycles to police departments and to the military. In the First World War, they provided the U.S. Armed forces with 20,000 bikes, and in the Second World War with more than 90,000. By the 1950s, they were once again the only American manufacturer. Many of their models, such as the Super Glide, the Low Rider, and the Electra Glide, became American classics and inspired a vibrant biker culture.

Japanese bikes were also at the vanguard of motorcycle innovation. They were the first to forsake kick-starting for electronic starters, and from the 1980s they dominated in development. Innovations included the first turbocharged production model, a 1981 Honda, and a resilient alloy frame, introduced on a 1988 Yamaha.

Big bikes became so massive that a reverse gear was devised for a 1988 Honda, whose six-cylinder engine developed more power than many cars. A radical new engine with oval, twin-plug piston chambers was introduced in the 160 mph NR-750, a 1995 Honda with carbon-reinforced fairing, titanium parts and a surface coating to improve airstreaming; at $78,000, it was the most expensive motorcycle yet.

The story of the bicycle

The bicycle also underwent high-tech upgrading after a quiet start. The classic English safety model, with same size wheels, chain drive, and a crankshaft at the base of the seat-post, was well established by 1900, and progressive improvements in gearing constituted the only major development through much of the century. An internal hub mechanism which could accommodate up to five gears was perfected in 1938.

Innovations such as the small-wheeled, folding Moulton had temporary fad appeal in the 1960s, but from California in 1981 came the mountain bike, with strengthened frame, low gearing, and fat wheels and tires; initially custom-built for a few adventurous spirits, it was taken up by major manufacturers as its popularity spread.

Costly titanium, and components made from alloys such as chromium-molybdenum, created lighter, stronger and more expensive bikes, with the aerodynamics of racing models coaxed into improvement with oval tubing

WORLD BEATERS The British Norton (top) and the American Harley-Davidson (above) are design classics and have attracted huge cult followings in the world of motorcycles.

and reprofiled handlebars. Drag was further reduced by replacing spoked wheels with slim carbon-fiber wafers in 1984, as new high-tech materials did for the conventional bicycle what it had done for the motorcycle.

SUPER BIKES British bicyclist Chris Boardman races at the 1992 Barcelona Olympics on his streamlined machine.

TRAFFIC CONTROL

CONTAINING THE CHAOS CREATED BY CARS HAS BEEN A SLOW AND TENTATIVE PROCESS

Turn-of-the-century city streets were noisome and chaotic, awash with manure and with bolting horses a constant danger. The gradual replacement of the horse was soon found to be a mixed blessing, however. In 1901, the first klaxon horn sounded—invented, ironically, by the man who was also responsible for the first electric hearing aid, Millar Hutchinson—and city streets have been noisy places ever since.

As the number of cars and trucks on the roads increased, something had to be done to improve road surfaces themselves. The problem was solved in Britain in 1907 by spreading them with coal tar. White showed up well on the new black-top, and by 1911 white road markings had made their debut in the U.S. as the center line safety strip.

Cat's-eyes, invented in 1934 by road contractor Percy Shaw was another British contribution to road safety. Shaw was driving home in heavy fog one night and was saved

EARLY GRIDLOCK The mass production of motor cars led in no time to traffic jams and exhaust pollution; this is Paris in 1923.

CLOCK LIGHTS Traffic lights in Berlin in 1931 had three colors, and motorists watched at which color the hand was pointing.

from going off the road by a cat whose eyes were reflected in his headlights. Shaw's "eyes" consist of a pair of glass prisms fitted over an aluminum reflector and encased in a rubber pad; they made him a fortune.

Heavy traffic

By the 1930s, the Germans were already speeding along a growing network of autobahns—motorways. The first autobahn, designed in 1921 by Karl Fritsch, appropriately doubled as a racetrack. The American version was the parkway, which encircled urban areas with entrance and exit roads instead of intersections, and was fringed by stands of trees and shrubs. The first, the Bronx Parkway, opened in New York in 1925.

One of the factors driving these changes

POLICE STOP

The inventor of radar was an early victim of the radar-gun speed trap. Sir Robert Watson-Watt was on his way to a speaking engagement— appropriately enough to discuss radar—in Canada in 1954, when he was stopped for speeding by a highway patrol. Watson-Watt identified himself and pleaded for mercy, but he was made to pay his fine on the spot.

was the development of increasingly heavy transporters. In 1915 the Michigan blacksmith and wagon-maker August Freuhauf hitched a wagon behind his Model T Ford to improvise transport for his pleasure boat, thereby initiating the dominance of the highways by tractor-trailers. The development in 1930 of a diesel engine for road vehicles by British engineer Cedric Bernard Dicksee, followed in 1934 by the advent of eight-wheeler trucks, hastened the switch of heavy goods from rail to road.

1901 The first klaxon horn

1914 First electric traffic lights appear in U.S.

1921 First autobahn designed in Germany

1934 Cat's-eyes invented

1938 The world's first breathalizer —the "Drunkometer," invented by an American, Dr. R. N. Harger

Road safety

Despite all the new roads, the increased volume of traffic posed problems, particularly in towns. On August 5, 1914, a concerned citizen of Cleveland named Alfred A. Benesch became responsible for the erection of the first electric traffic light; a bell rang when it changed. Amber (now yellow) was added in New York in 1918, after red-green sets had proved too abrupt for the city's criss-cross street grid. Britain was slow to introduce traffic lights—the first set did not appear there until 1927—but was the first country to come up with the "zebra" crossing markings, introduced in 1951.

Where to put all the cars posed a mounting problem, too. This was solved in part by stacking them: the multistory parking garage was the brainchild of a Massachusetts garage owner in 1928. The parking meter was the bright idea of Oklahoma newspaper editor Carlton Magee. An experiment in 1935 was successful enough for Magee to set up a company to manufacture them.

As cars increased in speed, new limits had to be set. The standardization of a 55 mph

ROADS THAT DRIVE CARS

It's a bank holiday, and cars are streaming bumper-to-bumper along the highway, so you let go of the wheel and sit back to read a book, or to chat with the driver ahead. This vision of the future was realized in September 1994, when four cars were grouped together in a "platoon" on a test road in California at over 50 mph, 12 feet apart.

Since the 1980s, the prohibitive cost and the environmental damage caused by highway construction have spurred efforts to develop "smart" roads capable of steering cars through magnetic sensors and radar. The idea is to have roadside computers control the platoons while on-board computers control the cars, with the two systems in constant interaction. Among many challenges, the scientists have yet to perfect a computer program that can cope with magnetic distortions caused by the metal in bridges. The entire on-board computing could be accomplished using a single microchip, with data-space to spare for advertising from hotels and restaurants along the route, and could add less than $500 to the car's cost. One stumbling block to the introduction of a "smart" highway is the question of legal liability. Who faces charges in the event of an automated crash?

FLOW PLAN Officials eye a 1936 design for a German autobahn, including the cloverleaf design that allows motorways to meet head-on and to merge traffic without pause.

speed limit, set in 1973, helped reduce the United States highway fatality rate from 5.21 per 100 million miles driven in 1969 to 3.46 a decade later.

Seven years before that, Congress had made a major step in the movement toward safer driving by establishing the National Safety Bureau, later renamed the National Highway Traffic Safety Administration (NHTSA), which was responsible for setting safety standards for all cars and trucks manufactured after January 15, 1968. The NHTSA required, among other standards, collapsible steering columns and door side-beam reinforcement bars to absorb impacts from the side. By the 1990s, however, many speed limits were raised to 65 mph—cars had become more maneuverable, and thus safer, and higher speeds were shown to be more fuel-efficient.

Coping with congestion

Feverish road construction had been the early response to the traffic explosion but, from the 1960s, invention turned to means of control rather than accommodation. A first attempt at relieving congestion with an automated system was made in Chicago in 1965, when 7 miles of choked highway were fitted with ultra-sonic monitors, each feeding data into a central computer that triggered stop-and-go lights on access roads. In 1986, a European consortium launched Pro-

metheus, a project to develop a computer-guided driving system aimed at relieving congestion and improving safety. At the same time, research in the United States began into automated traffic lanes; these would be equipped with magnetic markers spaced along the road and would control a vehicle through its on-board computer.

In 1992, development started on an Intelligent Vehicle Highway System (IVHS), combining "smart card" computer technology with a radio transmission system. This would enable drivers to pay fines or tolls without stopping, to summon help, to check road and traffic conditions ahead, or simply to communicate with one another.

A pilot stretch of "intelligent" roadway, laced with fiber-optic cables and embedded with probes and sensors, was being constructed in Virginia by the mid-1990s.

TICKING WARDEN By the 1970s, parking meters—an American invention of the 1930s—had become a familiar sight on streets worldwide.

FINDING OUR WAY

FROM INSTINCT AND EYESIGHT TO PINPOINT NAVIGATION BY SATELLITE BEAMS

At the turn of the century, navigators were still relying on the ship's compass to find their way—and, after the first air flight in 1903, pilots depended on nothing more than instinct and landmarks on the ground. However, in 1901, the U.S. Navy had conducted a successful experiment with radiotelegraphs (which transmitted and received messages by wireless telegraphy) over a range of 21 miles. Shore stations were set up, and by 1903 about 50 merchant vessels were equipped with wireless telegraph for receiving information about the weather and the position of other vessels. This initiative in making navigation less hazardous was complemented in 1908 by the first practical gyroscopic compass, produced in Germany. Like a spinning top, the gyroscope maintains its position in space regardless of movements around it; furthermore, the gyrocompass is unaffected by metals and points to true—rather than magnetic—North. The instrument was soon perfected by American inventor Elmer Sperry.

The sinking of the *Titanic* in 1912 concentrated scientific minds, and it was with a view to detecting icebergs that the French scientist Paul Langevin used quartz crystals in 1915 to transmit very short sound waves, which then bounced back from any object in the vicinity. The principle of sending out and then listening to the echo of ultrasonic pulses lay behind the development in the 1920s of Sonar (Sound Navigation Ranging) as a means of underwater detection.

Meanwhile, the Swiss-American engineer Frederick Kolster developed an experimental radio-compass system with transmitters on the New Jersey coast. Navigators had only to note in quick succession the bearings of two signals in order to determine their position roughly. By 1928 the U.S. was webbed with a network of radio stations that guided a pilot from point to point.

The coming of radar

Radar was typical of many modern inventions in that it came about through the effort of many minds over many years. In a patent of 1928, the TV pioneer John Logie Baird described "a method of viewing an object by projecting upon it electromagnetic waves of short wavelength" and believed, with some reason, that he had invented radar. However, the more generally accepted story is that, around 1930, some British Post Office engineers became puzzled by the way in which short-wave radio receivers suffered interference whenever a plane flew by. Their report was filed away, only to become part of top-secret research that, from 1935, led to the development of radar (Radio Detection and Ranging) by a team headed by Robert Watson-Watt. Radar was designed to detect the approach of enemy aircraft at a distance —by timing how long the echo of a radio pulse sent by a transmitter took to be picked up by a radar antenna. The echoes, and their location, appeared as oscillations on a line of light on a cathode-ray screen. By the Battle of Britain in 1940, the network of radar installations around southeastern England was capable of spotting enemy warplanes more than 70 miles away; and by 1941, radar could be installed in aircraft, too. Postwar developments included Marconi's early warning and height-detection radar system, installed at Heathrow Airport in 1950. In 1967, a BEA Trident inaugurated the first blind-landing system

THE "DEATH RAY" THAT BROUGHT DELIVERANCE

The members of Britain's Air Defense Committee were hoping for a death ray when they asked the physicist Robert Watson-Watt to look into the military potential of electromagnetic waves. Impossible, they were advised. Would they be satisfied, instead, with a way to locate enemy aircraft at a distance? They were, and the result was radar. Watson-Watt's team worked at speed, for the Germans were researching it already. On February 26, 1935, Watson-Watt hitched his apparatus to an antenna and traced, with a little green blob on a cathode-ray screen, the path of a Heyford bomber. Here is his description:

"Late in the afternoon of February 25, 1935, a Morris with a biscuit-colored caravan body bearing the royal monogram was driven out of the gate of Dutton Park, which was shared amicably by cows and radio researchers. Dyer was at the wheel, A.F. Wilkins was leader of the expedition and the sole passenger. Up to the Bath road, on Iver and Uxbridge way, through Fenny Stratford and Towcester, till the Daventry masts were in sight. Then a discreet reconnaissance, and the caravan turned westward into a grassland field not far from Weedon. A rudimentary antenna was rigged, the receiver was checked over, and Wilkins and Dyer slept an untroubled, if unduly brief, sleep.

"A.P. Rowe had been given plenary powers as the sole eyes and ears of the Air Ministry. Early on the 26th I picked him up in London and drove him in my treasured Daimler . . . Wilkins had everything running sweetly, and we showed Rowe the full-screen vertical line from the Daventry ground ray. . . . Then we waited. The hum of the Heyford became audible, and we watched him fly by at about 6,000 feet towards Daventry. His instructions were to shuttle at that height to-and-fro on a 20 mile long beat from Daventry, on a course up and down the center line of the radio beam. He made only a fair job of holding the requested course, not one of his four runs took him right over our heads, but three passed very close. Then the little stub started to grow steadily, till it was a little over an inch long, then it waned and waxed between a half inch and an inch and a quarter in length; steadied again near full length, and waveringly dwindled as we listened to the diminishing drone of the engine. We calculated that when he was eight miles away the screen was still revealing his presence by its response to the energy reflected by the Heyford. Rowe and I, not showing any detectable signs of excitement or elation, bade goodbye to the demonstrator, walked to the Daimler and drove off briskly.

"What Rowe thought is on the record; here it is, by kind permission of the Ministry which we were, from that moment, to serve together till victory was achieved: 'It was demonstrated beyond doubt that electromagnetic energy is reflected from the metal components of an aircraft's structure and that it can be detected.'"

RADAR RESEARCHER Robert Watson-Watt invented radar in 1935.

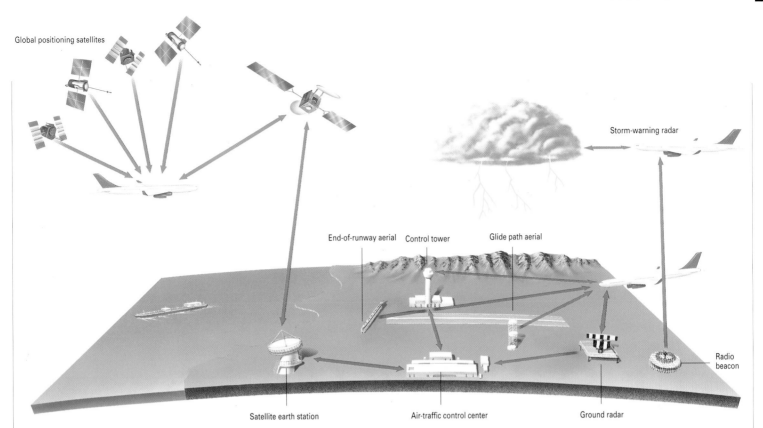

Global positioning satellites

Storm-warning radar

End-of-runway aerial   Control tower   Glide path aerial

Radio beacon

Satellite earth station   Air-traffic control center   Ground radar

for civilian aircraft. The instrument landing system used today consists of two radio beams, one horizontal and the other vertical; when the aircraft is aligned in the center of these two, it is in line with the runway.

In response to the needs of its underwater nuclear fleet, the United States developed Inertial Navigation, a form of direction-finding so precise that in 1958 the *Nautilus* was able to traverse the North Pole in a 96 hour, 1,800 mile journey beneath the ice pack. Then, in 1960, it launched Transit I, the world's first navigation satellite. Ten years later, work began on the Global Positioning System (GPS), a globe-girdling array of 21 satellites, whose multiple signals reduced the margin of error in position-finding, anywhere on Earth, to just 75 feet.

Tomorrow's world

By this time, computers were helping traffic controllers to manage crowded flight paths better. In 1981, Sodar (Sonic Detection and Ranging) made its debut at Frankfurt Airport to measure wind gusts and air currents stirred by aircraft movements. By the 1990s, a computer-based Traffic Alert and Collision Avoidance system was being developed, capable of monitoring all movements near an airport and ordering evasive action.

The adaptation of the Global Positioning System for civilian use spurred the invention of a spate of precision-navigation receivers for private pilots and yachtsmen. There were also battery-operated handheld models like the Scout, which ensured that the loneliest hiker need never get lost. GPS satellites in the mid-1990s were

FLYING AIDS A modern airliner has a precise fix on its location, can feel its way around in bad weather and follow a programmed glidepath to an automated landing.

performing scores of chores, including guiding supertankers into their berths. Sophisticated car systems under development included the Japanese Navmate, which it was possible to program to any destination. A satellite-directed computer then took over and pointed the way, correcting any mistakes made by the driver. By 1995, designers in the United States and Japan were even working on a GPS receiver the size of a wristwatch.

AIMING BY RADIO BEAMS In 1941, a radio-locator reports to an antiaircraft battery the position of incoming enemy airplanes.

DASHBOARD PILOT The computer-assisted Carminat navigation system was launched by Renault in 1995. The driver had only to follow street-by-street directions on screen.

1960 Launch of Transit I, the world's first navigation satellite

1970 Work starts on the Global Positioning System

1981 Sodar installed at Frankfurt Airport

TRAINS LOSE THEIR STEAM —BUT GATHER SPEED

WHEELS ON RAILS REACH THEIR MAXIMUM POTENTIAL AND THEN VENTURE BEYOND

During the 20th century, the train recovered from the brink of technological extinction to become once again a potent transport force, thanks to traction and track advances of revolutionary dimensions. The globe-girdling railway network that had been a wonder of 19th-century enterprise and engineering reached its apogee in 1904 with the completion of the Trans-Siberian Railway, linking Moscow with Vladivostok on the Pacific coast. Meanwhile, 70 years of advancements in steam locomotion had culminated in Wilhelm Schmidt's invention in Germany of superheating. Introduced in 1902, this improved performance by raising steam temperature and reducing moisture.

Steam, electricity and diesel

Although steam reigned supreme for the time being, the electric train was showing promise and diesels were already on the drawing board. Electricity's clean power had

CONTINENTAL BRIDGE A train crosses the Utka River in Russia; completion of the Trans-Siberian Railway in 1904 linked Europe with the Pacific rim.

led to its adoption by the London Underground in 1890. Electrical power produced quick acceleration and the kind of high speeds that enabled a locomotive to set a record of 124 mph in Germany in 1902—but it also had disadvantages. The capital cost of electrification was high and it therefore had to be used intensively.

Internal-combustion systems did not develop sufficient power to challenge steam until the advent of the compression-ignition diesel engine. The first diesel locomotive was built by the Sulzer company in Switzerland in 1912. Diesel was still not a match for steam, but a marriage of diesel technology and electricity produced the diesel-electric power unit (in which a diesel engine generates current for electric transmission), which was first tried in Sweden in 1913.

The rival technologies continued to proceed in hopscotch fashion. In 1915 the Hungarian Kalman Kando built the first electric locomotive capable of tapping the high-voltage public electricity supply by converting alternating current (AC) to direct current (DC) through a transformer and rectifier. Nine years later, the

THE STEAM TRAIN'S FINEST HOUR

On May 26, 1934, a gleaming new diesel-electric locomotive pulled into Chicago, having sped from Denver in 13 hours – half the normal time—and hit a top speed of 112 mph along the way: this was the Chicago, Burlington and Quincy Railroad's streamlined Zephyr, promoted as "a symphony in stainless steel."

The following year, the London and North Eastern Railway's chief engineer Sir Nigel Gresley unveiled the A4 class of steam locomotive, a streamlined development of his A1 Flying Scotsman. One of the A4's distinguishing features was its wedge front, which minimized any drag without causing turbulence to passing trains. On July 3, 1938, Mallard, an A4, touched 125 mph

FASTEST EVER The British Mallard set the speed record for steam power in 1938.

traveling through central England—the all-time world record for steam traction. "I gave Mallard her head and she just jumped at it like a live thing," said driver Joe Duddington. Mallard ran until 1963, clocking more than 1.4 million miles.

first diesel-electric locomotives ran in the United States. The first diesel passenger-train was put into operation in 1934, and the first unit specifically designed for freight service came into use in 1941. The 1930s saw an increase in speeds, spurred by public

thirst for ever-faster services. Streamlining was introduced and, with it, steam surged to an ultimate 125 mph, achieved by a British train in 1938. In the United States, the demands of miles-long freight trains and long mountain routes led to the development of bigger steam engines, culminating in the 1940s with Union Pacific's Big Boy class, with an articulated undercarriage enabling it to negotiate turns: at 540 tons, this was the heaviest land vehicle ever constructed.

From the 1950s, however, an abundance of cheap oil encouraged diesel development

STEAM DREAM This artist's vision of steam-power was inspired by U.S. trains of the 1940s.

CRAWLING TO A STOP

A never-stopping commuter train was demonstrated in London in 1925. The train maintained a modest speed of 16 mph and slowed down to a crawl at the line's stations. The experiment was not repeated.

---

in scores of countries, including the United States. By the late 1970s, there were more than 27,000 diesel units in operation throughout the country, accounting for almost all of America's railway motive power. At the same time, Britain developed an experimental High Speed Train (HST), consisting of two powerful 1680 kW diesel-electric locomotives, one pulling and the other pushing the passenger cars. The train was quickly dubbed the 125, in tribute to its top speed of 125 mph.

The triumph of electricity

France and Japan, on the other hand, favored electrification. In France, engineers had shown in 1955 that a super-fast electric train could reach 200 mph. Further research and heavy investment paid off in 1981, when the first Train à Grande Vitesse (TGV) began running between Paris and Lyon on a purpose-built line with gentle, sweeping curves and a clever use of gradients to induce a roller-coaster plunge over hills. On a test run in May 1990, a TGV hit 320 mph.

The Japanese, too, made history with a high-speed service designed to compete with air travel. The first Shinkansen, or bul-

let train, sped from Tokyo to Osaka on October 1, 1964. The 320 mile electrified track was built to maintain scheduled speeds of up to 130 mph. In 1992, an advanced bullet train, the Super Hikari, came into operation in Japan.

Tomorrow's train

In the 1980s, steam enthusiasts had their hopes raised briefly, and in vain, by American experiments in the use of low-smoke coal and by trials in South Africa of a computer-controlled steam locomotive. However, with wheels on rails approaching their maximum potential, research had now turned to magnetic levitation (maglev): trains float a fraction of an inch above the track, held there and push-pulled by a stream of magnetic impulses from a linear induction motor.

In the U.S., plans for maglev systems have been developed by several states, and a study commissioned by the federal government in 1993 supported the initiation of a national maglev program. As the 1990s ended, however, these plans were still well in the future.

SPEED DREAM The French TGV (top) and the Japanese Shinkansen (above) tested the frictional limits of wheels running on rail. The future may lie with magnetic levitation, already used in Sydney, Australia (below).

1964 First Shinkansen, or bullet train

1979 The "125" enters service
1981 TGV runs between Paris and Lyon

INTO THE AIR

FROM THE FIRST FALTERING FLIGHT IN **1903** TO SUPERSONIC TRAVEL IN LESS THAN **100** YEARS

The world paid little attention when two bicycle dealers named Wilbur and Orville Wright achieved powered flight on December 17, 1903. Their craft was a box-kite contraption powered by a homemade gasoline engine, which was connected by bicycle

TAKE OFF In the only photograph of the first powered flight in 1903, Orville Wright is at the controls while Wilbur stands to the right.

chain to a pair of propellers. In four tries before five witnesses, one clicking a camera, the Wrights' "Flyer" skimmed the sands of the North Carolina coast near Kitty Hawk for a best distance of 852 feet, before a gust of wind tumbled the craft apart. At this stage, however, the future of air travel

seemed to lie with the powered balloon, or airship, of a rigid-framed type championed by the German Count Ferdinand von Zeppelin and first flown over Lake Constance in July 1900. Controlling such an ungainly craft as the 420 foot prototype airship, LZ1, demanded improvements—in particular, increased power—but by October 1909, the Count had inaugurated the world's first commercial airline, flying his zeppelins sedately between five German cities.

The Wright brothers had, meanwhile, returned home to Dayton, Ohio, and created in their much sturdier Flyer III, a maneuverable biplane that could stay aloft for half an hour or more. The pilot was able to maintain stable flight and to turn by "wing-warping"—literally changing the shape of the wings by tugging on wires attached to the wing tips. Their first functional airplane flew on June 23, 1905, but the Wrights' passion for secrecy limited their contribution to subsequent aircraft development. This was concentrated in France, where late in 1905 enthusiasts set up the first aircraft factory at Billancourt, near Paris. Breakthroughs included the invention of the joystick control column and wing flaps, or ailerons, to control banking, and the first crude monoplane, built in 1906 by

WHO INVENTED THE AIRPLANE?

The origins of manned flight are the subject of intense nationalistic rivalry, although Sir George Cayley in 19th century England is often acknowledged as the "father of aviation" in that he designed the first practical craft and proposed the use of an internal combustion engine to propel it. Russian claims rest upon Alexander Mozhaiski, who built a steam-powered plane that flew 65 feet in 1884. And the French can point to Felix Du Temple, who patented a steam-plane in 1857 and managed to get it off the ground—from a sloping ramp—in 1874. However, French pride is focused upon Clément Ader, who in 1900 piloted a steam-powered monoplane on a flight of about 165 feet. Recognition of the Wright brothers is based on the fact that theirs was the first sustained and controlled flight. This, too, is disputed by the Germans who wish to give the honor to Gustave Weisskopf, who emigrated to the United States and changed his name to Whitehead. Whitehead is said to have flown half a mile in 1901, followed by flights of up to 7 miles over Long Island Sound in January 1902. But witnesses were never interrogated and none had a camera to record the event.

Romanian-born Trajan Vuia. All these developments came together at 4:35 on the morning of July 25, 1909, when Louis Blériot took off from Baraques, near Calais, in an improved monoplane of his own design and landed with a bump in Dover 37 minutes later. "England is no longer an island," wrote one alarmed commentator.

LIGHTER THAN AIR The Hindenburg airship at Lakehurst, New Jersey, weeks before it burst into flames in 1937, killing 35 aboard.

1903 Wright brothers achieve powered flight

1909 Louis Blériot flies across Channel
1910 First flight of the seaplane

1919 First nonstop Atlantic crossing

1933 Maiden flight of Boeing 247

1937 Frank Whittle tests the first jet engine

1949 First jet airliner takes to the skie

MARINE AVIATION A German Dornier DO X arrives in New York harbor in 1931; flying boats offered luxury but proved too slow.

Purpose-designed engines and more aerodynamic airframes increased speeds and improved reliability. Instrumentation was added in 1910, with the invention of an airspeed indicator and the installation of an in-flight radio telegraph.

The dominant power unit in these early years was the air-cooled Gnome, a rotary engine that spun with the propeller. Invented in France in 1907, the Gnome's major asset was its light weight. It was responsible for another French first, when Henri Fabre converted a Gnome-powered biplane of the Wright type into a seaplane by replacing the wheels with floats. On March 28, 1910, he managed to take off in the Mediterranean, thereby inaugurating an era of marine aviation.

Streamlining the modern plane

Planes were assuming a more familiar shape. In 1912, Louis Poulman constructed his Tubavion in the hope of securing a military contract. The lightweight plywood frame formed a tapering cylinder. Freed from internal bracing, a single skin of wood now carried the load, thus becoming the first monocoque, or single-shell, fuselage.

In Russia, under the patronage of the Czar, 28-year-old Igor Sikorsky was design-ing the first multi-engined aircraft. The Bolshoi had a 92 foot wingspan and was equipped with a couch, armchairs, and cooking facilities for its maiden flight on May 13, 1913. The timing was not propitious. With the advent of the First World War the following year, Sikorsky's airborne hotel was converted into the world's first four-engined bomber.

War quickened aircraft development. In Germany, Hugo Junkers devised the first all-metal monoplane with low, cantilever wings that anticipated future designs. And in Britain, with the advent of peace, the Vickers-Vimy bomber, which had been delivered too late to fight, made the first nonstop Atlantic crossing in 1919. The Vimy was powered by two Rolls-Royce engines, which had to be overhauled every 100 hours.

Experiments in pressurization that would enable flying at high altitude began in 1920, and the first pressurized cabin was installed

FIRSTS IN REFUELLING

The first in-flight refuelling was accomplished on November 12, 1921, by American Wesley May. He jumped from the wing of another plane with a can strapped to his back, and poured fuel into the tank. The more conventional method, by aircraft-to-aircraft hose, was accomplished over San Diego on June 26-27, 1923. The process was repeated 15 times in the course of setting an endurance record of 37 hours 15 minutes in a De Havilland DH4B.

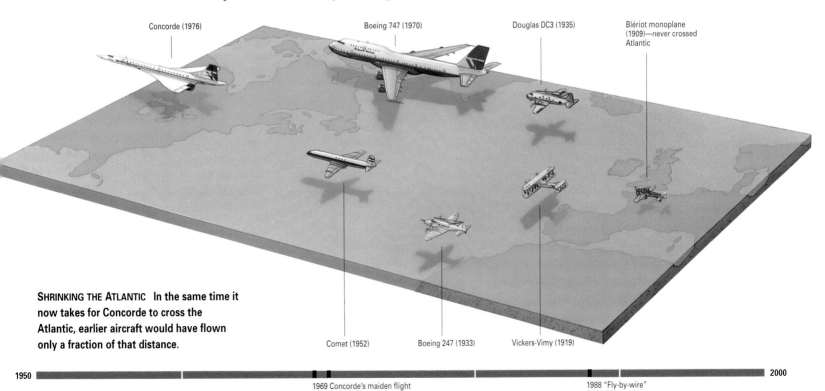

Concorde (1976) Boeing 747 (1970) Douglas DC3 (1935) Blériot monoplane (1909)—never crossed Atlantic

Comet (1952) Boeing 247 (1933) Vickers-Vimy (1919)

SHRINKING THE ATLANTIC In the same time it now takes for Concorde to cross the Atlantic, earlier aircraft would have flown only a fraction of that distance.

in a British aircraft, the De Havilland DH4, in 1922.

Airships continued to offer competition by sacrificing speed for comfort and the kind of range that enabled a zeppelin to cross the

North Pole in 1929. But the lighter-than-air hydrogen with which they were filled required only a spark to ignite, and the tragedies that resulted committed them to oblivion within a few years. Seaplanes, much

FIRST JET AIRLINER The De Havilland Comet went into service in May 1952 (top); an engineer inspects one of its engines (above).

enlarged as flying boats, offered airship-style luxury coupled with the convenience and sense of security that came with being able to put down in remote places, at a cho-sen shore, river or lake. By 1929 such planes included the biggest aircraft to date, the Donier DO X, which boasted a bar, smoking and sitting rooms, bathrooms and sleeping quarters; one of these carried 169 people on a test flight.

The modern airliner was born in February 1933 with the maiden flight of the Boeing 247. This low-wing, twin-engine monoplane with retractable landing gear, de-icers on leading edges and autopilot, cruised at 189 mph and was able to climb on one engine. Within a month, it was in service with United Airlines and cutting cross-America times to under 20 hours. But it was soon superseded by the legendary (and still flying) Douglas DC3, which did the same job better. The 21 passenger DC3, which became known around the world by such fond names as the Gooney Bird and the Dakota, was the first transport plane to conquer the Himalayas. More than 13,000 were built.

By now, the piston aircraft—with

an engine similar in principle to an automobile's internal-combustion engine—had reached its operational limits, but a fundamentally different solution existed. The jet engine was to be some 80 percent more efficient than the piston engine.

The coming of the jet engine

In 1930 a Royal Air Force cadet named Frank Whittle patented a jet engine. Lack of encouragement so delayed its development in Britain that the first jet to fly was German, with a power-plant designed by Hans von Ohain. "The hideous wail was music to my ears," rejoiced planemaker Ernst Heinkel when the He 178 took off from Rostock on August 27, 1939.

Jet design was too new a technology to play much of a part

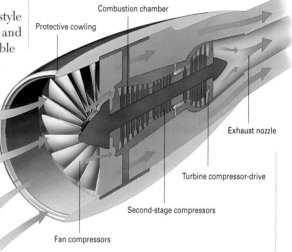

JET THRUST The gas turbine, or jet engine, gulps in air which is compressed, mixed with fuel and then ignited. The thrust exerted by the hot, expanding exhaust gases provides the motive power.

in the Second World War, but Britain seized the initiative soon afterwards. Based upon an invention of A.A. Griffith, who in 1920 had thought of using jet exhaust to turn a plane's propellers, the first turboprop, the Vickers Viscount, had its maiden flight in July 1948. A year later, the first jet airliner took to the skies. Its four engines enabled the De Havilland Comet I to cruise at 490 mph making the world a smaller place. And in 1970, Boeing, the Seattle builder, consolidated its dominance with the wide-body 747, the first "jumbo" jet, capable of cruising near the speed of sound with 500 passengers aboard.

TESTING THE FIRST JET ENGINE

British engineer Frank Whittle conceived the idea for the jet engine when writing a student paper and he patented it as a 23-year-old in 1930. Here he describes testing the first one on April 12, 1937:

"I signalled for an increase of speed of the starter motor, and as the tachometer indicated 2000 rpm I gradually opened the main control valve. For a second or two the speed of the engine increased slowly and then, with a rising shriek like an air-raid siren, the speed began to rise rapidly, and large patches of red heat became visible on the combustion chamber casing. The engine was obviously out of control.... This incident did not do my nerves any good at all. I have rarely been so frightened. The next evening, after an alteration to the fuel system, we tried again. This time things were even more alarming. The engine accelerated out of control from about 1500 rpm.... Though I switched off the fuel pump, the speed rose rapidly. Sheets of flame belched from the jet pipe, and clouds of fuel vapor jetting from leaking joints were ignited. Flames were leaping and dancing in midair above the engine. The personnel, alerted by the earlier experience, disappeared even more rapidly. Later that evening Laidlaw [combustion chamber expert], who was staying at the same hotel in Rugby, insisted on my drinking considerable quantities of red wine to calm my nerves."

JET PIONEER Frank Whittle with a Proteus jet engine.

1900

1903 Wright brothers achieve powered flight

1909 Louis Blériot flies across Channel
1910 First flight of the seaplane

1919 First nonstop Atlantic crossing

1933 Maiden flight of Boeing 247

1937 Frank Whittle tests the first jet engine

1949 First jet airliner takes to the skies

1950

In pioneering trans-national plane building, the Concorde was a hard-earned triumph over historic rivalry and conflicting methods. British firms made the engines and electronics, French firms the afterburners and hydraulics. The slim delta-wing craft, with an aluminum alloy skin, carried 100 passengers at twice the speed of sound, cutting the transatlantic flight time to under three hours. But its high fuel consumption and the boom it made as it broke the sound barrier limited its appeal. Only 14 entered commercial service, from 1976 onward, and they were permitted to break the sound barrier only over the ocean.

Design priorities now switched to improving efficiency. The first jet engines had been noisy, dirty fuel-guzzlers. A solution to this problem was provided by the fan jet, first developed in 1958 by Pratt and Whitney. It was adopted by the new generation of big jets, making them quieter and more fuel-efficient.

Vastly improved safety was matched by a greater capacity to investigate the rare crashes, thanks to the Red Egg, a virtually indestructible cockpit recorder of flight data and pilot conversation. Invented by Australian chemist David Warren, it soon became popularly known as the "black box."

WIRED WINNER Engineers work on the wide-body interior of the European Airbus, the first computer-controlled airliner.

Executive jet travel for the affluent made its appearance in the 1970s with a spate of small twin-engine designs. Typical of these was the Learjet, but the ultimate thrill became possible in the mid 1990s with the advent of the first private supersonic jet, the BD-10. This twin-engine two-seater built by the American Jim Bede weighed just 250 pounds and, at less than 29 feet from tip to tail, could be parked in a garage. Yet it could reach almost twice the speed of sound and climb 20,000 feet in a minute.

Flying into the future

The BD-10's secret lay in its wing design and in the light, strong materials used. In 1986 the strength and reliability of new ultra-light composites were showcased in the Voyager, a craft created by the American Burt Rutan. It flew nonstop around the world, logging

SONIC BOOMER   Despite its breathtaking speed and grace, the Anglo-French Concorde was never a commercial success.

24,987 miles without refuelling.

Only when the Europeans started to work in consortium did they finally challenge American ascendancy in civil aviation. In April 1988 the "fly-by-wire" A320 Airbus went into service as the first airliner in which computers could do the work of pilots.

Computer-control reached a new dimension with the Boeing 777, a twin-jet jumbo created inside a computer, using new three-dimensional modelling technology. Its 8 million parts were designed, modified and assembled, and the prototype flown, entirely in simulation. The actual 777 that resulted in June 1994 was fully computer-controlled, made unprecedented use of new composite materials, and had engines capable of producing 40 percent more power without any increase in noise.

Passenger care also advanced. In-flight audio tapes had been joined in the 1970s by movies, and in the mid-1990s the firm of GEC-Marconi devised a computerized cabin system with seats equipped with individually controlled interactive videos. Passengers could now select from an array of entertainment, play games with one another, make phone calls, shop, work, or do business.

American firms spent a billion dollars researching a rival to Concorde, but it never flew off the drawing board. They opted, instead, to pursue travel at many times the speed of sound as a long-range goal. By the late-1990s, both the United States and the Europeans were researching space planes able to loop beyond the atmosphere and achieve remarkable flight times, such as New York to Tokyo in 180 minutes.

1950

1969 Concorde's maiden flight
1970 First "jumbo" jet

1988 "Fly-by-wire"
A320 Airbus enters
service

2000

JUMPS AND SPIRALS

OVERCOMING THE PROBLEMS OF VERTICAL FLIGHT: FROM FLYING TOPS TO HELICOPTERS AND JUMP JETS

The helicopter had existed in the form of flying-top toys for hundreds of years before the dawn of the 20th century. However, the first manned takeoff was not accomplished until November 13, 1907, when the Frenchman Paul Cornu who, like the Wright brothers, was a bicycle dealer, managed a 20 second hover aboard an ungainly contraption powered by a bulky engine. It fell to bits upon landing.

The complex demands of helicopter design proved so daunting that little headway had been achieved by the 1920s, when the Spanish inventor Juan de la Cierva added a free-spinning four-blade rotor above the cockpit of a standard monoplane to create the autogyro. The rotor was not connected to the engine, and it was the airflow caused by the craft's movement through the air that kept the rotor blades spinning; these exerted a lifting force even when the engine

FLYING TOP   The autogyro, invented by Juan de la Cierva in 1919, became popular in the 1930s and then once again in the 1990s.

was turned off, enabling the craft to make a steep, but safe, descent.

Cierva made his first flight on January 9, 1923, and by 1928 he was flying the English Channel with a passenger in an improved model, in which the rotor had entirely replaced the conventional aircraft wing. Hundreds of Cierva autogyros were built in the 1930s, but interest waned when he suffered a fatal crash in England in 1936. This happened to coincide with the development of the first practical helicopter. On June 26, 1936, German engineer-designer Heinrich Focke flew his prototype Fa-61. Two counter-rotating, variable-axis rotors solved the persistent helicopter problem of directional control.

Modern helicopters and jump jets

In the United States, Russian emigré Igor Sikorsky invented the modern helicopter by balancing a single main rotor with a small one on the tail. His highly maneuverable VS-300 flew for the first time on September 14, 1939, and spawned hundreds of helicopter types, from one-man midgets to fearsome war machines. Jet power proved highly

WHIRLYBIRD MAN   Igor Sikorsky took more than 30 years to perfect the helicopter, which achieved its potential in the 1950s.

adaptable to the helicopter and gave it a much-needed boost in power. The first turbojet helicopter flew at Villacoublay, France, in April 1951, and Aérospatiale's Alouette II of 1955 established the type's popularity.

The notion of using the brute thrust of a jet engine to lift an aircraft vertically had engaged British scientists from 1941 and led to the Flying Bedstead, a test rig flown experimentally between 1954 and 1957. Further developments included the first VTOL (vertical takeoff and landing) aircraft, the Short SC1, and Hawker-Siddeley Harrier. The immense energy-demand of jump jets limited their development to military uses, but spin-off studies continued into VTOL commuter craft that might be capable of serving crowded urban areas. In 1991 a prototype hybrid took to the air. The twin-prop Osprey V-22, designed by Bell and Boeing, lifted off in helicopter mode; once in flight, the wing-tip engine assemblies pivoted forward 45 degrees to assume the position of a conventional aircraft.

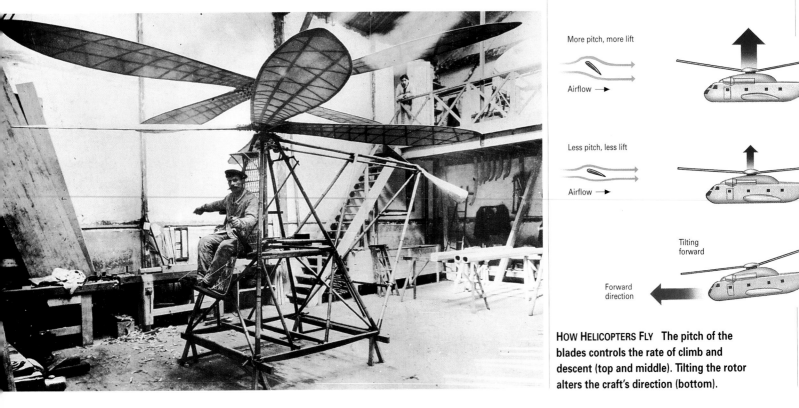

More pitch, more lift

Airflow →

Less pitch, less lift

Airflow →

Tilting forward

Forward direction

HOW HELICOPTERS FLY   The pitch of the blades controls the rate of climb and descent (top and middle). Tilting the rotor alters the craft's direction (bottom).

HOVERCRAFT AND WATER-SKIMMERS

FLOATING ON A CUSHION OF AIR RATHER THAN WATER REDUCES FRICTION AND WAVE RESISTANCE

The dream of creating a boat that skimmed over the water rather than ploughed through it was an old one, and early in the century a French count and an Italian airship designer both achieved it. Count Charles de Lambert had been working for more than 20 years on his theories when, in 1906, he fitted a flat-bottomed boat with an airplane engine and "hydroplaned" over calm water at a startling 38 mph. Enrico Forlanini did even better by exploiting the same laws of nature that produce lift in an aircraft. The result was the hydrofoil, a craft whose submerged wings, or foils, raised the hull out of the water, thus freeing it from drag.

The main problem with these early hydrofoils was their fuel consumption; but by 1937 a commercial one, designed by Hans von Schertel, was carrying passengers along the Rhine. From the 1950s, hydrofoils found a niche as express ferries around the world, particularly in the Soviet Union where, in 1957, the Raketa craft carrying up to 100 passengers was introduced. It would carry 20 million commuters a year on more than 150 ferry routes. These advances led to the development of the jet-foil—a hydrofoil powered by a jet engine. A 400 passenger jetfoil, with twin gas turbines powering the water jets, went into service in Hong Kong in 1974.

BUOYANT BRAINWAVE The air-cushion principle was highly adaptable; it could buoy up big seagoing craft like the cross-Channel hovercraft (above) or a Land Rover fitted for crop spraying (left).

WHATEVER HAPPENED TO THE DREAM?

The hovercraft, once heralded as the future of aquatic transportation, has had difficulty getting off the ground. Though it was initially a British invention, much of its development in recent years has taken place in the United States and in the former Soviet Union, where it reached its fullest potential as a military assault vehicle.

Spin-off inventions included the "hoverbed" for serious burns cases, designed by British surgeon John Scales in 1961, and in 1963 the Flymo floating lawn mower. Pallets with air cushions were also devised to help with the shifting of heavy loads in factories.

A small French-designed fiberglass hovercraft of the 1990s offered solutions to some of the craft's persistent problems with an improved aerodynamic rudder and a power-plant sealed to avert salt-water corrosion.

The modern hovercraft

A more radical solution was pursued by a British boat-builder named Christopher Cockerell, who had devised a way to float a hull on thin air. The theory of the air cushion vehicle (ACV), or hovercraft, had been propounded early in the 18th century by the Swedish philosopher Emanuel Swedenborg. Cockerell made it work. Wonder greeted the public unveiling in June 1959 of the first hovercraft, the SR-N1, and excitement intensified with the first English Channel crossing on July 25, the 50th anniversary of Blériot's flight. The craft was essentially a 7 ton doughnut with an engine in the middle that provided enough down-draft to keep it hovering above the water and enough thrust to send it scudding forward in a cloud of foam.

The addition of a rubberized "skirt" reduced pressure losses and allowed it to operate in choppier sea, but it was nine years before regular Channel services began with the very much larger SR-N4. An elongated version accommodating more than 400 passengers and 55 cars was introduced in 1978. However, the promise of the hovercraft as a mass transport vehicle was not fulfilled because of fuel and maintenance costs.

The wave-piercing catamaran, an enormous twin-hulled craft able to cut through choppy waters and carry more than 400 passengers and 80 vehicles, was devised in Australia by Robert Clifford and Philip Hercus in the 1980s.

A combination of boat and plane technology culminated in the Air Fish, a skimmer from Germany that is designed to glide like a large sea bird when close to the water. Its stubby wings deflect the airflow downward, enabling the craft to cruise at 74 mph, 3 feet off the water. The first production craft in 1995 was a two-seater powered by a motorcycle engine, but it was hoped that further developments would eventually enable cargo to be carried faster than by ship and cheaper than by aircraft.

REFITTING THE SHIP

VOYAGING LOSES ITS GLAMOR AS TECHNOLOGY MAKES A BUSINESS OF SEA TRANSPORTATION

Steam, and sometimes even canvas, were driving ships around the turn of the century, with 5,000 years of sailing technology culminating in 1909 in the launch of the six-masted schooner *Wyoming*, at 330 feet the longest wooden vessel ever. But new concepts were in prototype. Most revolutionary of all was the adoption of the steam

ATLANTIC QUEEN The *Queen Mary* shortly before her launch on the Clyde in 1934. She could carry almost 2,000 passengers across the Atlantic in three to four days.

turbine—first demonstrated in 1897 by a tiny boat called *Turbina*, which scooted into Queen Victoria's Diamond Jubilee naval review at an incredible 32.75 knots, or nearly 40 mph, with flames leaping from its funnel. In 1901, the *King Edward* slipped down the Clyde River in western Scotland to become the first turbine-powered commercial vessel. Steam at very high temperature and pressure from the ship's boilers is guided through a series of vanes and blades, attached to a shaft; as it passes through, it causes the blades to rotate and the propeller shaft to turn. Navies and merchant fleets hastened to re-equip with turbines.

The marine diesel engine was not far behind the steam turbine. The engine was tried first in 1902 in a French canal boat,

called the *Petit-Pierre*. Two years later, the first diesel engine put to sea in the *Vandal*, a Russian tanker built in St. Petersburg for service in the Caspian. Economical running was the chief attraction of diesel power. The lighter and less bulky engines freed room for cargo; and from the 1930s, most cargo ships and all but the largest liners would be diesel-driven motor-ships.

Shipshape

At the same time, improvements in boiler performance greatly increased the power generated by steam turbines, and these, in turn, prompted improvements in hull design. In 1908, Sir John Isherwood patented a system of tank bulkheads, framed and girdered for strength, although this did not save the "unsinkable" *Titanic* when she was

ripped by an iceberg on April 15, 1912.

The rivet began to give way to the electric arc weld after the launch in 1920 of the *Fullagar*, the first welded ship, had demonstrated a clear advantage in construction time and vessel performance. New bow shapes were devised to cut through the waves more efficiently. The energy-saving

THE END OF THE GREAT LINERS

The 1930s were the halcyon days of the luxury Atlantic liner, with fierce competition between Britain, France and Germany driving the growth of the industry and stimulating ever-speedier ships. A benchmark was set early, with the launch in 1907 of the *Mauritania*, whose interior trim included sitting rooms and furniture in the style of Chippendale. With a speed of 25 knots, *Mauritania* held the coveted blue ribband for the fastest Atlantic crossing for more than 20 years.

Normandie, the first liner to exceed 1,000 feet in length, was launched in 1932 but was eclipsed within two years by the launch of the *Queen Mary*, which went on to set a new crossing record of three days, 20 hours, 42 minutes. The *Queen Elizabeth*, largest of all the great liners, was launched in 1938; she became a troopship during the Second World War before making her civilian debut in 1946.

LUXURY LIFE ON THE OCEAN WAVES The first-class smoking room of the *Queen Mary* (above) offered the latest in luxury and design. Right: the *Empress of Britain* (1937).

1900 ━━━ 1950

1901 First commercial vessel with steam turbines   1907 Launch of *Mauritania*   1904 First diesel-engined tanker   1931 Stabilizers on the Italian liner *Conte di Savoia*   1938 Launch of *Queen Elizabeth*   1934 Launch of *Queen Mary*

SUPERTANKER **A bow shot of the *Esso Northumbria* taken in 1975 captures the bulk and brute force of the supertanker.**

bulbous bow, invented by the Japanese and first employed in 1962, was the result of research dating back to 1929, when the liner *Bremen* was designed with a forward sweep at the waterline.

Nuclear power promised a new dawn, with its compact, long-lasting uranium fuel increasing the range of the ship. The Russians were first with the experimental ice-breaker *Lenin*, commissioned in 1959 and able to slice with ease through an ice-cap more than 8 feet thick; her three nuclear reactors and their protective shield weighed 3,000 tons. The Americans tried with the *Savannah*, the first nuclear-powered merchant ship, which began sea trials in 1962 and went into service the following year, only to be retired in 1967. By this time, Japan had the *Matsu* and West Germany the *Otto Hahn*—but to no avail. High running costs and public fears of radiation limited further developments.

Mass construction methods pioneered in the Second World War led, in the 1960s, to a new way of building ships. Hulls were pre-assembled in large segments, or modules, which were then brought to the yard by massive transporters and welded together. Marine engineers were also developing new kinds of

WIND-ASSISTED TANKER **A computer controls the angle of this tanker's rigid sails in order to maximize their efficiency; this Japanese innovation stemmed from rising fuel costs.**

ships to cope with the growth in trade. The shipment of liquefied gases in high-pressure tanks was inaugurated by the *Methane Pioneer*, which brought a consignment of natural gas from Louisiana to a terminal at Canvey Island, near London, in 1959. And from 1964, purpose-designed container ships, with cellular holds and deck-storage, were constructed, replacing the cargo ship.

Bulk transport

The first supertanker (typically carrying more than 75,000 tons of oil products) went into service in 1968, and in 1972 the first half-million tonner, the *Globtik Tokyo*, was launched. This floating behemoth, almost a quarter mile long, was powered by steam turbines geared to a single propeller shaft. The vessel was automated to the point where the control room only required the attentions of a pair of watch engineers.

In recent years, rising fuel costs have encouraged a surprising new tack. The last commercial sailing ship had been laid up in 1936, but from 1980 onward people looked to the wind once more. Japanese coastal vessels were fitted with masts bearing rigid foils that were constantly adjusted to wind direction by a computer-directed motor. Reductions of up to 50 percent in the fuel bill resulted in the venture being continued, while in France vessels with an experimental spinning cylinder, or turbosail, fitted to the mast have also achieved considerable savings.

1950

1959 First nuclear-powered vessel   1968 First supertanker enters service
1962 Sea trials of first nuclear-powered
merchant ship, the *Savannah*

2000

PLUMBING THE OCEAN DEPTHS

INVENTIONS THAT TURNED AN AREA OF IGNORANCE AND TERROR INTO A PLACE FOR WORK AND PLAY

For many years, divers in cumbersome, watertight suits and metal helmets had been restricted to depths of less than 65 feet, where pressure is double the atmospheric level. Any deeper and they risked "the bends"—excruciating and sometimes fatal decompression sickness, caused by gases concentrated in their blood forming bubbles as they surfaced. In 1928, Sir Robert Davis invented the submersible decompression chamber in which this could be controlled by gradually returning a diver to normal atmospheric pressure. French navy researchers continued to work on the problems of improving diver mobility, while containing the pressure hazard. By 1936 they had found the basis of a solution—in the form of a

DISASTER DISCOVERED The *Titanic*'s giant propeller looms out of the ocean-bottom gloom in a photograph taken from the porthole of the *Mir* submersible in 1991.

compressed air bottle and mask. In 1943, this became the brilliantly simple and effective aqualung, invented by Commander Jacques Cousteau in collaboration with Emile Gagnan, a control-valve specialist. The aqualung was to transform lumbering divers into the free-roving "frogmen" of the Second World War and made possible the postwar development of undersea oil fields.

Another means of exploring the world beneath the ocean was to travel there in

UNDER PRESSURE

The diver's decompression chamber has been reinvented as a medical tool. Trauma patients, such as earthquake victims, are placed in a chamber under pressure and fed pure oxygen, which helps the body to repair itself faster.

underwater vessels, or submersibles. In 1930, the American Otis Barton designed a hollow steel ball capable of withstanding the build-up of water pressure that had kept submarines near the surface. He called it a bathysphere and, that year, he and scientist C. William Beebe descended by cable to a depth of 1,368 feet. Three years later, they were winched down to 3,284 feet.

The early bathysphere was succeeded by the bathyscaphe, a deep-diving apparatus

EXPLORING THE UNDERWATER WORLD

A common valve used in gas cookers was key to the invention of the aqualung. Adapted, it enabled divers to regulate through their breathing the supply and pressure of air from their back-tank.

The scuba revolution which resulted was led at almost every stage by its primary inventor, Jacques Cousteau. In 1952, he helped invent underwater television equipment and put it to spectacular use in bringing the wonders of the deep into every home. An underwater "dolly" was invented in 1954, and also the first underwater 35mm camera. Cousteau also pioneered undersea archaeology with the first exploration of ancient wrecks.

By the 1990s, camera-housings capable of withstanding 600 times normal pressure were being constructed by the American Al Giddings. Coupled with high-intensity mercury-vapor lighting, used by Robert Ballard on a return visit to *Titanic* in 1991, this opened up great depths to universal scrutiny.

invented in 1948 by Swiss scientist Auguste Piccard. The U.S. navy took an interest in Piccard's work and, on January 23, 1960, Lieutenant Don Walsh and Piccard's son Jacques rode the *Trieste*, an improved bathyscaphe, 35,815 feet down into the Marianas Trench in the Pacific. This epic dive of almost 7 miles revealed that life existed even in the deepest part of the ocean.

Sealab, the first underwater research station, began to study the effects of prolonged deep immersion on teams of Americans. By 1966, in Sealab III, they were staying down for two weeks and more. Robot exploration began in 1970 with RUM (Remote Underwater Manipulator). This American submersible, with TV cameras and a retrieving claw, could crawl the ocean floor at depths of 10,000 feet, controlled by cable from the surface. *Alvin*, an American research submarine, was able to hover about 700 feet over the wreck of the *Titanic*, while its robot explorer Jason Jr. conducted the first investigation. The French responded with the *Nautile*, a crewed titanium sphere with cameras and carbon-fiber arms, which visited *Titanic* in 1987.

The same year, the Russians unveiled *Mir* 1 and 2, speedier research subs that could operate at depths of over 20,000 feet. In 1989, Japan's *Shinkai 6500* set a new submarine depth record of 21,320 feet, which opened as much as 98 percent of the ocean floor to possible exploration.

1900

1950

1928 Decompression chamber invented
1930 Otis Barton's bathysphere

1943 Cousteau
aqualung invented

1948 Bathyscaphe
invented

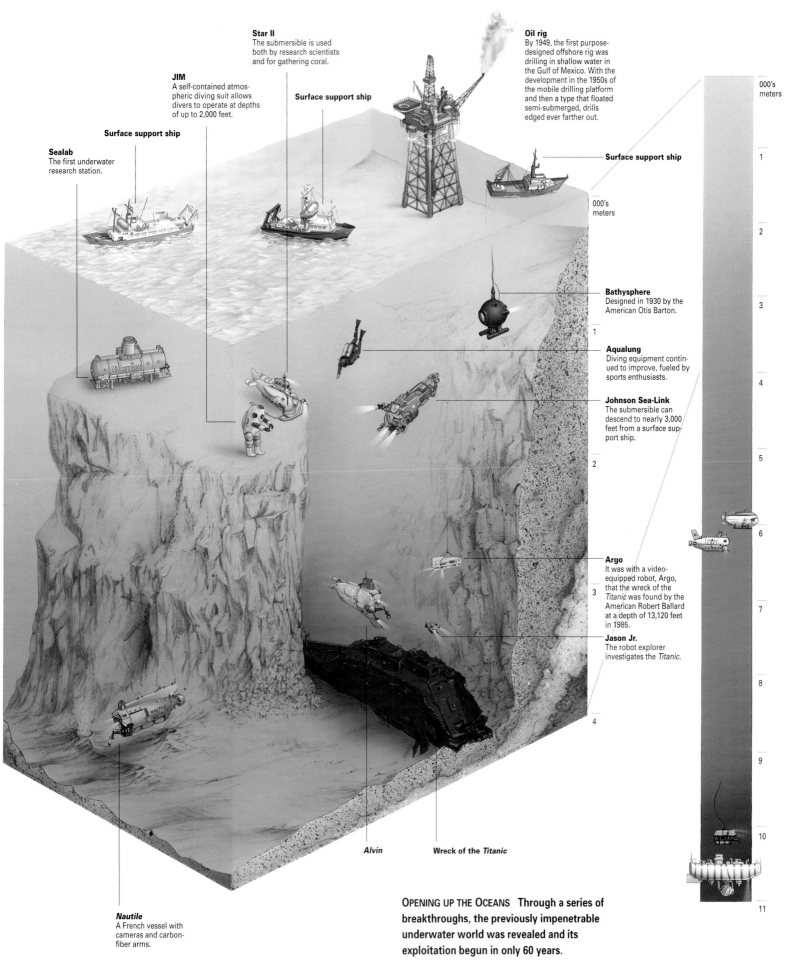

Star II
The submersible is used both by research scientists and for gathering coral.

JIM
A self-contained atmospheric diving suit allows divers to operate at depths of up to 2,000 feet.

Surface support ship

Oil rig
By 1949, the first purpose-designed offshore rig was drilling in shallow water in the Gulf of Mexico. With the development in the 1950s of the mobile drilling platform and then a type that floated semi-submerged, drills edged ever farther out.

Surface support ship

Sealab
The first underwater research station.

Surface support ship

000's
meters

1

000's
meters

Bathysphere
Designed in 1930 by the American Otis Barton.

Aqualung
Diving equipment continued to improve, fueled by sports enthusiasts.

Johnson Sea-Link
The submersible can descend to nearly 3,000 feet from a surface support ship.

1

2

2

Argo
It was with a video-equipped robot, Argo, that the wreck of the *Titanic* was found by the American Robert Ballard at a depth of 13,120 feet in 1985.

3

Jason Jr.
The robot explorer investigates the *Titanic*.

4

Alvin

Wreck of the *Titanic*

Nautile
A French vessel with cameras and carbon-fiber arms.

OPENING UP THE OCEANS Through a series of breakthroughs, the previously impenetrable underwater world was revealed and its exploitation begun in only 60 years.

3

4

5

6

7

8

9

10

11

1968 American drilling ship, *Glomar Challenger*

1987 *Mir* 1 and 2

ROCKETING INTO SPACE

FROM THE FIRST STRATEGIC WEAPONS TO ROCKETS THAT LAUNCH SATELLITES AND SPACECRAFT

A Russian schoolmaster named Konstantin Tsiolkovsky pointed the way into space. He began by constructing wind tunnels to study the effects of air friction and concluded, after years of calculation, that a multistage rocket fuelled by liquid oxygen could achieve the velocity required to escape Earth's gravity. His findings were published in 1903, the year of the Wright brothers' first fitful flight.

Liquid propulsion

Making reality of Tsiolkovsky's theories engaged many minds over the next half-century. Robert Hutchings Goddard, a physics professor living in Massachusetts, spent from 1909 to 1925 pondering and eventually building a rocket motor fuelled by petroleum spirit and oxygen. The oxygen

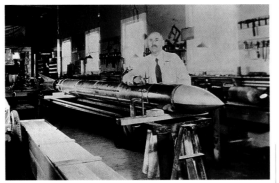

ROCKET SCIENTIST Robert Goddard (above) lived just long enough to see his vision cruelly realized in Nazi Germany's death-dealing V-2 rocket (above right).

carried on board enables the fuel to burn in the airless environment of space. As the gases created by the burning fuel escape through the exhaust, they exert a force in the opposite direction, just as a child's balloon flies across the room as air escapes through the nozzle. Following these principles, Goddard succeeded on March 16, 1926, in lofting the first liquid-propelled rocket almost 200 feet.

In 1929, he launched the first rocket with instruments—it carried a barometer, a thermometer and a small camera—and, in 1935,

one of his rockets reached 7,500 feet. Goddard's pioneering efforts were conducted in isolation, whereas Germany had a pair of visionaries named Hermann Oberth and Walter Hohmann, who in the 1920s worked out the principles of space flight and calculated the best orbits for reaching the planets. Oberth had a brilliant teenage assistant named Wernher von Braun. When he was only 22, in 1934, von Braun scored his first success with the A-2 series of prototypes for a long-range rocket fuelled by ethyl alcohol and liquid oxygen. Years of development culminated on October 3, 1942, with the successful launch of the A-4. This revolutionary 12-ton rocket achieved a height of 60 miles in a trajectory that took it up to 200 miles downrange at five times the speed of sound. Redesignated the V-2 (for Vengeance Weapon 2) and loaded with high explosive, it was the precursor of all space rocketry besides being the first strategic missile.

After Germany's defeat in the Second World War, captured V-2 rockets were shipped to the United States and fitted with instruments instead of explosives. Here, they were used for the scientific exploration of the upper atmosphere until the supply ran out in the early 1950s. Of longer-term benefit was the acquisition by the U.S. of about 120 German specialists including von Braun himself, along with their plans and concepts for three and four-stage rockets and even a space station.

A radio beep circling the Earth on October 4, 1957, stunned as much as it thrilled the world, for it signalled the Soviet Union's surprise achievement in launching the first artificial satellite: *Sputnik* (Companion). The 2 foot steel sphere was shot into orbit atop a Korolev rocket. Weighing 300 tons and exerting 514 tons of thrust at liftoff, the Korolev was far more powerful than anything

SURVEYING FROM SPACE

The first perfect world atlas was created in the mid-1990s by artist Tom Vansant, collaborating with scientists at the Jet Propulsion Laboratory in Pasadena, California. Inspired by photographs of Earth taken by Apollo astronauts on their way to the Moon, he selected the best 2,000 cloud-free shots from many satellite images and pieced them into a globe-girdling composite. The infra-red colors were altered to natural hues, and a panning video camera then filmed the complete composition.

the Americans had available at the time. American resolve to be first on the Moon, however, was demonstrated in November 1967 by the test launch of the Saturn 5, a three-stage monster designed by a National Space Agency team headed by von Braun. The Saturn weighed 2,900 tons and developed 3,400 tons of thrust at liftoff.

Saturns powered all the American manned flights from 1969 to 1973, by which time scientists had started to develop an aerospace craft—a rocket-launched glider capable of returning from space and landing like a conventional aircraft. *Columbia,* the

LAUNCH-PAD PARADE The space shuttle – without its strap-on fuel tank and booster rockets—is compared with previous rockets.

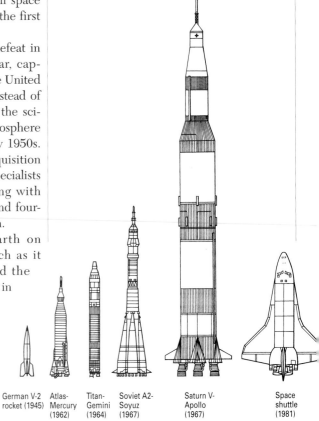

German V-2 rocket (1945) | Atlas-Mercury (1962) | Titan-Gemini (1964) | Soviet A2-Soyuz (1967) | Saturn V-Apollo (1967) | Space shuttle (1981)

SUPER BOOST Three on-board rocket engines, augmented by drop-away boosters, blast the shuttle *Columbia* 28 miles high within two minutes of liftoff.

first space shuttle, made its maiden flight on April 12, 1981. Three rocket engines in the tail were fed from a giant external tank filled with liquid hydrogen and oxygen, but much of the primary thrust came from a pair of solid-fuel booster rockets that blazed like fireworks. Small rockets maneuvered it in space and slowed its return to Earth, while more than 30,000 individually installed thermal tiles protected leading surfaces from the inferno of re-entry. The shuttle could carry a payload of up to 39 tons in its voluminous 60-foot long cargo bay, but it could not reach high orbit.

Europe rockets ahead

Meanwhile, the ten-nation European Space Agency was developing the Ariane series of rocket launchers, capable of placing communications satellites in high orbit. As the 1990s ended, the European upstart had gained for itself more than half of all commercial space business.

Ariane 5, which was assembled in France from components supplied by 70 companies in 12 nations, had a massive liquid-fuel main tank, with two 600 ton solid-fuel boosters providing 90 percent of the liftoff thrust. Despite the fact that the first rocket had to be exploded seconds after blastoff back in 1996, the program continued successfully.

WHO NEEDS ASTRONAUTS?

From *Sputnik* I, the first spacecraft launched into orbit, the relative success of space probes and robots has sustained the debate on the merits of costly manned flight. The Soviets set the pace, with the Luna probes of 1959, first to photograph the dark side of the Moon. In 1966, another Luna craft made the first soft landing on the Moon, ejecting a capsule that relayed television pictures back to Earth. A Soviet craft reached Venus in 1967 and, in 1970, another made the first Venus landing. While the U.S. was landing men on the Moon, Soviet robots were exploring the lunar surface.

But the United States also sent probes to parts of space where human explorations was not feasible. An American probe, Mariner 9, orbited Mars in 1971, to be followed by Voyager, Magellan, and Galileo probes to more distant planets. A Pioneer probe launched in 1972 was still sending back data in the late-1990s, more than 5 billion miles out.

On December 4, 1996, the U.S. launched the Pathfinder probe, which landed on Mars on July 4, 1997. Two days later, a small six-wheeled vehicle called Sojourner rolled down a ramp and on to the surface of the Red Planet, and through remote controls from earth, conducted valuable experiments on the chemical composition of the rocks and soil.

SPUTNIK I **The first man-made object to orbit the Earth.**

1957 Soviet Union launches *Sputnik* I

1967 Test of *Saturn* 5, which was to launch man to the Moon
1969 Man on Moon

1977 Launch of first Ariane rocket

1981 *Columbia* space shuttle makes its maiden flight

MAN IN SPACE

FROM THE FIRST LEAP INTO SPACE TO THE MOON LANDING TOOK LESS THAN 12 YEARS

Dogs led the way into space. Laika was first, carried into orbit aboard *Sputnik 2* on November 2, 1957, within a month of the first satellite launch. Although sensors signalled back to Earth vital information about a living creature's responses to extremes of rapid acceleration and then weightlessness, it was a one-way trip for Laika – for there was, as yet, no means of bringing a space capsule back to Earth. Belka and Strelka followed on August 19, 1960, and their safe return after 24 hours in orbit proved that the twin problems of automatic control and recovery had now been solved, and established the conditions for the first manned spaceflight.

On April 12, 1961, Yuri Gagarin, a 27-year-old Soviet pilot, circumnavigated the Earth in 108 minutes at an altitude of 203 miles aboard *Vostock (East) 1*. The craft consisted of a spherical pressurized capsule, 7 feet, 6 inches in diameter; this was placed on

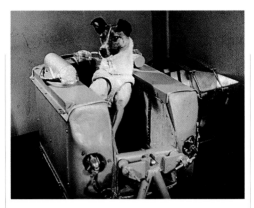

DOG IN SPACE Harnessed into a suitcase-like cabin aboard *Sputnik 2*, the dog Laika preceded man into space by four years.

top of a module that carried the oxygen supply, and was equipped with a retrorocket and tiny thruster rockets to brake *Vostock* and angle it for atmosphere re-entry. The craft landed by parachute.

The United States had embarked upon its Mercury manned spacecraft program in 1959, but it lagged the Russians by almost a year. On February 20, 1962, John Glenn completed three orbits and then splashed down in the Atlantic, within 40 miles of the plotted position. The cone-shaped Mercury capsule was an extremely tight fit for its lone occupant who, like his Russian counterpart,

remained strapped in throughout the flight. Improvements were now focused on the comfort of the crew during the flight and the maneuverability of the craft.

The two-man Gemini craft fitted with a propulsion unit made maneuvering in space possible for the first time. *Gemini 3*, with Virgil Grissom and John Young aboard, accomplished the first transfer from one orbit to another in March 1965 and, the next year, the *Gemini 8* crew accomplished the first space docking.

Life-support systems

With the world watching on television, Neil Armstrong and Edwin "Buzz" Aldrin stepped onto the lunar surface on July 21, 1969. It was the first of six manned landings over three years. The round trips lasted a minimum of eight days, mostly spent floating weightless in an Apollo cabin with a diameter of 9 feet, 6 inches. Food was dehydrated to save weight, either in bite-size cubes or

MOON MOTORING The later Apollo missions, such as *Apollo 17*, were equipped with a light, rugged lunar rover for exploring the surface of the Moon.

HUMAN SPACECRAFT Shuttle astronaut James van Hoften soars to work hitched to his Manned Maneuvering Unit, a backpack with jet control nozzles.

sucked through a tube. The bulky, pressurized space suit donned for the Moon visits was worn over water-cooled undergarments, forming a self-contained life-support system, complete with toilet facilities.

Space stations and shuttles

Once the Moon flights had been concluded in 1972, Apollo parts were fashioned into *Skylab*, America's first orbital station, which was launched the following year. *Skylab* was built into a Saturn V rocket stage with a 20-foot cross-section and fitted with two-level accommodation: a laboratory-workshop above living quarters. It had a bathroom, a

ROCKET MEN

The first "rocket man," according to Chinese records, was a man named Wan Hu, who, 500 years ago, strapped 47 rockets to the back of his chair, ignited them, and perished in the explosion. Dream became reality in 1961, when Wendell Moore invented the rocket-belt. Developed by Bell Aerosystems, it consisted of a rocket motor attached to the flyer's back and controlled by handlebars.

shower and ovens for heating up meals that included prime rib of beef. In February 1986, the Soviets launched their *Mir* orbiting station.

The problem with space stations and spacecraft until the 1980s was that they could be used only once. In 1981, however, the space shuttle *Columbia* became the first reusable space vehicle. It takes off like a rocket but glides back to land like an aircraft. Since 1983, some space shuttle flights have

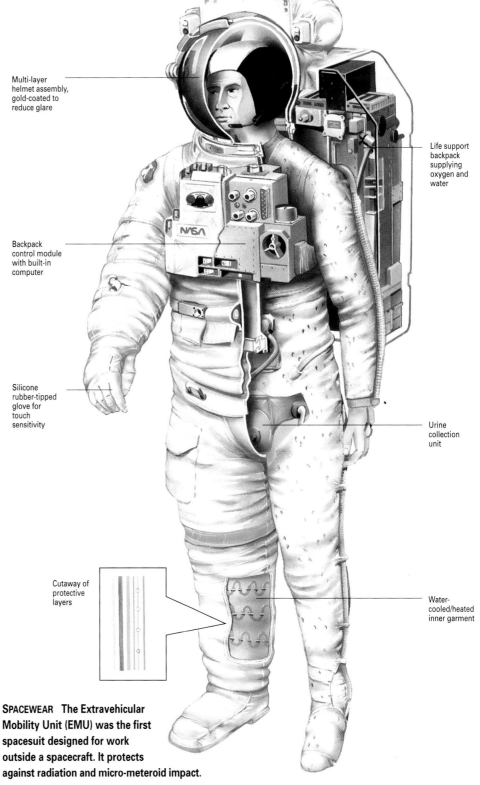

Multi-layer helmet assembly, gold-coated to reduce glare

Backpack control module with built-in computer

Silicone rubber-tipped glove for touch sensitivity

Cutaway of protective layers

Life support backpack supplying oxygen and water

Urine collection unit

Water-cooled/heated inner garment

SPACEWEAR The Extravehicular Mobility Unit (EMU) was the first spacesuit designed for work outside a spacecraft. It protects against radiation and micro-meteroid impact.

carried a European workshop-laboratory called *Spacelab* into orbit.

Four shuttle craft were flying by 1986, when growing doubts about the program's cost-effectiveness were compounded by a grounding order following an explosion that destroyed the shuttle *Challenger*, 73 seconds into launch on January 28, with the loss of all its crew members.

Shuttle flights resumed in 1988, with activity increasingly focused on a project to build a permanent outpost in space as an international research center. First projected by the United States in 1984 as the Freedom station, it was to consist of a number of laboratory modules and a crew module, all attached to a central spar, and serve as a launching platform for further space exploration.

1950 — 2000

1957 First living creature in space
1961 Yuri Gagarin orbits the Earth
1969 Man on Moon
1971 *Salyut 1*, the first (Soviet) space station in orbit
1972 *Skylab*, first U.S. orbital station
1983 *Spacelab* tried
1986 *Mir* orbiting station

MISSION TO PLANET EARTH

VOYAGES INTO OUTER SPACE BROUGHT EXCITING, ASTOUNDING—AND OFTEN BIZARRE—DISCOVERIES TO TERRESTRIAL MORTALS

From the launch of the first astronaut in 1961, the space program has been a major stimulus for invention. The outlandish and unlikely results have ranged from lunar rovers and zero-gravity toilets to soft drinks. This conscious move into commerce by the National Aeronautics and Space Agency (NASA) has meant the development of practical applications for space technology. Ventures extended from research into space-skimming, hypersonic airliners of the future to a bowling-ball balancer, derived from a flotation system used to balance the Voyager spacecraft. NASA called this its "Mission to Planet Earth." This mission includes giving a helping hand to a variety of research projects, as in the case of an acoustic refrigerator—freezing by sound

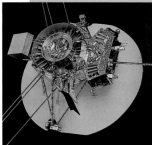

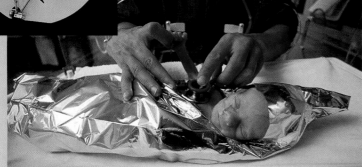

SPACE WRAP The thermal reflective qualities of space blanket material on spacecraft also ensure minimal heat loss of premature babies.

waves passed through compressed gas—flown in the shuttle Discovery and adaptations of space clothing. The latter goes back as early as 1971, when American stock-car racer Richard Petty experimented with a water-cooled "cold suit." Adaptations that followed included protective clothing for workers in steel mills and similar industrial environments, and a special suit for use in extremely hazardous situations, such as a nuclear or chemical plant explosion.

G-suits to protect astronauts from blacking out during high-acceleration launches led to the development of military anti-shock trousers (MAST) and civilian versions designed to save trauma victims by shifting blood from the lower body and maintain pressure in the brain and chest. The peculiar circumstances of the space environment and the necessity of closely monitoring an astronaut's condition also produced new medical equipment such as the piccolo portable blood analyzer.

A prime example of successful transfer technology was scratch-resistant sunglasses, employing a coating developed for space-helmet visors. Of more specialized appeal was a

machine enabling a person to be sustained indefinitely on his or her own purified waste water—something astronauts had been doing for years. The ceramic material that forms the space-shuttle's heat shield also began to find potential commercial applications in the 1990s, ranging from insulation for jet engines to a human bone substitute in artificial implants.

NASA's specialized needs often launched trails of invention whose end is still nowhere in sight. The need for a means of trapping meteoric dust particles led to the development of aerogel, a glass material so light and yet hard that it was dubbed "frozen smoke." As well as the flat trap that NASA was looking for, it could be made in a round or cube form, water-absorbent or water-repellent. It was hard enough for use as a sonic detector in auto-focus cameras and a form which conducted electricity could be used in the design of super-light batteries and small, fast computer circuitry. Further research focused upon the use of other materials to create, for instance, a polystyrene aerogel cup that kept coffee hot indefinitely.

Aerogel was the lightest thing ever made until bettered by a related material that was lighter even than air. This wispy "magic carpet" could be colored and had good insulation properties, yet static electricity was sufficient to lift it. It was biodegradable, it was even edible—but its potential uses remained the subject of debate.

PHOTO FINISH Auto-focus cameras were made possible thanks to a NASA invention known as "frozen smoke."

ECLIPSE OF THE SUN High-impact anti-glare visors worn by astronauts were adapted to produce sunglasses with similar attributes.

THE CHANGING FACE OF BATTLE

WHEN WAR BROKE OUT IN 1914, THE ARMIES TRAVELLED TO THE FRONT BY TRAIN BUT THEN HAD TO WALK TO BATTLE—NO FASTER THAN THE ROMAN LEGIONS 2,000 YEARS BEFORE. THE MAJOR WARS OF THE CENTURY HAVE BEEN THE MOTHER OF MANY INVENTIONS. TROOPS ARE NOW CARRIED BY HELICOPTER AND TANK; AND ENEMY POSITIONS ARE SENSED BY RADAR AND SATELLITE, AND THEN ELIMINATED BY LONG-RANGE MISSILES.

IN THE TRENCHES: THE FIRST WORLD WAR

HIGH EXPLOSIVES, MACHINE GUNS AND GAS TURN WARFARE INTO MASS SLAUGHTER

In the great battles of the 19th century, the fates of nations were decided in a single day. At the Battle of Sedan on September 1, 1870, the Germans humiliated France in an afternoon. Previously, at Trafalgar in 1805, a British naval victory over France and Spain had led to British supremacy at sea for a century.

It is hardly surprising that when war broke out in Europe in August 1914, each side believed that a quick victory would bring their soldiers home by Christmas. But

TRENCH WARFARE German troops prepare for a gas attack and the desperate assault across "no-man's-land" that will follow.

DEATH SPRAY Primarily weapons of defense, mass-produced machine guns reaped a daily harvest of death from 1914 to 1918.

new technology changed all that. Trains meant that each nation could mobilize and transport hundreds of thousands of men. Yet it was a new type of weapon, not numbers of men, that held the balance between France and Britain against Germany.

In 1884 an American, Hiram Maxim, had invented a gun that used the energy of its recoil to load a fresh bullet automatically. Known as a Maxim, or machine gun, it

MEMOIRS OF AN INFANTRYMAN

In his diary of the trenches, Private Charles Cole recalls his experience of one of the first tanks:

"Something was brought near to the reserve trench, camouflaged with a big sheet. We were very curious and captain said, 'You're wondering what this is. Well, it's a tank,' and he took the covers off and that was the very first tank. When we made the next attack we just had to wait for the tank to go by us and all we had to do was mop up and consolidate our trench.

"Well, we were waiting for the tank. We heard the chunk, chunk, chunk, then silence! The tank never came. . . . Well, we went over the top and we got cut to pieces because the plan had failed. Eventually the tank got going and went past us. The Germans ran for their lives. So the tank went on, knocked brick walls, houses down, did what it was supposed to have done—but too late! We lost thousands."

became the prototype for weapons designed in Germany, France and Russia. Any army advancing over open country was now dangerously exposed to machine-gun fire and, at the Battle of the Somme in July 1916, the British suffered 60,000 casualties in one day.

Early machine guns were too heavy to move easily, but, even in 1916, when lighter versions were in use, they remained weapons of defense rather than attack. The war on the western front became one in which whole armies were immobilized in trenches.

Poison gas

Germany's new tactic to break the stalemate was to send chlorine gas over to enemy trenches, in 1915. Before long, both sides were using

GAS PROOF A German medical orderly is hampered by his bulky breathing apparatus and oxygen supply.

 British Mark IV

 British Vickers Medium

Soviet T-34

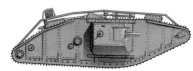

1914 Start of First World War   1918 End of First World War
1915 First use of chemical warfare

1943 Battle at Kursk involving 6,300 tanks

chemical warfare, progressing to ever nastier forms such as mustard gas. Such sinister methods were countered by gas masks.

The coming of the tank

It was the British who now thought they had the solution in the form of the tank (a code name given to conceal its real purpose). However, early versions overheated, gassed out their drivers or simply became stuck in the mud. Only at the Battle of Cambrai in November 1917 did a mass attack of 400

SHIPWRECKED Torpedo-armed submarines wiped out millions of tons of shipping and nearly won the war for Germany.

British tanks on level ground make a major breakthrough. By the second day most had broken down and the advantage was lost.

The submarine comes of age

Attention now turned elsewhere. Perhaps a nation could be starved into surrender, by sinking the ships that bring in food supplies?

For the first time in the history of war, the submarine came into its own—thanks to 20th-century developments in its design and weaponry. By 1914, a submarine could travel at ten knots submerged. In 1917, at the peak of the German campaign against ships supplying Britain, one in every four was lost to U-boats (from the German *Unterseeboot*, or "underwater boat"). Only by having ships sail in convoys were losses reduced.

Britain survived, and it was Germany that collapsed through sheer exhaustion after one final attempt to break through the trench system in 1918. The submarine had been the single weapon that came closest to winning the war.

GROUND ATTACK: HOW THE TANK WAS DEVELOPED

The tank has become one of the most successful 20th-century military inventions, spearheading ground attacks in a way that would be impossible for unsupported infantry alone. For maximum effect, a tank has to be fast, mobile over difficult terrain, well-armed and well-protected. Weighing the balance between heavy armor and speed, this combination has not been easy to achieve.

The use of a linked track, adapted first in 1916 from tractors, was crucial for propelling what was at first no more than an armored box. The first tanks, the British Mark 4s, were cumbersome and inefficient, and needed several men to operate them. Their engines, originally from tractors, quickly overheated under the strain of driving their weight over difficult ground. Even in ideal conditions, they travelled at less than 4 mph and had a total range of less than 37 miles. They were protected by riveted armor plates, but these could easily be blown apart by shells. And they had no turrets—the driver operated from the front, which inevitably restricted vision.

By the 1920s, faster, more sophisticated designs had emerged. The British Vickers Medium of 1925 had a speed of over 18 mph and a range of 155 miles, with a rotating central turret to enable the driver to see more clearly. Unfortunately, its armor was still its weak spot, and it wasn't until the 1930s that tanks became heavier and better armed. Most significant of all, however, was the revolution in strategy pioneered by the German Panzer divisions, in which tanks were used together in coordinated attacks.

During the Second World War, the Americans favored the M4 General Sherman, producing more than 50,000 of them. The Sherman was light (32 tons), relatively maneuverable, and had a speed of 25 mph, but was not well armored and was easily outgunned. Far more successful, however, was the Soviet T-34. It was extremely mobile even in snow—which gave it a crucial advantage over the German tanks in the Russian campaign. It was also frugal in its use of fuel. At the great tank battle at Kursk in July 1943—the biggest ever known, with some 6,300 tanks involved— the Russians' tank forces stalled a major German assault and turned the course of the war on the eastern front.

FRENCH LEAVE From 1915, France experimented in tank design — though the "landship' did not come into its own until the Second World War.

After the Second World War, tanks increased in firepower. The British Centurion tank, first developed in 1945 but continually upgraded, fired ammunition that could penetrate armor of double the thickness of before. Its combination of reliability, firepower and strong protective armor made it an excellent tank for warfare in open country. The Israelis used it in their defeat of the Egyptians in the Sinai Desert in 1967. One of the Centurion's drawbacks, however, was its weight and consequent loss of speed. The standard Soviet tank of the 1950s, the T-54, weighed 36 tons against the Centurion's 50, and could travel at nearly 31 mph compared with the Centurion's 22 mph.

The latest tanks have benefited from improvements in weaponry and maneuverability. A typical modern tank is the M1A1 Abrams, a 67 ton monster capable of 56 mph on firm ground. It is able to spot targets 2 miles away through their heat signatures; at 6,000 feet a hit is virtually guaranteed. (By contrast, Second World War tanks took an average 17 rounds to destroy a target at 2,100 feet.) Its shells either inject a jet of burning gas into the target or fire a dart that, according to a U.S. army document, strikes with the "force of a race car striking a brick wall at 200 mph, compressed into an area smaller than a golf ball." The M1A1 Abrams spearheaded the land attack in the Gulf War.

British Centurion

British Chieftain

American M1A1 Abrams

1950

2000

1966 Invention of the British Chieftain tank

1985 First M1A1 Abrams tank in the U.S.

ON THE MOVE: THE SECOND WORLD WAR

TANKERS, BOMBERS AND MISSILES BRING THE TERROR OF WAR INTO EVERY HOME

Among those who had won, the experiences of the First World War suggested that effective defense would always overcome successful attack. The French built a great complex of forts, the Maginot Line, along their border with Germany, confident this would prevent any renewed German onslaught. Yet they

were to be outwitted by technology. The Second World War turned out to be one of movement, with Germany and Italy overrunning most of Europe, and Japan conquering much of South East Asia and the Pacific. What had changed?

By 1939 the cumbersome tanks of the First World War had been transformed into more mobile, flexible machines. All nations had them, but the Germans coordinated them into large, armored Panzer divisions—which they used to punch a hole through opposing armies. This was known as blitzkrieg, or "lightning war." The tank had come of age.

Air wars

Blitzkrieg would not have had the same success without air support. Aircraft had been used in the First World War, mainly for reconnaissance, but there had been dramatic developments since then in their speed, range and versatility. The Panzer divisions

BLITZKRIEG MACHINE Germany's shrieking Stuka dive-bombers spread terror among civilian populations.

were backed by Stuka dive-bombers that shrieked their way down toward their targets. It was clear that no campaign could succeed without air supremacy, and this placed a premium on the fighter plane, too. Single-engine fighters, such as the German Messerschmitt Me 109 and the British Spitfire, could now reach about 348 mph and, with oxygen, fly as high as 30,000 feet. This made them a formidable match for the slower-moving bombers, and it was the failure of the Germans to destroy the Spitfire squadrons in the Battle of Britain in 1940 that led them to call off their planned invasion of Britain.

Aircraft need bases to launch from, and airfields were therefore among the first targets of any blitzkrieg attack. A revolutionary

development was the aircraft carrier, a mobile air base on the sea. The first aircraft carrier to be designed as such was the British HMS *Argus* (1918), but all the major navies soon realized their importance. The traditional naval engagement in which battleships pounded each other with heavy guns had become obsolete. A ship could now strike, through its aircraft, ten times as far as the range of its guns.

Picking a target

However, aircraft and their carriers could now be spotted through a British invention, radar—"radio detecting and ranging." It had long been known that radio waves could be "bounced off" objects and the echoes picked up, but it was not until the 1930s that the British scientist Robert Watson-Watt devised a reliable way of reading the "messages."

As with many inventions, effective coordination was the key to success. By 1939 the British had a string of radar stations along the southern coast, and it was these, linked to central operations rooms, which allowed incoming German aircraft to be tracked.

In the air, radar also helped Allied planes to find their targets. Originally assumed to be the decisive weapon of the war, the bomber had a problem in terms of accuracy. The British, armed from 1942 with the Lancaster bomber, preferred to bomb by night and to compensate for their lack of

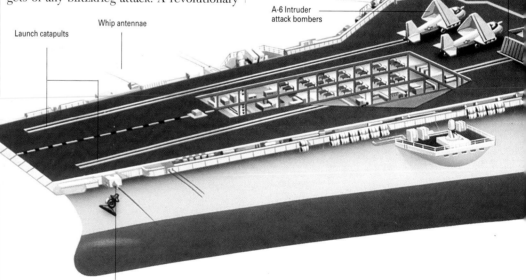

Jet blasts deflec

A-6 Intruder
attack bombers

Whip antennae

Launch catapults

Close-in weapons system

1900

1918 HMS *Argus*, the
first true aircraft carrier

1939 Outbreak of
Second World War
1940 Battle of Britain

1945 End of Second
World War

1950

CARPET BOMBING B-17 Flying Fortresses of the American Eighth Air Force unload over Germany. The B-17 was succeeded in 1944 by the B-29 Super Fortress.

microwaves, radar enabled bombers and fighter planes to pinpoint targets with greater accuracy—and even made it possible to detect submarines.

Rocket attack

At the end of the war the Germans perfected a weapon that might have saved them. As early as 1926, a liquid-fuelled rocket had been launched in America, and other countries had supported similar research. But in 1942, at the remote island of Peenemünde, where the V-1 flying bomb was also produced, the Germans were forging ahead in rocket design.

Peenemünde was ruthlessly bombed when the Allies learned of Germany's new miracle weapon, but the key scientists involved survived. By 1944 the V-2, the first ballistic missile, was finally ready to launch. This 12-ton monster, about 50 feet long, had a range of 200 miles and a ton of explosives in its warhead. Its liquid-fuel engine was so powerful that it could reach the speed of sound within 30 seconds. When it reached its target, just five minutes later, it hit the ground at well over 1,865 mph. There was

FLYING BOMB The German V-1 flying bomb anticipated the cruise missile by 40 years.

no defense against such weapons and, with the V-2s placed on mobile launchers, they were hard to eliminate by bombing. Over a thousand hit Britain between September 1944 and March 1945.

If the project—the importance of which had not been recognized by Hitler—had been supported earlier, Britain might well have been forced into surrender. As it was, the V-2 had little effect on the outcome of the war, but ballistic missiles were to change the character of warfare forever.

Navigation aid receivers

Surface search radar

Air search radar

Air search radar

E-2C Hawkeye early warning aircraft

F/A-18 Hornet strike fighters

F14 Tomcat variable sweep-wing fighter

Close-in weapons system

Arresting gear cable

SHIP TO SHORE: THE MODERN AIRCRAFT CARRIER

Modern super-carriers have steam catapults to boost the heavy jets up to flying speed for launching, and arresting gear cables to help them land. A nuclear-powered carrier also has a longer range, operates more consistently at high speeds, and has no smoke discharge to obscure the deck.

All these features are incorporated in the United States' *Nimitz* class carriers, first developed in the 1970s. These are enormous ships, almost like mini-towns inside, with room for over 6,000 crew, 89 aircraft and storage for 280,000 tons of fuel. Enormously expensive, in the future they may be rendered obsolete by mini-carriers designed for vertical takeoff aircraft.

accuracy by aiming at cities. The Americans favored daylight precision bombing, but their heavy bombers were vulnerable to fighter attack. As the technology developed in 1940 to incorporate more sensitive

1950   2000
1961 Invention of nuclear aircraft carrier
1963 First use of vertical takeoff aircraft
1985 USAF unveils Stealth Bomber, an aircraft invisible to radar

THE BOUNTY OF WAR

SPACE ROCKETS AND WASHING POWDER, HELICOPTERS AND NYLON STOCKINGS: WAR PROVES A CATALYST FOR COMPLETE TRANSFORMATION OF SOCIAL LIFE

Necessity being the mother of invention, nothing has ever stimulated the creative process so much as the ultimate crisis of global warfare—itself a concept of the 20th century. The two world wars spurred a spate of major advances, and the benefits of the intense technological competition of the subsequent Cold War and its spectacular space race were still being realized at the dawn of the new century.

The demands of the First World War brought about advances in explosives, steels, machine tools and mass production in general. Weather forecasting became a science: weather fronts are so called because their discovery dates from the war, when an analogy was drawn with the intractable fighting on the western front.

When not directly responsible for a breakthrough, the war often spurred the development of a creation existing in its infancy. Aviation was no more than a hobby until the First World War transformed it into an industry. Washing detergent was a development brought about by a shortage of natural fats, and the safety razor, the wristwatch (first worn by artillery officers) and mass-marketed cosmetics were among the many innovations that resulted from the war's transformation of social life.

The Second World War was the launch pad for space rockets and jet engines, computers and nuclear energy. It brought about the breakneck development of radar, and paved the way for the communications revolution and industrial automation. Faster and larger warplanes made the enormous advance of civil aviation possible from the 1950s onward; the German V-2 rocket and the electromechanical computers developed to crack enemy codes later played a key role in the subsequent attempts to conquer space.

The Second World War saw the development of the helicopter, four-wheel-drive vehicles and scuba gear and hastened the invention of improved plastics and other synthetic substances such as nylon. It also ushered in the aerosol can, packaged foods and even the ballpoint pen.

The ensuing Cold War ensured that there was no letup in an arms race now augmented by the space race. Rockets able to lob

A SAFER SHAVE Stubble removal could be a perilous activity in the midst of battle with a traditional cutthroat razor, First World War, 1917. Small wonder that safety razors became so popular with the troops.

nuclear missiles between continents could also place spy satellites in orbit, and out of such martial intent came the benefits of increased communications and the wonders of space exploration.

By the early 1960s, the U.S. government was funding more than half the research and development of American industry, largely in the interest of acquiring new weapons (a situation known as the military-industrial complex). At the same time, parallel efforts were being made in the Soviet Union—but they were to prove too much of a burden and eventually contributed to the USSR's collapse. The demise of the Soviets coincided with the most technologically challenging of all American military

ON THE COLD FRONT Weather forecasting became established as a science at the Bergen Geophysical Institute in Norway in 1917.

Labatt's
EST?
BREWERS   LONDON

programs, the Strategic Defense Initiative (known as Star Wars). As promulgated by Ronald Reagan in 1983, this called for the development of a satellite-based screen to protect the United States fully from enemy intercontinental ballistic missiles. Early experiments proved the task to be daunting and probably impossible without further scientific breakthroughs. But the full force of inventive genius had hardly been brought to bear when an ease in political tensions meant that the program was virtually scrapped. The civilian space program was also severely cut back.

The short, sharp Gulf War of 1991 provided a stage for showing off the latest "smart" technology, but the question still remained: could science maintain its rate of advance without the stimulus of war paranoia?

AIR FORCE Although invented in 1926 by Norwegian Erik Rotheim, the aerosol can was not developed commercially until 1941.

BREATHING SPACE Jacques Cousteau and Emile Gagnan's development of the aqualung in 1942 enabled a new method of underwater enemy attack and spawned a new sport—scuba diving.

REPLACING HORSE WITH HORSEPOWER The advantages of the truck over the horse and cart were fully appreciated after the First World War. By 1928, many companies had their own fleet.

LIFE IN THE SHADOW OF NUCLEAR WEAPONS

"AWE AND TERROR . . . WE KNEW A TERRIBLE THING HAD BEEN UNLEASHED"

In 1945 it was clear that Japan was near defeat. The country was being bombed without mercy and was unable to defend itself. Yet there seemed little chance of voluntary surrender, and it was feared that an invasion could cost a million American casualties. It was then that a new weapon, the atomic bomb, became ready. The decision to use it, one of the most controversial of the

THE DAY OF THE BOMB

Philip Morrison, a scientist working on the atomic bomb, recalls the day it was dropped in 1945:
"We heard the news of Hiroshima from the airplane itself, a coded message. . . . Then the people came back with photographs. I remember looking at them with awe and terror. We knew a terrible thing had been unleashed. The men had a great party that night to celebrate, but we didn't go. Almost no physicists went. We had obviously killed 100,000 people and that was nothing to have a party about. The reality confronts you with things you could never anticipate."

war, was taken by the new American President, Harry Truman. Within a few days of the bombing of Hiroshima and Nagasaki in August 1945, Japan had surrendered.

A-bombs and H-bombs

The atomic bomb (or A-bomb) was the culmination of several decades of work on atoms. It had been discovered, early in the century, that atoms were not the smallest unit of matter but contained a nucleus, which partly consisted of tiny particles, called neutrons. In 1938 a German, Otto Hahn, showed that if uranium was bombarded with neutrons, the uranium atom would split, and that this splitting —or fission as it was called—

BRAINS BEHIND THE BOMB Otto Hahn's discovery of nuclear fission was the first step in the development of the atomic bomb.

would release vast amounts of energy. In the process, other neutrons would be released which could, in turn, cause fission in surrounding atoms. This would result in a chain reaction and a further outburst of energy, which could be harnessed into the biggest bomb the world had ever seen. It took top scientists and $2 billion, coordinated in the Manhattan Project (1942-5), before a form of uranium—U-235—and plutonium were

THERMONUCLEAR EXPLOSION The dangers of radioactive fallout were still not fully appreciated in 1958, during Pacific tests.

1938 German Otto Hahn discovers process of nuclear fission

1945 Bombing of Hiroshima and Nagasaki

FIRST STRIKE When the bomb "Little Boy" was dropped on Hiroshima, below, it killed 80,000 people in an instant and condemned thousands more to a lingering death.

isolated as suitable materials for fission. The first atomic bomb was detonated in the New Mexico desert in July 1945; a few weeks later Hiroshima and Nagasaki lay in ruins.

Hardly had the Second World War come to an end than a new one began, the so-called Cold War between the United States and its allies, and the Soviet Union—which had developed its own atomic bomb by 1949.

By 1952, American scientists had perfected an alternative means of releasing energy in the hydrogen bomb. The H-bomb, as it was known, derived its massive energy from the fusion of the nuclei of hydrogen isotopes. Very high temperatures are needed to enable this fusion, which were supplied by exploding an atom bomb within the hydrogen bomb casing. The result was immensely more powerful and destructive than even the A-bomb.

Launching a nuclear attack

Along with the nuclear weaponry itself came self-propelled launchers, which were being developed in the West and the Soviet Union during the 1950s. Capable of reaching speeds over 18,630 mph, these intercontinental ballistic missiles could deliver their deadly freight to the most remote targets on earth. They were soon concealed in reinforced concrete silos, on planes or in submarines—to prevent detection—making it virtually impossible for a nuclear force to be destroyed.

Advancements in the 1960s meant that missiles were able to carry more than one warhead—the part that contains the explosive charge. Some of these MRVs—or "multiple re-entry vehicles"—carried as many as ten, the idea being that they would spread out and explode separately and increase the chances of hitting a single target. By the 1970s, it was possible for each warhead to have its own target (creating MIRVs, "multiple independently targeted re-entry vehicles"). All these developments created a stalemate between the two superpowers—

ON THE BUTTON The fire-control panel of a Thor nuclear missile housed in England. Both British and American commanders had to insert keys to enable a launch to proceed.

the uneasy world of MAD, "mutually assured destruction," in which each knew that a nuclear attack on the other would bring immediate retaliation.

In March 1983, President Ronald Reagan announced that he would break the stalemate by creating a defensive shield around the United States that would protect it from nuclear attack. This so-called Strategic Defense Initiative, soon nicknamed Star Wars, would have involved a complicated network of satellites and airborne antimissile missiles—a plan that, even as the 21st century was dawning, belonged to the world of scientific fantasy.

THE SUBMARINE REVOLUTION

The submarine, already an effective weapon in two world wars, has been revolutionized since 1945. In 1953, the new "teardrop" shape of the USS *Albacore* meant it could travel faster under water than on the surface. Then, in 1955, the world's first nuclear-powered engine, in the USS *Nautilus*, made it possible to travel thousands of miles without surfacing. The first missiles which could be launched from under water, the Polaris, were incorporated in the early 1960s. The Trident missile, operational in 1978, now has a range of several thousand miles.

SUBMERGED MIGHT A U.S. navy Polaris ballistic missile being fired from the submarine USS *George Washington*.

1953 Soviet Union tests its own hydrogen bomb

1957 Soviet Russia builds first intercontinental ballistic missile

1977 U.S. produces neutron bomb

STATE OF THE ART: MODERN TECHNOLOGY IN THE GULF WAR

SECRET WEAPONS IN A VOLATILE CONFLICT, WHERE NO ONE HAD ALL THE ANSWERS

In August 1990 Saddam Hussein, the dictator of Iraq, invaded and occupied the small, but oil-rich, country of Kuwait. The international community strongly condemned the occupation, not only on ethical grounds but also because of fears for Middle East oil supplies. When Saddam Hussein refused to move, a coalition of nations under United States leadership was formed to lead a counteroffensive from Saudi Arabia.

In form, this was to be a traditional war between two military forces, but in the weapons used it was anything but traditional. Iraq had bought widely, and often secretly, on the world market. The United States had a mass of new technological weaponry, much of which had never been used in warfare. What would happen was anyone's guess.

The strategy of the coalition, commanded by General Norman Schwarzkopf, was to destroy the enemy's communications and military infrastructure from the air so that Iraqi troops in Kuwait would be isolated, demoralized and easy to destroy in a land

THE COUNTDOWN Saddam's propaganda offensive was no match for such systems as the Patriot antimissile battery (below) and cruise missiles (right).

attack. Among its weapons was a cruise missile, which had never been used in conflict. Designed to be fired from a ship, at a cost of $2 million apiece, the Tomahawk had a computerized guiding system that enabled it to fly low and undetected for 500 miles. Only half of the missiles hit their targets, however, despite navy confidence in their accuracy.

The Americans also had their most up-to-date precision strike aircraft—the F-117 Stealth Fighters. Stealth had first been developed in the 1970s, but the F-117A was the latest version—constructed to absorb rather than reflect radar signals and so to reach its target unseen. Laser-guided bombs were designed to fit inside so that they, too, could not be detected by radar. These GBU-27 bombs, as they were known, were fired using laser-beam technology for precision

COMPUTER BOMBING

Computers have revolutionized the fighting of wars, but a single failure can cause chaos. At the beginning of the Gulf War, the computer system responsible for launching the Tomahawk missiles on the USS *Wisconsin* refused to accept instructions. In the end, the whole system had to be reprogrammed by hand with 24 pages of code. Only then, half an hour after schedule, were the weapons launched.

accuracy, and had a range of 6 miles. However, in practice, pilot error, clouds and enemy gunfire made 25 percent of the GBUs miss their target, with horrendous consequences for civilians.

The most feared of the Iraqi weapons were the Scud missiles (modified versions of a Soviet original). Although outdated, many

SPECIAL MISSION Flying low to knock out Iraqi airfields, the Panavia Tornado GR-1 suffered some of the heaviest losses.

were set on mobile launchers that could be dismantled, moved and set up again within 25 minutes without being detected. During the war, the Iraqis used them against their old enemy, Israel. The damage was slight, but Israel was poised to counterattack.

Determined to prevent any escalation of the war, the Americans hoped to shoot the Scuds down with their Patriot missiles. The Patriots had originally been designed to hit aircraft, but this version was capable of locking onto the flightpath of an incoming missile. As the Scuds plummeted back to earth at about 4,000 mph, the Patriot acted like a bullet aimed at another bullet. In the event, the Scuds had been so poorly adapted that many dissolved in flight. This confused the Patriots and only a small percentage of launches resulted in a hit.

The bombardment of the Iraqi forces began on January 17, 1991. Despite the sophisticated technology of the combined forces of the coalition, much of the damage

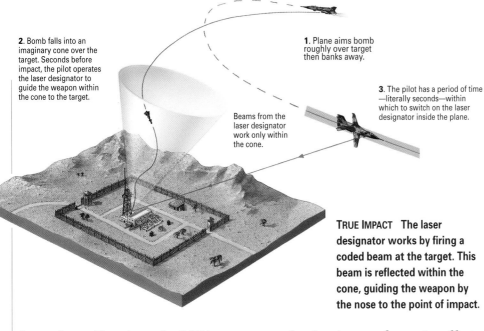

2. Bomb falls into an imaginary cone over the target. Seconds before impact, the pilot operates the laser designator to guide the weapon within the cone to the target.

1. Plane aims bomb roughly over target then banks away.

3. The pilot has a period of time —literally seconds—within which to switch on the laser designator inside the plane.

Beams from the laser designator work only within the cone.

TRUE IMPACT   The laser designator works by firing a coded beam at the target. This beam is reflected within the cone, guiding the weapon by the nose to the point of impact.

THE ENEMY WITHIN

The capacity to devastate an opponent through biological warfare has increased dramatically over the course of the century. Botulinum toxin, a type of nerve gas, is a bacterium which can cause respiratory failure within a few hours and damage the victim's nerve system irreparably before antitoxins can be given. A single missile warhead could contain enough toxin to contaminate an area of 1,428 square miles. Fearing that Saddam Hussein would use the toxin in the Gulf War, all troops were issued with protective clothing.

STEALTH STRIKE   The radar-evading F-117A fighter bomber (below) was designed to deliver bombs guided to their target by a laser beam for precision accuracy.

to the Iraqis was done, in effect, by traditional bombs. However, the overall strategy had proved to be effective. The ground attack began on February 24, and the Iraqi forces in Kuwait had capitulated within four days. They had lost 100,000 dead, with 65,000 captured. The coalition's casualties were 234 dead and 57 missing.

1950

1985 First
Patriot missiles
deployed by U.S.

1990 Iraq invades
Kuwait

2000

MILITARY MIGHT VERSUS THE HUMAN SPIRIT: GUERRILLA WARFARE

INNOVATION PROVIDES THE SPUR TO GREAT ENDURANCE AND DETERMINATION

One of the most widespread forms of conflict since 1945 has been guerrilla warfare: struggles of small bands of men against the military might of their rulers or invading armies. Described as the "war of the flea," successful guerrilla warfare saps the morale of an occupying army through continual low-level attacks.

Handheld weapons

One reason why guerrillas have been so difficult to defeat is that they have been able to draw on new portable weapons with immense power. One of the first was the American MI Bazooka, a rocket armed with a high-explosive antitank (HEAT) warhead. Innovations since include the Swedish Miniman, which can be fired from a glass-fiber tube and the British Swingfire, which weighs only about 26 pounds. Similar developments in surface-to-air missiles (SAMs) have

FLASHING BLADES   A brace of choppers airlifts supplies to support American forces during the Vietnam War.

resulted in equally portable—and relatively cheap—devices capable of destroying tanks and aircraft.

At the same time, automatic rifles and machine guns remain important weapons in the guerrilla arsenal. The Soviet Kalashnikov, based on a German assault rifle, is light, and reloadable from a detachable magazine—making it an ideal weapon to use on the move.

Helicopters in action

In the 1960s, the United States was drawn into supporting the government of South Vietnam against a determined guerrilla movement, the Vietcong. The United States had the most sophisticated technology in the world, but their enemy was a people that had been hardened by centuries of resistance to outsiders.

The linchpin of the American attack was the helicopter—with its ability to hover, take off and land in small spaces. Most successful of these was the Bell Huey Cobra, which could travel at 220 mph. It was armed with a Minigun, able to fire 4,000 rounds a minute, cannon, grenade launchers, rockets and missiles. Capable of carrying 14 fully equipped troops or six stretcher cases, it could lift casualties from a forest floor to the most modern of operating tables in 15 minutes—halving the number of those who died of their wounds.

The Vietnam War witnessed the creation of small antipersonnel mines, only about 1 pound in weight, which were made in the shape of stones or other casually discarded objects. Strewn over open country by helicopters, this speeded up the process of laying minefields.

As the conflict escalated, the U.S. took to using chemical means to clear the jungles of Vietnam in the hope of leaving the Vietcong nowhere to hide. They used napalm, which burns more slowly and can be propelled farther than pure gasoline, and the defoliant Agent Orange (named after the colored stripe of its storage drums). Only later were the human costs of such warfare counted, in terms of terrible burns, cancer, and skin diseases. In the event, all the superior

WAR OF THE FLEA Shoulder-fired Stinger missiles were supplied by the U.S. to Muslims fighting the Soviets in Afghanistan.

technology and strategic planning by the Americans turned out to be futile anyway, and the Vietcong remained throughout the invisible enemy.

❝❝ NAPALM INJURIES

A journalist, reporting on the Vietnam War, describes the effect of napalm: "In the children's ward of the Qui Nhon province hospital, I saw for the first time what napalm does. A child of seven, the size of an American four-year-old, lay in a cot by the door. Napalm had burnt his face and back and one hand. The burned skin looked like swollen, raw meat; the fingers of his hand were stretched out, burned rigid. A scrap of cheesecloth covered him, for weight is intolerable, but so is air." ❞❞

1900

1960 U.S. becomes involved 1973 U.S. pulls out of Vietnam
in helping South Vietnam
against Vietcong guerrillas

2000

A REVOLUTION IN RELAXATION

MOTION PICTURES, TELEVISION, AND VIDEO HAVE COMBINED WITH EVER-MORE SPECTACULAR SPECTATOR SPORTS TO CREATE A WORLD OF PASSIVE PLEASURES IN CONTRAST TO THE RECREATIONS OF THE PAST. AT THE SAME TIME, TECHNOLOGICAL ADVANCES—IN MORE SENSITIVE DEVICES AND NEW MATERIALS—HAVE ENHANCED THE PURSUIT OF SPORT AND ADVENTURE THAT TEST THE LIMITS OF INDIVIDUAL DARING AND SKILL.

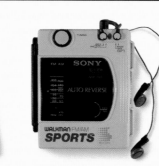

THE WHOLE WORLD IN YOUR HANDS

CAMERAS HAVE CHANGED SCORES OF EVERYDAY ACTIVITIES, AND EVEN OUR PERCEPTION OF LIFE

The camera has revolutionized modern news-gathering, advertising, astronomy, cartography, espionage, the judging of sports events and the accuracy of medical diagnosis and aerial bombing. But, most of all, it has transformed our concept of ourselves. "That's a beautiful baby," says a friend. "That's nothing," replies the proud parent, "you should see his photograph."

Cameras for the masses

The ambition of American George Eastman was to make the camera "as convenient as the pencil." And it was the invention of roll film (1889) that enabled him to construct a cheap, handheld camera, which gave reliable results

EARLY ACTION SHOT   A Kodak camera was used to take this photograph of a train crash, at the turn of the century, in Paris.

even to the untrained amateur. "You press the button—we do the rest," claimed his slogan. In 1900 Eastman's Kodak company launched a "box Brownie" camera that sold for $1. So simple that a child could use it, the box Brownie was designed to infect the rising generation with the photographic bug. The six-exposure film sold for just 15 cents. The following year, Kodak accounted for 80 percent of world sales of roll film.

Although successful experiments in color photography date back to the mid-19th century, the first patent for a simple, practical process, requiring no special camera, was issued to the French Lumière company, Europe's largest manufacturers of photographic materials, in 1903. Autochrome, as this process was known, involved scattering photographic plates with some 90 million microscopic colored granules of potato starch, which acted as filters allowing the passage of some rays in the light spectrum and blocking others. From 1906 onward, the St. James's Studio in London's Old Bond Street offered "natural color" portraits, using a different process of printing from three separate negatives, each representing a primary color. Agfa of Dresden devised their own color-plate process in 1916, and marketed it as Agfacolor in 1932. But it was not until 1936 that the first commercially successful color process for amateurs, Kodachrome, was marketed; usable only for transparencies, its appeal was limited, but Kodak color print film, available from 1942, proved an immediate winner.

Cameras for professionals

The Cirkut panoramic camera, launched in 1904 and manufactured until 1949, incorporated a motor-driven swivel movement which enabled the camera to photograph an entire school or college. A clockwork motor drive for handheld cameras, which eased the process of moving the film from frame to frame, became popular with photojournalists from 1934.

The Ensignette, sold by the English manufacturer Houghton from 1909, was the first small camera to use roll film. The development of faster, smaller film, requiring shorter exposure times while still giving a clear image when enlarged, opened the way for ever-smaller, more portable cameras. In 1913, a German researcher, Oskar Barnack, devised an experimental camera which used smaller, 35 mm film: this was the prototype Leica,

BEYOND BLACK AND WHITE   This three-color carbon print of a Miss Lena Ashwell was made in a London studio in 1907.

which was finally launched in 1925. Precision-made, compact yet capable of giving ultra-sharp negatives that could be enlarged considerably, the 36 exposure, handheld, tripod-free Leica soon became a

I WANT IT NOW !

When Dr. Edwin H. Land (1909-91) of Cambridge, Massachusetts, took a picture of his three-year-old daughter Jennifer, she demanded to see it instantly. And he thought, Why not?:

"... Within an hour the camera, the film and the physical chemistry became so clear that with a great sense of excitement I hurried to a place where a friend was staying to describe to him in detail a dry camera that would give a picture immediately after exposure." Land's brainchild, the first Polaroid camera, went on sale in the U.S. in 1948. It had no rival until Kodak launched one in 1976. In 1985

Dr. Edwin Land

Kodak withdrew from the field after a decade of court battles over patents, facing a bill for $1 billion in damages.

1900

1900 Launch of the "box Brownie"

1907 Autochrome plates marketed
1909 First miniature camera to use roll film

1925 Leica launched

1929 First functional flashbulb

1936 Kodachrome marketed

1947 Polaroid camera first demonstrated

1950

favorite with pressmen and other outdoor photographers; from 1930, some Leicas had interchangeable lenses, which enabled photographs to be taken from a wide variety of distances. Such developments enabled photographers to take pictures that were more spontaneous and less posed.

Although Kodak continued to dominate the mass market in the interwar years, more and more technical refinements came out of Germany, where, thanks to Zeiss lenses, Contax were outselling Leica by 1932. By 1935 there were German-made cameras with shutter speeds of ¹/₅₀₀th of a second.

Cameras from Japan

Japan's camera production, a paltry 36,700 units in 1930, was greatly stimulated by its war needs. During the Korean War, Western photographers became enthusiastic converts to Nikons, and by 1955 Japanese output had passed the 1 million mark. In 1963 Japan, producing 2.9 million units a year, surpassed

BIG SHOT A giant Nikon F3 was placed on the summit of the Matterhorn (above) in Switzerland, so that climbers could take photos of themselves.

SPY GEAR Miniaturized cameras and film spurred the development of concealed cameras.

Germany as the world's largest manufacturer of cameras.

In 1963, Kodak issued a new challenge with the Instamatic, the world's first commercially successful pocket-sized camera with easy-load cartridge film. But despite this, Japan's global supremacy was confirmed by its superiority in mass production and in the technological edge of its electronics industry, which enabled it to create "idiot-proof" cameras relying on automatic computer-chip-controlled features that allowed the average photographer to take professional quality photographs.

WHAT'S IN A NAME?

The Japanese Canon camera company was originally named after Kwanon, the Buddhist goddess of mercy. Market reaction to the name's religious overtones was unfavorable, however, and it was renamed Canon.

By 1990 Japanese camera manufacturers and their overseas subsidiaries were producing ten times their 1962 output, with the U.S. retaining supremacy only in a niche market. The Polaroid camera, which produced instantly developed photographs, was first demonstrated in 1947; the early cameras produced fuzzy images, but from 1963 onward the Polaroid format was available in color, becoming a firm favorite with party-goers and professional photographers alike.

SHOOTING WARS The 35 mm Leica achieved fame in the hands of war photographer Robert Capa (left), seen with colleague George Rodger in 1943.

SOUNDS OF THE CENTURY

FROM CYLINDERS, PLATTERS, AND TAPE TO COMPACT DISCS THAT INCORPORATE VISION

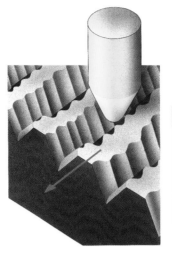

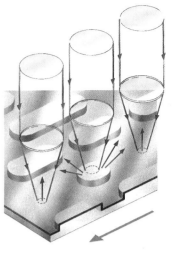

Record Player The stylus vibrates as it passes between the undulating walls of the groove, causing a magnetic coil to produce electric signals that re-create the original.

Tape Recorder The electric signals stored on the magnetic tape cause the replay head to produce electric pulses which, when amplified, re-create the original sound.

Compact Disc Player A laser beam aimed at the spinning disc is reflected differently off the flat areas and off the pits, or depressions. These reflections are detected and converted for amplification.

When, in the 19th century, the energetic American inventor Thomas Edison attempted to forecast the future uses of sound-recording apparatus, playing music was only one of several possible uses he foresaw: the others included the dictaphone, talking books for the blind, speaking clocks, teaching elocution, preserving threatened languages, distance learning, and immortalizing the last words of the dying. With the possible exception of the last, all these predictions have come true. But the

SOAKING UP THE SOUND Until the adaptation of the microphone in 1925, recordings were made using a large recording horn.

music business has eclipsed them all to become a multi-billion dollar global industry. Edison might have been forgiven for underestimating its potential—he was deaf.

From cylinder to disc

By 1900 there were already speaking clocks, talking dolls, recorded language courses, and coin-operated jukeboxes. Most of these used wax cylinder recordings, with a maximum

SONY WALKMAN

When Sony launched the Walkman, the name of which having been invented by Chairman Akio Morita, English dealers wanted to call it the Stowaway, Americans the Soundabout and Australians the Freestyle. Morita was adamant about his original choice—which entered the standard dictionary in 1986. Morita later declared that adding a word to the English language was his greatest single achievement.

playing time of two minutes. Recordings were also made on discs of hardened rubber, vulcanite and shellac; and it was discs such as these that came to predominate over cylinders, owing to their greater convenience in handling and to improvements in their sound quality and duration. The principle was the same, however. A recording stylus, attached to a revolving cylinder or disc, vibrated as it picked up sound from a horn; as it did so, the stylus cut a groove, which varied in depth (in the case of the cylinder) or in the pattern of wavy lines (in the case of the disc), according to the volume of sound. By reversing the process, the recorded sound could be reproduced.

In 1902 Enrico Caruso, the world's greatest tenor, made his first disc recording, and in 1903 the Gramophone Co. issued the first recording of an entire opera, Verdi's *Ernani*, on 40 ten-inch single-sided discs. The problem with producing these early discs was that the artists still had to sing into large recording horns. It was not until 1925 that Bell Telephone Laboratories made a major breakthrough by using a new microphone to turn sound into an electric current, which then controlled the V-shaped, groove-cutting tool. However, as most people's record players were still mechanically operated, they were quite unable to appreciate the huge leap forward in clarity and power of electrically-produced sound.

By 1979, digital recording was offering the next major step forward in sound quality. In the digital disc, sound is recorded not as grooves, but as millions of microscopic depressions, or pits, which are then detected and played back by a laser beam, or stylus, which never touches the surface. Compact discs (CDs), were marketed in 1982 in Japan

STORY OF SOUND The record player, tape recorder and CD player re-create electrically sound signals that have been recorded.

and 1983 in the United States. Far smaller than long-playing records (LPs), CDs offered double the playing time and were less vulnerable to damage. By 1993, the CD had all but replaced both records and tapes, accounting for over 70 percent of recorded music sales in the U.S. by 1997.

Tape technology

Visitors to the Paris Exposition of 1900 were able to record their voices on piano wire;

EASY LISTENING By 1960, listening to records had become a portable pleasure, with the introduction of battery-operated record players.

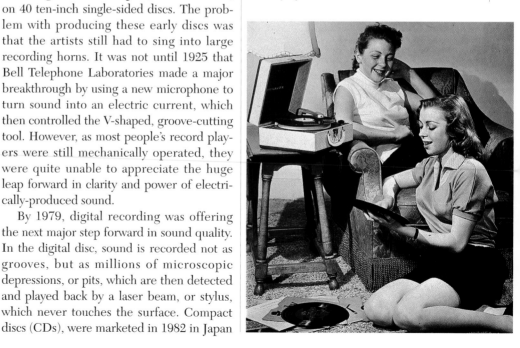

1902 Caruso makes his first disc recording

1925 Bell Labs develops electrical recording

1935 Magnetophone tape recorder exhibited

1948 Columbia launches vinyl LPs on market

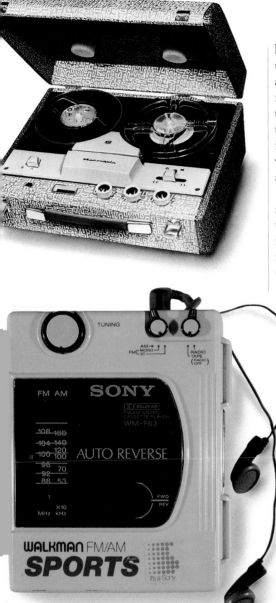

his Telegraphone so that it could record for up to 30 minutes, reproduce sound as clearly as an early telephone, and incorporate the reel-to-reel mechanism basic to modern tape-recorders. But he lacked the resources to develop it. Magnetic recorders gradually found a use in gadget-conscious offices and were taken up, first of all, by film companies and then by British radio.

The steel tape was unwieldy and very sharp-edged. Breaks were hand-soldered together, and it was said that the tapes ran so fast that radio engineers would cower in corners if they feared a breakage. However, German researchers were already developing a flexible tape, which combined an insulated base with a magnetic coating. The joint expertise of the electronics firm AEG and chemicals giant I.G. Farben produced what would now be regarded as a basic modern tape recorder, the Magnetophone, which sold out immediately when first exhibited at the 1935 Berlin Radio Show. Researchers, particularly in Germany, continued to improve tape machines throughout the Second World War, until radio listeners could no longer tell if a broadcast were live or recorded. In July 1945, an American soldier, John Mullin, tracked down four German machines, still intact, and shipped one back home to San Francisco. Mullin's fortune was made when Bing Crosby decided to abandon discs in favor of tape to record his popular radio shows.

Cassette players

With Crosby's backing, a new tape industry was born, at first in the United States; and by 1950, American buyers could choose from more than 25 different models of tape recorder. Originally intended for in-car entertainment, the cassette (in which the narrow, magnetic tape is self-contained in a case) was devised by George Eash of Cleveland in 1956 and was available in Ford cars from 1965 onward. By then Philips had developed a much smaller,

mini-cassette (1961), which was introduced to the world, with an appropriate player, in 1963. To encourage the widespread adoption of what is now the standard audio cassette, Philips allowed other manufacturers to use its patent without charge. The market for audio-cassette recordings received a huge boost in 1979 when the Japanese company Sony launched the Walkman, a tiny personal tape player that could be worn with headphones, while doing anything from jogging to housework.

Sounds electric

The 20th century has also witnessed the proliferation of electric musical instruments, in which the sound is picked up electronically and then transmitted to an amplifier—such as the electric guitar, pioneered in the United States in 1935 by the Rickenbacher Company.

West German radio engineers began experimenting in 1951 with generating electronic sounds, which they assembled on magnetic tapes to create artificial music. But American engineer Robert Moog short-circuited this laborious process by combining all the equipment into a single device, the "synthesizer," perfected in 1965; a version based on a guitar, rather than a keyboard, appeared in 1978. In 1971 the Allen company brought out the digital organ, which re-creates the sounds of different instruments. By the late 1980s, machines would be able to recreate the sound of an entire symphony orchestra.

DOWNSIZING The compact Stuzzi tape recorder of the 1960s (top) weighed a hefty 18 pounds; it preceded the Sony Walkman (first launched in 1979) by only a dozen years.

and so it was that the Austrian Emperor Franz Joseph became the first monarch to be magnetically recorded, on a device invented by Danish Valdemar Poulsen.

The principles of magnetic recording are much the same today: a wire (or tape) is wound around a magnet, and magnetized in a pattern that varies according to the sound picked up and converted into tiny electric currents by a microphone; when the wire is wound past the magnet a second time, the electric currents it produces correspond to those generated initially and reproduce the original sound. Poulsen radically improved

ELECTRONIC MUSIC The synthesizer was invented in 1965; Japan's first modular synthesizer, consisting of individual modules or features that could be combined in any number of ways, was built in 1976.

1951 First taped language course

1956 First book recorded on tape goes on sale

1965 Moog "synthesizer" perfected

1979 Digital recording developed
1979 Sony launches Walkman
1982 CDs marketed in Japan

1983 CDs marketed in the U.S.

THE SILVER SCREEN

FROM THE COMING OF SOUND AND COLOR TO COMPUTER-GENERATED ANIMATION

Motion pictures were largely invented out of technologies devised for some other purpose. Electric power was intended for industry; light bulbs for illuminating the home; and Celluloid, the essential base for film stock, was initially used as a cheap substitute for ivory in the manufacture of billiard balls and false teeth and, later, to make detachable collars for men's shirts. Creative in its powers of adaptation, rather than of invention, the movie business has periodically used new technologies to renovate, and occasionally re-invent, itself—in terms of how films are produced and viewed.

Motion pictures were born in Europe but grew up in America. The first commercial cinema projecting moving scenes taken from

SILENT STAR As this French poster from the 1920s shows, the English comic actor Charlie Chaplin mimed his way into the world's heart.

life was opened in a café basement in Paris in 1895. From 1914, however, the focus of the film business shifted to the United States. In the first decade after the war, movies were still made to be accompanied by live music or, in special instances, by phonograph records which synchronised with certain scenes in the film.

The coming of sound

The invention in 1927 of a film stock that could simultaneously record both image and sound revolutionized the industry—with consequences that went far beyond aesthetics. Stars whose careers had been built on looks, expression and gesture were discarded if they lacked the voice and verbal skills to make the transition to the new medium. And the film which incorporated the odd musical scene by means of records or live accompaniment gave way to the full-blown musical. In *Sunny Side Up* (1929), which set new box-office records for the Fox company, the

male lead sings "If I had a Talking Picture of You" to a framed photograph—which comes to life and sings back to him. As well as building its action around set-piece songs, the same film also reinforced its visual imagery with the sounds of Irish, Italian, and Swedish accents and with background noises made by traffic, dogs, children playing, and all the normal cacophony of a city's streets.

From now on, scriptwriters revelled in the opportunity to supplement visual gags by means of dialogue peppered with wise-cracks, puns and crosstalk. In Britain and

other English-speaking countries, filmgoers heard American accents, many for the first time in their lives, from Gary Cooper's laconic Western drawl to James Cagney's fast-paced New York snarl and Katharine

MAKING MOVIES TALK Alfred Hitchcock, covering his ears, directs *Blackmail*, the first British talkie, at Elstree film studios in 1929.

Hepburn's careful Connecticut vowels. At first, cameramen had to work inside sound-proofed, padded boxes so that the microphones would not pick up the whirring sound of the camera. At one extreme, sound led to the abandonment of formerly favored costume textiles, such as tulle, which rustled so much that it interfered with the recording of the actors' words. At the other, it required the reconstruction of the movie theater itself. "Picture palaces" built with acoustics

TALKIE TRIUMPH Crowds gather to *hear* Al Jolson sing in *The Jazz Singer* (1927), whose success signalled doom for the silent screen.

1917 Two-color Technicolor first used in a feature film

1927 Image and sound recorded simultaneously

1930 Full-color film from Technicolor

suitable for a full-scale orchestra were modified or replaced by a new architecture designed to minimize sound reverberation and to maximize the clarity of the dialogue.

The coming of color

Just as silent films invariably had sound accompaniment of some kind, so, from the first decade of film-making, many black and white films had at least some elements of color. Laborious hand-tinting was used initially, but in 1906 the British photographer George Albert Smith invented a two-color process, Kinemacolor. The original Technicolor process, also two-color, was first used for an American feature film in 1917. In 1930, Technicolor at last produced a film that gave full color, but the coming of sound held back further improvement because the dyes used in tinting film restricted the quality of sound reproduction. As a result, full color was used for less than one film in ten until the late 1940s.

Technicolor film recorded red, blue and green images on three different strips, a process requiring a special beamsplitter camera that the studios had to lease from the Technicolor company. Technicolor's market leadership was not finally undermined until the 1950s, when the Eastman Kodak company introduced Eastmancolor, a single-film, "mono-pak" process that did not require a special camera. As TV switched to color in the 1960s, Hollywood all but abandoned black and white.

The big screen experience

In 1948 Americans occupied 90 million movie theater seats a week; by 1951 that figure had plummeted to 51 million. The challenge from television convulsed Hollywood into a frantic search for a viewing experience that could not be replicated in the home. "Cinerama," a wide-screen system, spearheaded the counteroffensive. It promised films that were bigger, better, more colorful and more "real." However, Cinerama also required expensive conversion work on existing movie theaters to accommodate

EXPANDED HORIZON When projected, the compressed image on this strip of CinemaScope film is stretched and expanded on the wide screen.

three projectors, a much bigger screen—and fewer seats. Getting a decent payoff for this outlay encouraged some movie-houses to run the same title for as long as two years. Travelogues with thrilling natural effects, such as ski runs or whitewater rapids, lent themselves best to the novel format; but it proved ill-suited to intimate dramas, and the installation costs were simply too great for it to become the industry standard. Three-dimensional systems, on the other hand, were much cheaper to install but, although one producer vowed to throw effects at the audience "until they start throwing them back," the effects were often unconvincing, and audiences disliked wearing the glasses needed to view them.

CinemaScope used a lens system which compressed an image horizontally when photographing it and "stretched" it back out

SHOCK! HORROR! THRILL! A New York audience wears glasses with polarized filters to view a three-dimensional movie.

when projecting it. The technology had been around since the 1920s, but it was not until 1952 that 20th Century-Fox introduced the system, claiming that "objects and things

appear to be part of the audience." Its superwide screen activated the viewers' peripheral vision in a way that resembled normal visual activity. The resulting effect was less one of looking through a frame and more one of looking into a space.

The very first Western, *The Great Train Robbery* (1903), terrified audiences who found that the onrushing locomotive was coming directly at them. Ever since its

SPECIAL EFFECT "Superman" Christopher Reeve soars over Manhattan, thanks to a "zoptic" illusion created by a pair of zoom lenses, developed in 1978.

beginnings, film has eagerly developed its capacity to outdo live theater—and, subsequently, the small screen—in simulating battles, flight, explosions, and monsters. The success of James Bond, Jaws, Star Wars, Superman, and Batman movies underlines the soundness of this strategy. In recent years, the computer has played a key role in the creation of special effects. The real stars,

for example, of *Jurassic Park*, which grossed over $50 million in its first three days, were the computer-animated dinosaurs, even though their 54 action sequences took up only six minutes of the film's playing time.

1952 Wide-screen CinemaScope introduced

CARTOONS: FROM CHALKBOARDS TO COMPUTERS

THE "FUNNIES" CAME TO LIFE, FRAME BY PAINSTAKING FRAME, AND WERE THEN DIGITIZED

When Walt Disney launched Mickey Mouse's career in *Steamboat Willie* at the Colony Theater in New York, on November 18, 1928, the art of animation already had a history stretching back three decades. The earliest film-makers had discovered that, by tinkering with sequences of single-frame exposures, they could produce startling trick effects, such as a disappearing ghost or a bottle of wine that mysteriously poured itself without human assistance. Films about haunted locations were hugely popular in England, America and France.

An art is born

Thomas Edison's studio took a first step toward artist-animated films in 1905 by experimenting with title-sequences which appeared to move. In 1906, American James Stuart Blackton made *Humorous Phases of Funny Faces*, which used the single-frame technique to animate hand-drawn chalk sketches and cardboard cut-outs. The result was short, crude – and influential.

From 1908 onward, the animated cartoon developed rapidly through the efforts of pioneers such as the Frenchman Emile Cohl and the American Winsor McCay. Cohl, a caricaturist, dramatist and photographer, who was 51 years old before he first saw the inside of a movie studio, completed more than 250 animated films between 1908 and 1921, but died in poverty and obscurity. McCay, a successful comic-strip cartoonist who also did a vaudeville act, translated his creations from the old medium of print to the new one of screen, and moved from the *New York Herald* to Blackton's Vitagraph Corporation of America. Gifted with a surreal sense of humour, McCay exploited the comic possibilities of crocodiles, mosquitoes and a dinosaur called Gertie, and created bizarre locations such as Slumberland in which anything could happen. Cohl was a workaholic, and McCay had an infinite capacity for taking pains: so both were temperamentally suited to the labor-intensive effort of making animated films as single-handed artisans.

The Henry Ford of animation

A breakthrough in productivity, however, was achieved by John Randolph Bray, known as the Henry Ford of animation. Bray achieved fame and fortune by turning the recently invented Teddy Bear into a comic-strip character. He then gathered a team of artists to turn out the mass of drawings required for a succession of films, and filed patents to protect the various drawing, tracing and painting techniques he was evolving. But it was Earl Hurd who patented the really crucial next step—"drawing upon a series of transparent sheets" of Celluloid. This meant that only the actual moving parts of a drawing needed redrawing for each successive frame, while the stationary setting could be re-used over and over again.

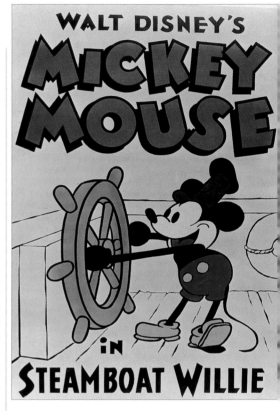

MICKEY'S FIRST MOVE *Steamboat Willie* moved animation into a new era in 1928 by synchronizing the movement of the characters' mouths with their voices.

By 1920, animation was sufficiently mature for caricaturist Edwin G. Lutz to produce the authoritative account, *Animated Cartoons; How They are Made, their Origin and Development*. And, in 1922, *Life* magazine's Robert E. Sherwood ranked Felix the Cat alongside Charlie Chaplin and Buster Keaton as one of the all-time movie greats. Meanwhile, in Kansas City, Walt Disney,

BEWARE! GENIUS AT WORK

Although cartoons portray a world in which the normal laws of physics and constraints of nature can be defied or even turned inside out, their creators base their work on a keen observation of everyday reality, as an article in the *Motion Picture World* of March 26, 1927, made clear:

"A movie cartoonist has to be more than just a little bit crazy, he must in most cases be a raving maniac. In the beginning he must have the endless source of perfectly silly ideas and then in order to work them out so as to provoke laughs in the theater, he has to have the qualities of a butcher, a carpenter, musician, actor, soldier . . . God only knows what a vast number of things a movie cartoonist has to study and observe before he can do his day's work. In fact, everything from how a snake makes love, to cooking a Spanish omelette in an Irish restaurant. It is not unusual in a cartoon studio to see several artists doing high dives off their desks, or playing leapfrog, maybe doing a dry swim on the floor while several others stand by and watch to study the timing of the action."

ANIMATED FILMS In Germany in the 1920s, Lotte Reiniger used jointed marionettes that she made herself in her animated films of fairy tales.

1906 Blackton's *Humorous Phases of Funny Faces*

1928 Mickey Mouse featured in *Steamboat Willie*

1937 *Snow White and the Seven Dwarfs*

CARTOON KING Walt Disney—a name synonymous with cartoons—was responsible for some of the best-loved characters such as Mickey Mouse, Donald Duck, Pluto, and Snow White (inset).

who could not afford, on his wage as a maker of lantern slides, to buy Lutz's book, had borrowed it from the library.

European makers of animated films had been outclassed in business terms by the 1920s, but they continued to produce much experimental work. The French made instructional films about tuberculosis and alcoholism, for example, and the Swedes films about sex education.

In Germany, Lotte Reiniger pioneered the animation of jointed, flat marionettes, filmed as delicately moving, spiky figures against a silhouette background of misty, mountainous landscapes; after three years of hard work, she produced an hour-long fairy-tale, *Die Abenteuer des Prinzen Achmed* (*The Adventures of Prince Ahmed*), which was premiered in Paris in 1926. Other animators worked with clay puppets, whose limbs and expressions could be painstakingly moved

between one shot and the next. And, in the Soviet Union, the propaganda potential of cartoons was hailed by producer Dziga Vertov as "the incarnation of the inventor's dream . . . It is possible to realize . . . what is unrealizable in life . . . Sketches in movement. Immediate future projects. Theory of relativity on the screen."

A golden age

In 1923 Walt Disney became the first cartoon producer to work out of Hollywood, issuing *Alice's Day at the Sea* as his first production that year. Five years later, with *Steamboat Willie*, he became the first to make a film specifically for showing with synchronized sound—thus moving animation into a new era. No great talent with a pencil himself, Disney proved to be an exacting taskmaster of those who were. There was plenty of competition against which to measure the technical and commercial quality of his studio's output. Universal had Woody Woodpecker; Paramount had Felix the Cat, Popeye, Betty Boop, and, in the 1940s, Superman.

However, Disney trumped them all with *Snow White and the Seven Dwarfs* (1937), the world's first full feature-length cartoon, which received a rapturous reception and won him both a Special Award Oscar and an honorary degree from Yale as the "creator of a new language of art, who has brought the joy of deep laughter to millions." If *Snow White and the Seven Dwarfs* had been produced by a single Cohl or McCay working alone, it would have taken 250 years to produce. But Disney had 570 artists

BETTY BOOP When creating Betty Boop, the Fleischer brothers filmed a real actress, and then traced the film stills to achieve realistic movement.

to produce its 250,000 drawings. He soon consolidated his coup with *Pinocchio* (1940), *Fantasia* (1940), and *Dumbo* (1941).

After Disney

A quarter of a century after Walt Disney's death in 1966, his magic factory was still going strong. In 1991, *Beauty and the Beast*, a Disney production, became the first cartoon to be nominated for an Oscar as Best Picture.

The most significant advance since Disney's death has been the advent of computers. These are used to speed up the production process by eliminating much of the repetitive work that is involved in re-drawing complicated scenes that have only minor variations. Computers can also be used to modify drawings created in the traditional manner—for example, by extending them, or moving or rotating them through space.

DISNEY RIVAL Popeye was a creation of the Fleischers, who worked for Paramount.

COMPUTER CARTOON Disney's *Toy Story*, released in 1996, was the first feature-length cartoon to be computer-generated.

TV BROADCASTING IS BORN

TELEVISION HAS UNITED THE 20TH-CENTURY WORLD BY ENTERING ALMOST EVERY HOME

I f there is such a thing as a global village, television is the town square around which its inhabitants gather. Thanks to television, hundreds of millions of people across the world can watch the Olympics, a royal wedding or a spacecraft launch as they actually happen; or enjoy weekly drama or situation comedies. Mundane activities, such as the management of traffic and the surveillance of supermarket shelves, have been transformed by television technology. Television can also be used to monitor the inside of a nuclear reactor or to search for a shipwreck on the seabed. But, most fundamentally of all, politics, advertising, education, and entertainment have been revolutionized by the advent of "the tube."

Flickering into life

The concept of television existed half a century before the reality. The two most crucial inventions, both German, were already in existence by 1900. Paul Nipkow's "electrical telescope," a pierced scanning disc that dissects an image into lines, was patented in 1884. The series of light and dark areas in the lines is detected by a photoelectric cell;

TELEVISION PIONEER John Logie Baird uses a pair of ventriloquist dolls to demonstrate his "televisor." By July 1930, he was able to transmit sound and images simultaneously.

TELEVISION FILM In the film *Trapped by Television* (1936), Hollywood portrays its own impression of what a television camera might look like.

this then activates a lamp, which projects the same sequence of light and dark onto a screen through a second disc, rotating in time with the first. The other German invention, by Ferdinand Braun in 1897, was the cathode-ray tube, a vacuum tube of glass containing an electrode that when heated, emits a stream of electrons. These then bombard the fluorescent end of the tube, creating a spot of light. Braun's device was to form the basis of today's televisions. Work to develop these fundamental breakthroughs into a practicable system for transmitting and reproducing images proceeded simultaneously in the United States, Britain, Germany, Russia, and Japan, coming to fruition only in the 1920s. Between 1923 and 1931, Russian-born American Vladimir Zworykin produced the iconoscope, the world's first television camera, which converted an optical

image into electrical pulses. In 1926, John Logie Baird, a Scot, applied for a patent to use Nipkow discs as part of a mechanical television system, which he first demonstrated successfully in an attic laboratory. The same year, Kenjiro Takayanagi used an electronic system to transmit and receive the image of a Japanese character.

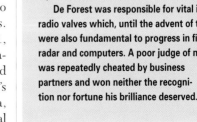

WRONG ROAD FORWARD

In 1935 John Logie Baird's misplaced faith in mechanical, rather than electronic, systems of image reproduction (which eventually frustrated his career) received powerful support from American electronics pioneer Dr. Lee De Forest:

"Improvements in television will not come by way of the cathode ray tube. They will come by way of mechanical reproduction. I know, I travelled all over Europe last year and saw all their equipment, but I am still convinced that the cathode-ray tube does not hold the solution to the problem, that it lies in mechanical reproduction."

De Forest was responsible for vital improvements in radio valves which, until the advent of the transistor, were also fundamental to progress in films, television, radar and computers. A poor judge of men, De Forest was repeatedly cheated by business partners and won neither the recognition nor fortune his brilliance deserved.

1900

1926 World's first TV demonstration
1928 U.S. begins experimental broadcasting
1931 First practical electronic camera

1950

1949 First Cable
TV service
inaugurated

Within less than a decade, the dull, fuzzy, flickering images produced by the earliest mechanical TV systems had been improved by the advent of the electronic camera, which used an electronic beam to scan images, rather than cumbersome discs.

Reaching the masses

Systematic broadcasting could now begin. Experiments began in the United States in 1928 but regular broadcasting began in Britain in 1932, with British radio initially using an improved Baird system, and then in 1936 switching to an electronic Marconi-EMI system. 1939 marked the first regular television broadcasts in the United States, and two years later, a 525-line,

EMERGING MARKET   Television sets went from being very utilitarian to fine pieces of furniture, the mark of sophisticated decor.

30-image-per-second standard was adopted. However, apart from a few electronics buffs who constructed their own sets, only the wealthy were able to watch television, since the price of a set made it a rich man's toy. The outbreak of World War II shelved further development of civilian broadcasting.

After the war, however, sales of television sets boomed on both sides of the Atlantic. Television reached 17 million American homes by 1951, as audiences fell in love with shows like "The Honeymooners" and Milton Berle's "The Texaco Star Theater." By 1960, a television set had the place of honor in over 80 percent of the nation's living rooms.

New media

Color TV began in the U.S. in 1951, but was not available until 1967 elsewhere. By that date, the continents had been linked by Telstar (1962), a relay satellite, and world TV ownership was nearing the 200 million mark.

SATELLITE TV   The first live television transmission across the Atlantic was made via the communications satellite, Telstar, in July 1962.

As satellites became cheaper and increased in number and capacity, media entrepreneurs recognized in them the opportunity to increase the number of TV channels. Viewers willing to pay subscriptions could receive alternative programming via their satellite dishes, in addition to what was on offer from local broadcasting systems. In the name of consumer choice, the way was opened for broadcasting almost anything from highly professional religious programs to sports to extremely amateur pornography.

American experiments with cable TV, in which programs are relayed to the home along cables sunk underground rather than by reception through a television antenna or satellite dish, date back to 1927. The first service was inaugurated, for a mountain-ringed town in Oregon, in 1949. But it was the advent of optical fiber cables in 1970 that led to the real expansion of cable systems, which were now capable of carrying dozens of channels simultaneously.

Portable televisions date from 1984 and interactive TV from 1990. The integration of the Internet into the livingroom television set in the late 1990s finally made the promise of "on-demand" customized programming a looming reality, but with social consequences still unknown. In the United States, viewers can use interactive TV systems to shop or to play games on their sets.

MAN OF MANY PARTS

John Logie Baird, the television pioneer, also invented a medicated fitted bandage and a glass razor. In 1928 he recorded images on gramophone discs, thus creating the first video system. In the same year, he also made the first transatlantic TV transmission and demonstrated a color TV system.

The cumulative effect of these trends has been to fragment audiences and thus, paradoxically, to undermine the socially integrating function which television had seemed to offer at first.

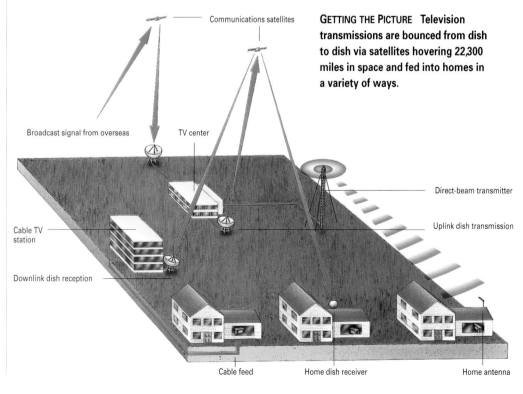

GETTING THE PICTURE   Television transmissions are bounced from dish to dish via satellites hovering 22,300 miles in space and fed into homes in a variety of ways.

Communications satellites

Broadcast signal from overseas

TV center

Cable TV station

Downlink dish reception

Direct-beam transmitter

Uplink dish transmission

Cable feed

Home dish receiver

Home antenna

1951 Color TV first broadcast in U.S.   1962 Transatlantic television relayed by satellite   1990 Interactive TV

VIDEO: FROM RE-CREATION TO RECREATION

THE VIDEOTAPE PHENOMENON: CHEAP AND INSTANT MOVIE-MAKING FOR EVERYONE

Video, like the camera, has passed from the hands of the professionals into those of the amateurs—but in a matter of years, rather than decades. Originally developed for film and broadcasting companies, video technology has found a wide range of applications in education and training, security and surveillance, advertising and public information, and home entertainment. Video technology allows banks to record the faces of customers, housewives to learn the arts of Oriental cooking, and football coaches and boxers to analyze the weaknesses of their opponents.

In the early years of television, there was no means of recording performances—

EARLY SURGE Britain's Vision Electronic Recording Apparatus (VERA) took two years to develop and was already dated when launched in 1958.

programs were broadcast live, with the participants giving a repeat performance if necessary. Although tape recorders were capable of storing sound, they could not cope with the complex electronic signals that constitute a television image. In 1956, however, the Ampex corporation of California launched the first commercially viable video recorder; and on the very same day, 3M announced the birth of the first magnetic videotape. This worked on the same principle as the tape recorder, in which the signal is recorded electromagnetically on a plastic tape coated with iron dioxide.

Struggles for simplicity and standards

Although the Japanese firm Sony marketed the first video recorder for the general public in 1964, public acceptance was hindered by its weight, cost and the challenge of threading tapes through an intimidating forest of rollers and heads. By 1969 Matsushita, JVC and Sony had developed the first user-friendly U-matic video cassette, with the tape housed in a plastic box. Competition now revolved around the size, and capacity, of the tape itself. Of the two rival formats, Betamax lost the battle in the marketplace to VHS (Video Home System), which now accounts for over 80 percent of world sales; and in 1982, some leading manufacturers pledged common support for an 8 mm standard format.

In 1982, Sony launched the Betamovie, the world's first camcorder for home movie enthusiasts, combining a video camera and a video cassette recorder. Tied to the Betamax cassette, the Sony model looked as if it might be immediately superseded by more compact 8 mm versions. In 1985, however, Sony brought out its own, two-speed Video 8, and in the same year also, the Handycam, a very simple, "record only" device, weighing in at under 3 pounds. JVC responded with its own model, incorporating autofocus and playback facilities. The simple-to-use, handheld

VIDEO GAMEBOX An advertisement for a portable Nintendo Game Boy claims that you simply have to slot in the cartridge, and then play any one of 80 games on the video display unit.

video was initially hailed by some as a technology that would allow non-professionals to challenge Hollywood in producing their own authentic representations of reality. In practice, the gap between the quality of images and sound produced by ordinary video technology and the quality demanded by professional broadcasters remained large. And most camcorder users stuck to weddings, graduations, and home videos of their travels and family occasions.

Video discs

The television pioneer John Logie Baird experimented with storing images on discs, rather than tapes, as far back as 1928, calling his system Phonovision. But even in 1965, Westinghouse's Phonovoid system could only store still images. Teledec, the first commercial video disc (1970), which was marketed in 1974 by the Anglo-German consortium of AEG-Telefunken-Decca, was a commercial failure. Philips, on the other hand, incorporated laser technology into their Laservision (1972), but were slow to bring it to market, taking until 1980 to launch in the United States, and 1982 in Europe. In 1987 Sony and Philips took a further step forward with a Compact Disc Video (CDV), which offered excellent pictures and digital hi-fi sound. Laser discs in CDV format, mostly carrying feature films, were first marketed in 1990.

The persistence of manufacturers in this field has been matched only by the reluctance of the public to accept what they are being offered. One explanation may lie in the alternative attraction of ever simpler and cheaper tape formats; another in confusion caused by manufacturers' competing formats; and a third in unwillingness to invest in expensive hardware which may rapidly become obsolete.

Slaves of the screen

By the 1980s, parents, teachers, and social critics identified video games as the computer-age equivalent of the Pied Piper of Hamelin, bewitching their children into a hypnotic state without actually having to tempt them out of their bedrooms. In 1990 the *Journal of the American Academy of*

Child and Adolescent Psychiatry carried an article on "Pathological Preoccupation with Video Games," accusing manufacturers of deliberately promoting the children's dependence on the medium.

The first video game, "Star War," developed at the Massachusetts Institute of Technology in 1962, required such costly and cumbersome equipment that it seemed to have no commercial future. However, the market took off when "Space Invaders," launched by the Japanese Taito Corporation

in 1978, and PacMan took amusement arcades by storm. As VDUs (Visual Display Units) became cheaper and more compact, people were able to play these games at home. The next logical development was Nintendo's paperback book-sized, handheld Game Boy (1989), the Walkman of video games, which rendered the player free to move about while playing. By the early 1990s, one in three American households owned one, and by the late 1990s, that number was past the one-in-two mark.

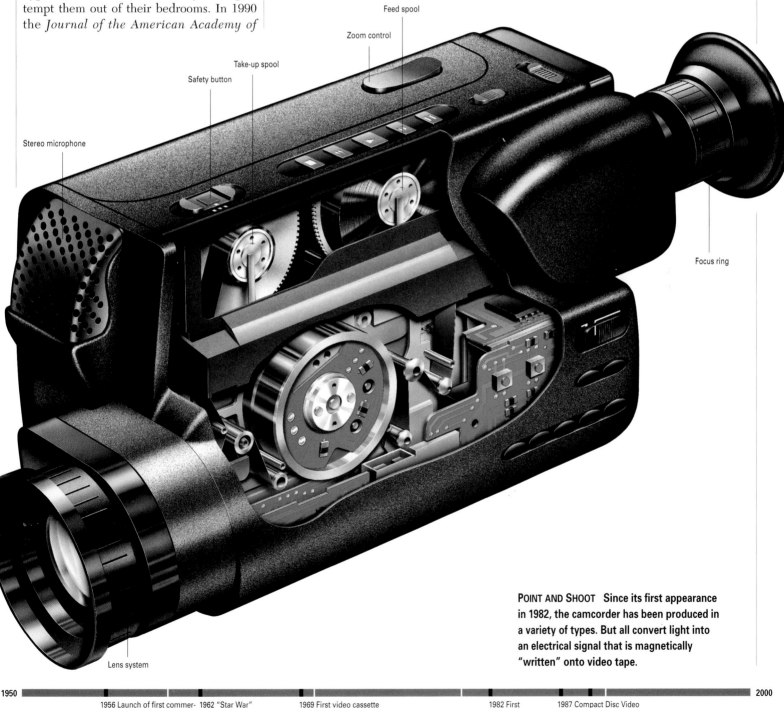

Feed spool

Zoom control

Take-up spool

Safety button

Stereo microphone

Focus ring

Lens system

POINT AND SHOOT Since its first appearance in 1982, the camcorder has been produced in a variety of types. But all convert light into an electrical signal that is magnetically "written" onto video tape.

1956 Launch of first commercially viable video recorder and first magnetic videotape

1962 "Star War" video game developed

1969 First video cassette

1982 First camcorder

1987 Compact Disc Video
1989 Nintendo's Game Boy

THE UPS AND DOWNS OF DO-IT-YOURSELF

DOMESTICATION OF MACHINE TOOLS SPAWNS A WHOLE NEW INDUSTRY, HELPING US TO SHAPE OUR WORLD FROM THE COMFORT OF THE GARDEN SHED

Stimulated by the development of electric tools and gadgetry designed specifically for home use, "do-it-yourself" (DIY) became a whole new industry from the 1950s. And the catalyst was the lightweight electric hand drill. Portable drills had existed since the turn of the century, when Wilhelm Fein of Stuttgart in Germany invented the first. Then, in 1917, Duncan Black and Alonso Decker, inveterate American inventors whose previous patents included a press for printing bank notes, produced a much-improved version with a trigger switch and a fan-cooled motor. However, at 24 pounds its use was limited to industry. It was not until after the Second World War that light-weight drills became available for home use. Constant refinement led to pistol-grip drills that increased their speed according to the amount of pressure applied.

The plastics revolution brought a cascade of cladding and sticking materials, such as epoxy resins and other improved types of fixative. Nothing in nature gripped like superglue, a family of synthetic adhesives properly known as cyanoacrylates, or CA. Their unique powers of attachment were discovered by chance when two Kodak chemists, Harry Cooper and Fred Joyner, were studying the light-refracting properties of a new material. The sample ruined an expensive piece of laboratory equipment, and it was only later that Cooper and Joyner appreciated the significance of their discovery. The first CA adhesive went on sale as "Eastman 910" in 1958.

The Workmate, a transportable, foldaway workbench—an essential item for the home "do-it-yourselfer"—was invented in 1968 by a Briton, Ronald Hickman, who joined forces with the Black & Decker company in the U.S. for its launch.

Some keen odd-jobbers were ready to tackle anything, including the assembly of their own cars. Designer Colin Chapman pioneered the trend in 1957 with the Lotus Elite, a sports car sold in kit form. By 1973,

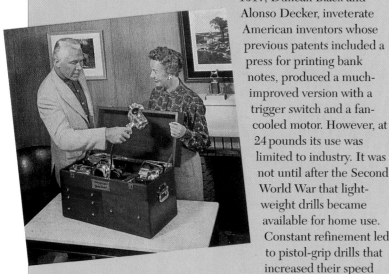

TREASURE CHEST In 1959, a Black & Decker tool set came in a polished mahogany box, with the emphasis on craftsmanship as much as DIY.

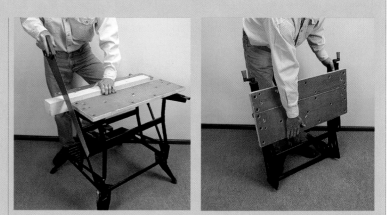

HOME HELP The Workmate transformed any part of the house into an instant workshop, and opened up DIY to a new generation from 1968.

the Sinclair company was offering pocket calculators in this challenging manner.

By this time, the electronics boom had made the lives of do-it-yourselfers considerably easier by automating many home tools. But technology's advance was double-edged. Sophisticated electronics thwarted domestic attempts at repair, and spelled doom for millions of home mechanics who liked to "fix" their cars. In the 1990s, many systems in new cars were controlled by computers whose programming was a closely guarded manufacturer's secret. Hope sprang from Chicago, however, where a company developed commercial software to interface with the car computer—thereby turning any home computer into a do-it-yourself diagnostic tool.

KITSCH CAR The craze for building your own car started in the late 1950s. This Jeffrey, 1974, incorporated a 1500cc Ford engine.

TRS 301

A CENTURY OF SPORT

TECHNOLOGY REVITALIZES TRADITIONAL SPORTS AND SPARKS NOVEL NEW ONES

The classic sports—baseball, tennis, football (both American and British), and hockey had all been formalized by 1900, and with the exception of basketball, no new sports have rivalled them in terms of popular participation. But new technologies have at least transformed the performance limits of some of them.

In particular, advances in materials science have afforded contestants better protection in ball and contact sports, such as baseball and football, and safer climbing on mountains. The leather soccer ball now has no laces to cut a player's face when heading it, and is treated with a water repellant so that it stays the same regulation weight throughout the game. Golfers have benefited from steel-shafted clubs (authorized for competition use from 1929), tennis players from steel and then graphite rackets (rather than wooden ones), and runners and jumpers from "aerodynamic" footwear. Track times have improved since the 1970s with the replacement of cinder surfaces by rubberized ones. Ball-throwing machines have added a new routine to training in baseball and tennis. Skaters and skiers have benefited from machines to make artificial ice (1949) and snow (1976). Under-water swimming has been revolutionized by the aqualung (1926) and frogman's flippers (1927).

But most of the really novel "sports" of the present century have been essentially individualistic, often more concerned with style than with competition. Craze-prone California has been an especially creative center, being responsible for the invention of beach volleyball (1940s), skateboarding (1960s) and the mountain bike (1973), and for popularizing rollerblading (1980s).

Sea speed

Although surfing had been practised by the Polynesians in the 18th century, it did not reach America until the 20th—along with several other water sports. The first water-skis consisted of two curved pine boards used by American Ralph Samuelson on Lake Pepin, Minnesota, in the summer of 1925. And in the 1960s, American surfers developed the sport of windsurfing (unaware of the independent invention of the sailboard by Briton Peter Chilvers in 1958).

The sky's the limit

The first free-fall parachute jump was made in 1924 by United States Staff Sergeant Randall Bose—for a bet. Parachuting has been practiced by soldiers and adventurous sportsmen ever since.

Hang-gliding dates back to 1948, when NASA engineer Francis Rogallo developed a

DAREDEVIL SPORTS Skateboarding (top) evolved out of ocean-surfing, while hang-gliding (above) was devised by NASA engineers; both took off in the 1960s.

flexible, woven-wire wing, but he was unable to find backers for further development. In 1964 another NASA engineer, Australian Bill Moyes, perfected a 48 square foot delta-wing design, and in 1969 his countryman, Bill Bennett, demonstrated its potential by flying over the Statue of Liberty. Motorized "ultra-light" hang-gliders appeared simultaneously in 1975 in Australia, France and the U.S., enabling would-be flyers in flat regions to participate.

More a "dare" than a sport, bungee-jumping began in Britain around 1980 and spread to the United States and Australia, although some people believe that it originated hundreds of years ago on the Pacific island of Vanuatu. Jumpers usually leap from bridges or cranes. In 1991 Australians invented a horizontal variant, bungee-running, which required contestants to run at full strength from a padded wall before bouncing back.

SAILING ON A BOARD Windsurfing was a development of the 1960s, which became a passion in the surfers' paradise of Hawaii.

1924 First free-fall parachute jump
1925 Water skis

1948 Hang-gliding originates

1958 Sailboard originates

1980 Bungee-jumping

TOYS AND GAMES

BRIGHT IDEAS ARE TURNED INTO FORTUNES, BUT SOME ENJOY ONLY FLEETING SUCCESS

Some of the world's most ingenious toys and games—from building blocks and board games to mind-stretching puzzles—have been the products of 20th-century inventiveness. Whether temporary craze or enduring success, all have achieved their spectacular international success through equally innovative marketing techniques.

Building for success

The 1910s saw skyscrapers sprout up across the American skyline. No wonder, then, that one of the most popular toys of the decade allowed children to recreate that very phenomenon in their own homes. In 1913, the year of the Chrysler Building's completion, a former Olympic gold medallist and medical doctor named A.C. Gilbert invented the Erector Set, a set of motorized toys made of steel parts, which could be built into elaborate constructions. In contrast to the modern allure of Gilbert's invention, in 1916, John Lloyd Wright, the son of the famous architect Frank Lloyd Wright, created a set of interlocking wooden toy logs, that harked back to the prairie days, called Lincoln Logs. Similar building sets were popular in Europe, such as a construction toy consisting of metal components, nuts and bolts, invented by the Briton Frank Hornby in 1900, and marketed as Meccano seven years later.

The emergence of Lego interlocking building blocks waited on the availability of cheap mass-produced plastic moldings. Invented in 1955 by Ole Kirk Christiansen, a Danish cabinet-maker turned toy-maker, it derived its name from *leg godt,* meaning "play well." By 1979, Lego components had come to account for one percent of Denmark's entire industrial export earnings.

Word game

The first crossword puzzle, devised by Liverpool-born Arthur Wynne, appeared in the weekend supplement of the December 21, 1913, issue of the *New York World*. The 32 clues were undemanding (for example, "opposed to less," "the plural of is"), but the feature proved popular enough to become permanent and to lead to the publication in 1924 of a first book of crossword puzzles, complete with attached pencil. By the end of 1924, four crossword books had become best-sellers, and crossword motifs had begun to adorn women's dresses, handbags, shoes and jewellery. Dictionary sales soared. The craze soon reached pathological proportions. One man became so absorbed in a puzzle that he refused to leave a restaurant; he welcomed the ten-day jail sentence he received because it allowed him to spend more time solving puzzles. In recent years, new variations on the crossword theme have appeared, incorporating cryptic puns, anagrams, literary references and even the obscure jargon of various sports.

Scrabble's success story

The passion for word games has guaranteed the enduring success of Scrabble. In the 1930s, unemployed architect Alfred Butts, a crossword fanatic, devised Lexiko, originally a game with letter tiles and racks but no board or tile-values. Undaunted by rejections, Butts added these new elements, renamed his game Criss-Crosswords and, in 1946, changed it to Scrabble. Finally launched in 1949, Scrabble caught on only slowly at first, selling 8,500 sets a year by 1951. Then the

HABIT-FORMING By offering sets in ascending size, Meccano inventor Frank Hornby pioneered the "repeat purchase" marketing strategy.

CROSSWORD COSTUME In this fanciful French fashion illustration, a model displays a dress based on the theme of "Les Mots Croisés," or crossword puzzles.

chairman of New York's Macy's department store, a keen Scrabble player himself, ran a promotion that started a nationwide craze. The press reported that other Scrabble fans included the Indian premier Jawaharlal Nehru, the composer Oscar Hammerstein II, and the Hollywood movie mogul Darryl F. Zanuck. By 1954 Scrabble had crossed the Atlantic and sales were passing the 5 million

MINIATURE GOLF

The world's first 18 hole miniature golf course was laid out at Fairyland Inn on Lookout Mountain, Tennessee, in 1926 and almost immediately eclipsed all other diversions for guests. Hotel owner Garnet Carter patented his obstacle course in 1929 under the trade name Tom Thumb Golf, and midget links soon sprang up all over the Southern states.

mark; and dictionary publishers experienced a boom like the one sparked off by the crossword craze of the 1920s. Scrabble is now manufactured in 24 different languages.

Monopoly matters

The world's best-selling board game was devised in 1933 by unemployed American salesman Charles Darrow, who sketched the original board (showing his favorite holiday resort, Atlantic City) on the oilcloth used to cover his family's kitchen table. Unlike Scrabble, Monopoly was an instant success, enabling players to revel in a cutthroat capitalist fantasy through the depths of America's worst depression.

Darrow asked a box manufacturer to make up 5,000 copies of his game and, even though he sold them at a hefty $10 each, he was unable to keep pace with demand. So he approached the leading board-game manufacturers Parker Brothers of Massachusetts, who turned it down on the grounds that it contained no less than "52 fundamental playing errors." The company soon reversed this initial rejection, and by February 1935 was churning out 20,000 sets a week. Since then,

PINBALL BLIGHT Religious reformers wanted pinball banned; a critic (in the hat) confronts players in a Los Angeles drug store in 1939.

85 million sets have been sold in 19 languages and 32 countries.

Pinball parlors

The pinball machine, launched in 1930, was a mechanized version of a 19th-century parlor game called bagatelle. Its inventor, David Gottlieb, sold a staggering 50,000 Baffle Ball machines in his first year of production in the United States, and in 1931 two rival

machines, Bally-Hoo and Whirlwind, each sold even more. In 1933, electric circuitry was introduced and the brightly lit machines were to be found in bars, cafes, amusement arcades and special "pinball parlors." By the 1940s, preachers and politicians were denouncing pinball as a disgraceful vice, seducing American youth into gambling at an impressionable age. In the 1950s, the game was exported to Japan where, as pachinko, it is played in 15,000 parlors.

Wham-O wizardry

In 1957, a Frisbee craze swept America as college students hurled 9 inch plastic flying discs to each other during class recesses (the Frisbee took its name from the flat tins used by the Frisbie Pie Company, which Ivy League students had used as a skimming toy for years before its plastic imitator was invented). Having sold millions of Frisbees at 79 cents each, the Californian Wham-O Manufacturing Company followed up their success with a plastic version of the bamboo hoop used by Australian schoolchildren in gym classes. Twenty-five million "Hula Hoops," at $1.98 each, were sold in the first four months after its 1958 launch. The craze was short-lived, however, and Wham-O had to wait until 1965 for its next great coup: the "Super Ball," a supersensitive, plum-sized, high-resiliency synthetic ball that would bounce so high and so long that it seemed to defy physics. Eventual sales topped 7 million.

The Rubick cube

Invented in 1974, an ingenious puzzle called the Rubik cube had a similarly blazing—if relatively brief—burst of popularity, making a millionaire of its creator, Hungarian Erno Rubik, a professor of architecture, in the process. Using universal ball-and-socket joints, which allowed movements of 360 degrees,

BEST SELLER Monopoly, the cutthroat capitalist fantasy of an unemployed salesman, turned its inventor into the first board-game millionaire.

Rubik combined 27 colored cubes to make one large cube whose multicolored surfaces had to be manipulated until each face presented a single color. This could involve working through 43,252,003,274,489,856,000 possible patterns.

Cube-mania became cited as the cause of a variety of human distresses, ranging from strained tendons to, of all things, divorce! Worldwide sales of the cube topped 100 million, and more than 50 books were published illustrating solutions, proving once again the appeal of fads.

MODEL CONCEPT Barbie (shown here in 1959) was the first doll in adult form and the first with a change of wardrobe. She was named after the daughter of her creators.

1900

George Eastman's Kodak company launches the handheld, simple-to-use box Brownie **camera**.

Frank Hornby devises a new construction toy that consists of metal pieces held together by nuts and bolts; it is sold as **Meccano** in 1907.

TRAIN MAN The Hornby name became synonymous with clockwork trains.

A Norwegian named Johann Waaler invents the **paper clip**.

1901

The first visibly modern car—Daimler's **Mercedes**—takes to the road.

King Camp Gillette files a patent for the **disposable razor blade**; manufacture begins in 1903.

British engineer Hubert Cecil Booth patents the **vacuum cleaner**.

1902

Italian-born Guglielmo Marconi receives the first **transatlantic signal** — in Newfoundland.

Weighing in at 1½ tons, the "Ivel" is the first **lightweight tractor**.

1903

The Dutch physiologist Willem Einthoven invents a forerunner of the **electrocardiograph** — which makes it possible to monitor irregularities of the heart.

Two bicycle dealers, Wilbur and Orville Wright, achieve **powered flight** at Kitty Hawk, North Carolina.

1904

The **Trans-Siberian Railway** links Moscow with Vladivostok.

French civil engineer Eugène Freyssinet develops **prestressed concrete**, which makes for lighter, stronger load-bearing beams.

Ira Rubel, in New York, invents **offset printing** — a process in which the image is transferred from the inked plate onto an intermediate rubber surface before being rolled onto the paper.

The British company Courtaulds produces an **artificial silk**, which was later to be called rayon.

1906

An **electric-powered washing machine**, designed by American Alva Fisher, appears on the market.

Reginald Fessenden makes the first **radio broadcast**—a Christmas greeting to ships off the coast of Massachusetts.

1907

American engineer Lee de Forest patents the **triode valve**, which was to hold the key to future radar, television, and computer development.

ROYAL MAIL The first letter is flown by air in 1911 to George V.

Five years after the technique had been invented—in Germany—the first photograph is sent by **facsimile transmission**, from Paris to London.

Frenchman Paul Cornu achieves the first manned takeoff in a **helicopter**.

1908

Swiss chemist J.E. Brandenberger

produces a cellulose film that was manufactured four years later as **Cellophane**.

The first practical **gyroscopic compass** is produced in Germany; the instrument is later perfected by American Elmer Sperry.

American William Coolidge produces a **tungsten filament** for use in light bulbs.

George Hale installs a 60 inch reflector mirror on a **telescope** at Mount Wilson, California.

1909

Fritz Haber, in Germany, produces **synthetic ammonia** from nitrogen and hydrogen; it was later used to make explosives and fertilizers.

German Count Ferdinand von Zeppelin inaugurates the world's first **commercial airline**, plying his airships between five German cities.

Leo Baekeland invents the first synthetic polymer—the forerunner of all modern plastics—**Bakelite**.

1910

The Italian tenor Enrico Caruso sings live on radio from the Metropolitan Opera House to audiences gathered in some of New York's smartest hotels: the first **outside radio broadcast**.

American engineer Chester Beach designs an electric motor that leads to the development of the **domestic electric food mixer**.

1911

American **Willis Carrier** invents the air conditioner—will take twenty years to become popular.

1912

Neon lighting is used in advertising for the first time —to promote Cinzano vermouth.

Charles Belling in Britain develops the first effective **electric heater**; six-bar Belling Standard heaters were an instant success.

The first **diesel locomotive** is built by the Sulzer company in Switzerland.

DIESEL DAYS A diesel locomotive was made in Switzerland in 1912.

1913

Englishman Harry Brearley develops **stainless steel** by adding chromium to steel. Krupp in Germany improved the formula in 1914 with a mix that included a little nickel.

Work is finished on the Woolworth Building in New York; for the next quarter of a century, it is the tallest **skyscraper** in the world.

Henry Ford builds a moving assembly line at his Detroit plant for making the Model T; similar **mass-production** techniques were developed in France in 1919 by Citroën, and in England in 1924 by Morris Motors.

American Irving Langmuir improves the tungsten bulb by filling the bulb with an inert gas, resulting in the now-familiar **incandescent light bulb**.

William Burton, of Indiana, patents a new process for **refining oil** called thermal cracking. It doubled the yield of petrol from crude oil and improved the quality of the product.

In New York, Mary Jacob files a patent for a "backless **brassiere**."

1914

The first **electric traffic light** is erected in Oakland, California.

Lawrence Sperry demonstrates the first **automatic pilot**, flying over Paris with his hands over his head; it would take almost 30 years before the autopilot was adopted in civil aviation.

1915

Chemical warfare is used for the first time during the First World War, when the Germans release chlorine into a trench manned by French Algerians. The trench was held only after Canadian reserves made improvised gas masks from handkerchiefs soaked in urine.

1916

A **tele-typewriter** to send written messages over phone lines is invented in Chicago, but it was not until 1931 that a system was launched nationally by Bell Systems. Called Telex (for "teleprinter exchange"), it gradually spread worldwide to the benefit mainly of business and newspapers.

Clarence Saunders opens the first **self-service store** in Memphis, Tennessee.

1917

Tanks start to show their potential as weapons of war during the Battle of Cambrai in the First World War.

Albert Einstein proposes how, when atoms are hit by radiation, they might be triggered into emitting radiation of their own; this is the theory behind the **laser**.

A wartime shortage of natural fats, from which soaps had previously been made, hastens the invention of the first artificial soap, or **detergent**, in Germany; it is called Nekal.

With airfields among the targets of enemy attack during war, HMS *Argus*, the first dedicated **aircraft carrier**, is launched.

1919

The British physicist Ernest Rutherford shows, in the first observed **nuclear reaction**, that the nucleus of an atom can be broken by bombarding it with particles.

1921

German Karl Fritsch designs the first *autobahn*, or **motorway**.

1922

German chemist Hermann Staudinger proposes a theoretical basis for the plastics industry by revealing how **polymers** can be created artificially by stringing together smaller molecules. This eventually led to the development of polystyrene, PVC, polythene, polyurethane and a host of acrylics and polyesters.

SAILING THE SKIES A book jacket of 1920 features an airship.

The **"Baby Austin" 7**, which anticipated modern mini-cars by a couple of generations, is designed by Herbert Austin, with the declared aim of "knocking the motorcycle and sidecar into a cocked hat." Under the slogan "The Motor for the Millions," the Baby Austin does for Britain what the Model T had done in America.

The first **water-skis**, consisting of two pine boards, are used by Ralph Samuelson on Lake Pepin, Minnesota.

1924

London watchmaker John Harwood designs the first **self-winding watch**, with a mainspring that was rewound as the wearer moved.

American William Mason discovers the first **hardboard** — tough, weather-resistant Masonite.

1925

Bell Telephone Laboratories develops **electrical recording**.

The compact, precision-made **Leica** camera is launched.

1926

An **electric steam iron** is launched by the Eldec Company, U.S.

John Logie Baird uses Nipkow discs to demonstrate a **mechanical television system** to members of the Royal Institution.

Robert Goddard launches the first **liquid-propelled rocket**.

Garnet Carter and his wife lay out the first **miniature golf course** at their hotel in Tennessee.

1927

The thermostat, a bonded strip of two metals that switches the electric current on and off according to temperature, is incorporated in an **automatic central-heating system**.

Film stock is invented that can simultaneously record both image and sound, thereby heralding the age of the **"talkies."**

1928

Walt Disney launches the career of **Mickey Mouse** in *Steamboat Willie*; Mickey was originally going to be called Mortimer.

WATER SPORT Americans enjoy water-skiing in 1923.

The wonder drug that was to change the world, **penicillin**, is discovered by the Scottish bacteriologist Alexander Fleming.

Juan de la Cierva flies the English Channel in a **rotor craft**.

A commercial **transatlantic telephone service** is launched, but it is very expensive.

1929

Inspired by an illustration in a veterinary journal, the German doctor Werner Forssmann inserts a catheter into a vein in his own arm until it reaches his heart. This pioneering experimental technique opened up the future possibilities of **heart surgery**.

MOTOR LUBRICANT First marketed in 1901, oil was served in jugs by the garage attendant of the 1920s.

A new understanding of the brain is made possible by the German psychologist Hans Berger and his **electroencephalograph**.

1930

American Otis Barton designs the **bathysphere**, a hollow steel ball that withstands pressure under water.

Michael Cullen opens one of the first **supermarkets** in New York.

American chemists Thomas Midgley and Albert Henne produce the first **fluorocarbon** for refrigerators; the next year, Electrolux refrigerators are mass-produced in Sweden.

Full-color movie film is introduced by Technicolor.

1931

Karl Jansky, in the United States, traces interference on the transatlantic radio-phone link to the constellation Sagittarius; his discovery leads to the development of **radio telescopes**.

American physicist Ernest Lawrence invents the **cyclotron**, which he uses to treat his mother's cancer.

Vladimir Zworykin produces the first practical **electronic television camera**: the iconoscope, which converts an optical image into electrical pulses.

Ernst Ruska builds the first **electron microscope** in Berlin, with 12,000 powers of magnification.

1932

American Harry Jennings invents a **folding wheelchair** for his friend, Herbert Everest. It is so successful that their company, Everest and Jennings, dominates wheelchair design for the next 50 years.

COLOR FILM In *The Wizard of Oz* (1939), Kansas is filmed in black and white, while the land of Oz is shown in Technicolor.

1933

The modern airliner is born in February, with the maiden flight of the **Boeing 247**.

Two British scientists working for ICI produce **polythene**.

American Charles Darrow invents **Monopoly**, the world's best-selling board game.

1934

Cat's-eyes are invented by British contractor Percy Shaw; they make a major contribution to road safety.

1935

Physicist Robert Watson-Watt heads a team that develops **radar** to detect the approach of enemy aircraft.

American researcher Wallace Carothers invents **nylon**, the first wholly synthetic fiber.

Parking meters are tested successfully in the U.S.

The first recognizably modern **tape recorder**, the Magnetophone, is exhibited at the Berlin Radio Show.

1936

The German engineer Heinrich Focke flies his prototype Fa-61, the first practical **helicopter**.

Kodachrome, a commercially successful color film for amateurs, is put on the market.

1937

Frank Whittle tests the **jet engine**, heralding a new era for the airplane.

The Nestlé company in Switzerland develop the first successful **instant coffee**, Nescafé.

Snow White and the Seven Dwarfs becomes the first full **feature-length cartoon**.

1938

Chester Carlson duplicates the first, blurred **photocopy** image.

The first practical plastic **contact lens** is developed.

1939

Fluorescent lighting—an effect created by coating the inside of the tube with phosphors—is an instant success at New York's World Fair.

The insecticide **DDT** is patented by Swiss chemist Paul Muller.

American William Heubner devises a **photocomposition machine** that projects characters onto film at the tap of a key.

1940

Henry J. Kaiser masterminds **"Liberty" cargo ships**. Because these ships were built faster than the Nazi U-boats could sink them, they helped to supply wartime Britain.

1941

A working **aerosol can** is developed for spraying insecticides.

Agricultural machine manufacturer Massey-Harris goes into production with the first **combine harvester**.

1942

The German Wernher von Braun's **V-2 rocket**, a 13 ton monster with a ton of explosives in its warhead, becomes the precursor of today's long-range rockets.

In a squash court at University of Chicago, Italian physicist Enrico Fermi improvises the first **atomic pile**. The world entered the nuclear age.

FIGHT FOR FREEDOM Liberty ships consisted of prefabricated sections welded by a workforce of 250,000, a quarter of them women.

Galvanized by the Japanese attack on Pearl Harbor, the U.S. government funds the Manhattan Project. Top scientists and $2 billion come together in a desperate race to develop an **atom bomb** before Germany. Hiroshima and Nagasaki are the victims of their success.

1943

Sausage skins and a beer barrel are the unlikely materials used by the Dutch doctor Willem Kolff to improvise a **kidney dialysis machine** during the Nazi occupation of the Netherlands.

Jacques Cousteau collaborates in the invention of the **aqualung** for deep-sea divers.

The British mathematician Alan Turing's **Colossus** is proclaimed as the first computer; it is used to decode enemy messages.

1945

The **ballpoint pen**, originally patented by Laszlo Biro, is launched commercially in the United States and becomes an instant success.

1946

French swimsuit designer Louis Réard creates the two-piece **bikini**.

1947

The **Polaroid camera**, producing instantly developed photographs, is demonstrated for the first time; color becomes available in 1963.

1948

The giant **telescope** on Mount Palomar, California, initiated by George Ellery Hale, is completed.

Columbia launches **plastic vinyl LP records**. Plastic, developed during the Second World War, replaces shellac as the main material for discs and allows record grooves to be smaller and closer together. This, in turn, enables discs to play longer.

1949

The first **jet airliner**, the De Havilland Comet I, takes to the skies.

Scrabble is launched in the U.S. By 1954 it had crossed the Atlantic, and sales had exceeded 5 million sets.

1950

Ralph Schneider and Frank McNamara launch the Diners' Club **credit card**.

1951

Color TV available in the U.S., though few stations broadcast in color.

1952

America explodes the first **H-bomb** at Eniwetok Atoll in the Pacific Ocean.

An American surgeon, Charles Hufnagel, implants the first **artificial heart valve**.

The first clinical test of the **pacemaker**, in Boston.

1953

The question of how to keep the heart motionless for surgery—without killing the patient—is solved by American doctor John Gibbon with his **heart-lung machine**.

Cambridge team James Watson and Francis Crick announce that they have cracked the genetic code—solving the mystery of human evolution. This discovery paves the way for the new science of **genetic engineering**.

1954

The first civil **nuclear reactor**, at Obninsk in Russia, produces enough electricity to meet the needs of a town of about 6,000 people.

Nonstick frying pans are developed by the French engineer Marc Grégoire.

1955

Dane Ole Kirk Christiansen invents **Lego** plastic building blocks.

Mass inoculations of Jonas Salk's **polio vaccination** turn the tide in fighting a much-feared disease.

Frozen fish fingers are launched; **frozen food** had been developed by Clarence Birdseye in the 1920s, and precooked frozen food in the 1930s.

The world's first **nuclear-powered submarine**, the USS *Nautilus*, makes it possible to travel thousands of miles without surfacing.

Dr Narinder Kapany, at Imperial College in London, demonstrates how **fiber optics** work; over the next 40 years, they transform the world of telecommunications.

Sony launches the world's first **transistor radio**.

1956

Univac launches the first **second-generation computer**, which uses transistors.

Ampex of California launches first commercially viable **video recorder**; 3M launches first magnetic videotape.

The first **transatlantic telephone cable** is laid.

Calder Hall, the world's first **industrial-scale nuclear reactor**, opens at Sellafield in the North of England.

NUCLEAR POWER   The cube-shaped building houses one of the original Sellafield nuclear reactors.

1957

The first **giant radio telescope** is built, at Jodrell Bank in England.

A craze for throwing 9 inch plastic discs, known as **Frisbees**, sweeps college campuses in the U.S.

1958

A light, cheap **aluminium can** is developed in the U.S.

As part of the U.S. space program, a satellite is launched into space with a **silicon solar panel**. Unexpectedly, it worked so well that it cluttered up the airways for five years.

1959

The English boat-designer Sir Christopher Cockerell shows the first **hovercraft** to the public.

The Soviet Union commissions a **nuclear-powered vessel**, the experimental ice-breaker *Lenin*.

TUNED TO THE STARS   The giant dish at Jodrell Bank in England reflects and focuses astronomical radio waves.

Alastair Pilkington announces the float-glass process, which makes flaw-free **glass** of a uniform thickness.

1960

Norethynodrel—the mass-market **oral contraceptive pill**—goes on sale in the U.S.

In California, Theodore Maiman demonstrates his ruby **laser**; the laser was to find applications in surgery, machining and communications.

The world's first experimental **communications satellite**, Echo I, is launched.

1961

A Soviet pilot, Yuri Gagarin, becomes the world's first **spaceman**; he orbits Earth aboard *Vostock 1*.

Albert Sabin's oral **polio vaccine** ensure that generations of future children are immunized for life.

1962

At Massachusetts General Hospital, two surgeons regraft the right arm of a 12-year-old boy in one of the first examples of **microsurgery**.

1963

Kodak produces the **Instamatic**, the world's first commercially successful camera with easy-load cartridge film.

MAN IN SPACE   A portrait of Yuri Gagarin, the Soviet cosmonaut.

1964

The first **Shinkansen**, or bullet train, speeds between Tokyo and Osaka.

IBM 360 series marks the transition to third-generation computers, using wafer-thin **silicon chips**.

1965

Following years of research by the Bell Telephone Company, the world's first **electronic exchange** is operating in New Jersey.

London designer and boutique owner Mary Quant creates the **miniskirt**.

Early Bird, the world's first **commercial communications satellite**, is launched over the coast

of Brazil; in 1969 it relays pictures of the first manned Moon landing.

1967

Heart transplants become a reality when South African surgeon Christiaan Barnard undertakes pioneering surgery in Cape Town. The patient survived for only 18 days, although he died of a lung infection rather than as a result of tissue rejection.

Hydroelectric principles are put to work in an estuary, when France decides to build the **first tidal barrage**—on the River Rance in Brittany. Turbines work round the clock as the tide ebbs and flows. To date, Canada has the only other commercial installation in the world.

1968

Americans Jim Drake and Hoyle Schweitzer develop the **sailboard** in its definitive form, with keel, articulating joint and wishbone boom. In 1982, however, a British court credits Briton Peter Chilvers with having invented the sailboard in 1958.

1969

The **Patient Operated Selector Mechanism** (POSM)—known as Possum—opens a new world to the totally paralyzed. Developed at Stoke Mandeville Hospital in Britain, it allows patients to communicate or

ORBITING EARTH The Russian *Mir* space station was launched in 1986, 15 years after the first one.

control their environment by electronic means.

Moon landing: with one small step, Neil Armstrong makes one giant leap for mankind.

The first **supersonic airliner**, Concorde, makes its maiden flight.

1970

Development work starts on the **Global Positioning System**, a globe-girdling array of 21 navigation satellites.

The **microprocessor**, which incorporates all the essential parts of a computer on a chip, is invented; it gave birth to the microcomputer and to mass-computing in general.

Boeing introduces the wide-body 747, the first **jumbo jet**.

1971

The Soviet spacecraft, *Salyut 1*, becomes the world's first **space station in orbit**; the U.S. follows in the next year with *Skylab*.

The first **digital watch** is produced in Dallas, Texas.

First **Computerized cargo-handling** comes into operation at London's Heathrow Airport.

1973

Work finishes on the twin towers of the **World Trade Center** in New York, each rising to 1,353 feet.

1974

Hungarian professor of architecture Erno Rubik invents the **Rubik cube**.

In response to the Middle East oil crisis, President Richard Nixon gives scientists the go-ahead to investigate alternative energy sources. This gives **solar power** the research resources needed to start to fulfill its potential.

1977

The first **autofocus camera** in the popular price range makes its debut.

The U.S. develops the **neutron bomb**, a nuclear bomb that can kill people without causing destruction to cities and industries. Public opposition was so great, however, that it was never put into production.

Europe's first geostationary weather satellite, **Meteosat**, is launched.

Bell Telephone installs the world's first commercial telephone system using **optic cables** in Chicago.

1978

Development in the U.S. of the **Quickie wheelchair**, an ultra-light model using hang-glider technology, brings new freedom to thousands of disabled people.

In vitro fertilization methods pioneered by Drs. Patrick Steptoe and Robert Edwards in Britain result in the birth of the first test-tube baby, Louise Brown. Her mother was unable to conceive naturally because of blocked fallopian tubes.

1979

The **mobile cellular phone** is launched.

Sony launches the **Walkman**, a small personal cassette player.

Digital recording is developed, and, in 1982, **compact discs**, in which the sound signals are detected and played back by a laser beam, are marketed in Japan. By 1991, sales of CDs outstrip sales of records and tapes.

G.N. Hounsfield, of the British electrical company EMI, shares the Nobel prize for medicine for his work on developing **CAT scans**.

LASER LISTENING Since 1979, the compact disc has eclipsed other means of sound reproduction.

More than 315,000 **Microcomputers** are sold in the U.S., an increase of 80% over the year before.

Canada's **Anik B satellite** inaugurates the world's first television service beamed directly into people's homes via a dish antenna.

Two Canadians, Chris Haney and Scott Abbott, come up with the initial idea for the game **Trivial Pursuit**. Some 50 million sets have been sold.

1980

IBM in the U.S. and NEC in Japan perfect a process of laser-scanning **bar codes**.

Microsoft provides the operating program for IBM's desktop personal computer.

Rollerblades are invented by two American students, as a summer training device for ice hockey players, with the ice skates replaced with aligned rollers.

1981

The first **TGV** runs between Paris and Lyon on a purpose-built line.

In the U.S., *Columbia*, the first **space shuttle**, makes its maiden flight on April 12.

Atom-by-atom exploration of matter is made possible by the **scanning tunnelling microscope**, or STM, which registers each atom as a bump as it scans the surface of a sample.

Government investment in the search for alternative sources of energy lies behind the development of the first two **wind farms**, in Altamont and Tehachapi, California. By the late 1990s, California was generating half the world's wind energy.

1982

Insulin—which occurs naturally in humans—is produced by **genetic**

engineering for the treatment of diabetes.

Sony launches the Betamovie, the world's first **camcorder**.

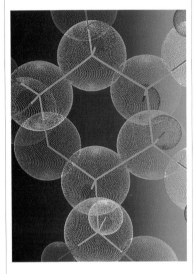

INVENTING INSULIN A computer graphic shows part of the molecule of human insulin.

The **PC4 post-coital pill** becomes available in Europe. Dubbed the "morning after" pill by the media, the PC4 could be taken up to three days after unprotected sex to prevent conception.

1984

A baboon's heart is **implanted** in a California infant born with a birth defect. She lives 20 days.

Apple launches the first graphics-based **Macintosh** computer.

1985

Desktop publishing becomes a reality with the launch of PageMaker, the first design software developed for a personal computer.

Fuji uses cheap plastic lenses to give the world the first **disposable camera**.

The Home Shopping Network, the first **TV sales channel**, is transmitted in the U.S.

SUPER TOWER Most aspects of NEC's headquarters in Tokyo are computer-controlled.

Scientists at the University of Leicester in Britain develop the genetic marker —a means of positively identifying a suspect from the slightest trace of blood or body fluid, a single hair or a few skin cells. The first conviction based on DNA evidence —or **genetic fingerprinting**—was made in Britain in 1987.

1986

RU486 abortive pill is invented in France; available outside France only on the black market until 1990.

1987

Disposable contact lenses become available. They can be discarded after a short time (anything from one day to one month) to avoid problems caused by deposits on the surface of the lens.

Solar-powered cars race across Australia, from north to south, in the first race of its kind, the World Solar Challenge.

1988

The **Super Phoenix**, a fast breeder nuclear reactor, becomes operational in France. It is seen as a safer and more efficient means of producing nuclear power.

The first **wave power device** is installed offshore in Scotland. Although the technology is only in an

embryonic state, it is capable of delivering enough electricity to power a small town. Its immediate future lies in generating power for island communities.

A man is fitted with a plutonium power-sourced **pacemaker** that has a battery life expectancy of 20 years. The very first pacemakers (fitted in the early 1960s) were expected to last only a couple of years.

DuPont announces that it will stop production of chloroflourocarbons (CFCs), used in aerosols and as refrigerants, but thought to damage earth's **ozone layer**, as discovered by satellite photos taken above Antarctica.

1989

The American artist Jason Lanier realizes the potential of the computer-generated artificial environments that had been developed by the U.S. Army and NASA for flight simulators and similar training tasks. Crude **virtual reality** systems were soon adapted for video games and amusement arcades. Other applications included medicine, and architectural and interior design. An interior designer could take clients on a tour through their future home, and surgeons could develop their skills in realistic simulation or even—with a system in prototype by 1995—could operate on real patients from a remote location.

Nintendo produces the handheld video **Game Boy**.

1990

From lighting to security, most functions of the **Super Tower** —NEC headquarters in Tokyo— are controlled by computer.

The shuttle *Atlantis* places the **Hubble Space Telescope**, capable of detecting stars 50 times fainter than any visible from Earth, into orbit.

Genetic engineering is used to treat humans directly. In Maryland, doctors remove defective white blood cells from a four-year-old, modify them and then reinsert them.

1990s

During the 1990s, research has continued in a whole range of areas that intimately affect how we live—in the food that we eat, the clothes we wear, the way we work, travel and shop, and even our sources of everyday entertainment. Only time will tell how far-reaching in their effects these inventions will be.

For the first time, **genetic engineering** has produced disease-resistant crops and man-made strains of mice; the new science even offers the prospect of new foodstuffs, such as a rot-resistant tomato and non-stringy celery. Scientists can also improve on nature by genetically engineering new natural textile fibers.

Bell Labs has created SAM (Speech Activated Manipulator), a seeing, talking, touching **robotic device** that can understand simple spoken instructions; the aim is to extend robotic capability in places, such as a radiation-contaminated area, that humans cannot enter.

VIRTUAL VIOLENCE A child wears a virtual reality helmet and fires a fake gun in an amusement arcade.

In 1992, work started on an **Intelligent Vehicle Highway System** (IVHS), which combines "smart card" computer technology and a new radio transmission system. It would enable drivers to pay tolls without stopping, summon help in the event of a breakdown, check road and traffic conditions ahead, and to communicate with each other. In other ways, the motor industry had turned full circle with a race to develop a practical, pollution-free **electric car** —a quest partly abandoned almost a century before.

Millions of people are making purchases from a home computer – in a process known as **cybershopping**.

INDEX

ACKNOWLEDGMENTS

Abbreviations:
T = Top; M = Middle; B = Bottom;
R = Right; L = Left

CB = Corbis-Bettmann
HG = Hulton Getty
ROC = Robert Opie Collection
SPL = Science Photo Library
SSPL = Science & Society Picture Library
UB = Ullstein Bilderdienst

3 SSPL, L, LM; SPL/Labat/Lanceau, Jerrican, RM; ROC, R. 6 CB, ML; Quadrant Picture Library, BR. 7 Arcaid/Nick Meers. 8 SPL/Jon Wilson, TL; John Howard, BR. 9 Architectural Association Slide Library/ Valerie Bennett; Topham Picturepoint, L; SSPL, LM; Anthony Blake Photo Library, RM; SPL, R. 10 CB, ML, R. 11 HG, TR, BR. 12 Architectural Association Slide Library/Koji Murakoshi, T. 12-13 Arcaid/ Richard Bryant. 13 Arcaid/Alex Bartel, TR. 14 AKG London, M; HG, BL; Illustration Matthew White/Philips Lighting, BM. 15 HG, TL; Arcaid/Alex Bartel, BR; ROC, TR. 16 SSPL, BL; ROC, TR. 17 Ransome, ML; Katz Collection; Illustration Matthew White, BR. 18 ROC, TR; UB, M; SSPL, BL. 19 CB, TM; SSPL, BL; AKG London, BM. 20 The Advertising Archives, TL; The Interior Archive, BR. 21 Rolex Watch Company, BL; SPL/David Parker, BM; Topham Picturepoint, TR. 22 Roger-Viollet, BL; UB, BM; SSPL, TR. 23 CB, T; Topham Picturepoint, BR. 24 HG, TR; AKG London, BL. 25 SPL/Dr Jeremy Burgess, ML; HG, R; Illustration Roy Williams/Du Pont, R. 26 ROC, ML, BM. 27 HG, L; Superstock, R. 28 Library of Congress, B; The Advertising Archives, MR. 29 SPL, TR; Library of Congress, BR. 30 SSPL, T; Anthony Blake Picture Library, B. 31 ROC, TM, RM; Magnum/David Hurn, B. 32 The Advertising Archives, T; Library of Congress, B. 33 SPL/Astrid & Hanns-Frieder Michler, TR; Anthony Blake Photo Library, BL. 34 HG, BL; Telegraph Colour Library, RM; Dr Leslie Bowie, TR. 35 SPL/Bruce Iverson; SSPL, L; Jean-Loup Charmet, M; SPL/Labat/Lanceau, Jerrican, R. 36 Jean-Loup Charmet, BL; Popperfoto, BR; Mirror Syndication International, MR. 37 Superstock, TL; ROC, TR. 38 CB, T; AKG London, BL; Image Bank/GK & Vikki Hart, BM. 39 Magnum/Richard Kalvar, R; SSPL, TM, TR. 40 Mirror Syndication International, BL; Mary Evans Picture Library, TR. 40-41 Topham Picturepoint. 41 CB, M, BR. 42 SPL/Hank Morgan, TL; SPL/Sheila Terry/Rutherford Appleton Laboratory, MR; SPL/Geoff Tompkinson, BL. 43 SPL/Bruce Iverson, TR; SPL/Will & Deni McIntyre, BR. 44 National Motor Museum, Beaulieu, ML; Image Bank/M. Rosenfeld, BL; HG, BR. 45 SPL/R. Maisonneuve, Publiphoto Diffusion, TR; ImageBank/Kay Chernush, B. 46 HG, B. 47 SPL/Dale Boyer/NASA, TL; SPL/Hank Morgan, ML; SPL/Labat/Lanceau, Jerrican, BR. 48 SPL/Philippe Plailly, TR; John Frost Historical Newspaper Service, ML; Illustration Martin Woodward, BR. 49 SPL/ NASA, ML; SPL/Roger Ressmeyer, Starlight, B. 50 SPL/Roger Ressmeyer, Starlight, B. 51 SPL/Jeremy Trew, ML; Illustration Matthew White, B. 52 SPL/ Manfred Kage, MR; Illustration Colin Woodman, TR. 53 SPL/R. Maisonneuve, Publiphoto Diffusion; SSPL, L; CB, LM; SPL/Terranova International, RM; ONE 2 ONE, R. 54 HG, TR; Mary Evans Picture Library, M; SSPL, BR. 55 CB, TR; UB, BL; Toucan Books Archive, TL. 56 AKG

London, TR, BR, BL. 57 HG, BL; BT Archive, BM; ONE 2 ONE, BR. 58 Illustrated London News Picture Library, TR, L, BL. 59 Illustrated London News Picture Library, TM, TR, B. 60 CB, BL; SPL/NASA, BR; Illustration Kevin Jones Associates. 61 SPL/Terranova International, TL; SPL/NOAA, R. 62 HG, TR, BL, BR; Jean-Loup Charmet, ML. 63 NSF/The Virtual Publishing House Ltd, TR; The Virtual Publishing House Ltd, MR; SPL/David Parker, ML. 64 Topham Picturepoint, TR, M; John Frost Historical Newspaper Service, BL. 65 SPL/Ben Johnson, M; SPL/Malcolm Fielding, MR; SPL/Alex Bartel, B. 66 SPL/Hank Morgan, ML; Illustration Michael Robinson/BICC Cables, BR. 67 SPL/Scott Camazine; Rex Features, L, RM; Mary Evans Picture Library, LM; SSPL, R. 68 HG, BL, M; SPL/CNRI, TR. 69 SPL/CEA-ORSAY/ CNRI, TL; SPL/Simon Fraser, Dept of Neuroradiology, Newcastle General Hospital, TR; SPL/P. Saada/Eurelios, BR; Illustration Kevin Jones Associates/Toshiba Medical Systems, BM. 70 SSPL, TR; SPL/Chris Priest, RM; AKG Photo, BL. 71 SPL, TR; SPL/David Campion, TM. 72 SSPL, BL; Illustration Matthew White/ Gambro, BR. 73 SPL/Dept of Clinical Radiology, Salisbury District Hospital, TR; SPL/Hank Morgan, BL. 74 Popperfoto, TR; HG, MM; Mary Evans Picture Library, BL. 75 Rex Features, M; SPL/Philippe Plailly/Eurelios, BR. 76 SPL/David Parker, BL; Illustration Kevin Jones Associates/ Johnson & Johnson Orthopaedics, TR. 77 Sygma/Christine Spengler, TL; Sygma, BM; Rex Features, BR. 78 CB, BL; David Constantine/Motivation, TR. 79 Allsport/ Clive Brunskill, RM; Rex Features/Chris Harris, B. 80 HG, BL; Illustration by Michael Robinson, BR. 81 SPL/John Mead; Rural History Centre, University of Reading, L; BIOS/J.P. Delobelle, M; National Motor Museum, Beaulieu, R. 82 CB, ML; BP Photo Library, B. 83 John Frost Historical Newspaper Service, TL; Illustration Kevin Jones Associates/Chevron U.K. Ltd, R. 84 Rex Features, MM; Illustration Roy Williams, BL. 84-85 BIOS/J. P. Delobelle. 85 Katz Pictures/Viktor Rudko, BM; CB, BR. 86 Mirror Syndication International, TR; SPL/Peter Menzel, MR, BL. 87 Environmental Picture Library/Martin Bond, TR; Magnum/Leonard Freed, R. 88 Environmental Picture Library/Martin Bond, TM; SPL/James Stevenson, TR; Still Pictures/Carlos Guarita/Reportage, ML. 88-89 SPL/Peter Menzel. 89 BIOS/M. Coupard, MR; Illustration Martin Woodward/Nova Scotia Power Inc, TR. 90 Rural History Centre, University of Reading, BL. 90-91 Popperfoto. 91 Still Pictures/Pierre Gleizes, TL. 92 CB, ML; Still Pictures/Mark Edwards, BL; The Natural History Museum, London, MR. 93 Image Bank/Barrie Rokeach; Jean-Loup Charmet, L; Image Select, LM; Genesis Space Photo Library, RM; Popperfoto, R. 94-95 Illustrations Matthew White. 95 SSPL, MR. 96 Superstock, MR; Jean-Loup Charmet, BL. 97 UB, T; Magnum/ René Burri, MR; The Advertising Archives, BL. 98 HG, TR; National Motor Museum, Beaulieu, B. 99 Popperfoto, TR; Pictorial Press/Andrew Morland, MR; HG/Neal Simpson, BR; HG, ML. 100 UB, TR; Mary Evans Picture Library, BL. 101 UB, TR; Popperfoto, BR. 102 National Portrait Gallery, M. 103 HG, BL; Gamma/FSP, BR; Illustration Kevin Jones Associates/Royal Institute of Navigation/Civil Aviation Authority, T. 104 HG, MR; Popperfoto, B. 105 The Advertising Archives, TL;

Magnum/Richard Kalvar, TR; Topham Picturepoint, MR; SPL/Alex Bartel, BR. 106 The Mansell Collection, ML, B. 107 Popperfoto, TL; Illustration Martin Woodward, B. 108 Topham Picturepoint, TM; HG, M; Popperfoto, B; Illustration Martin Woodward, MR. 109 Aviation Photographs International, TR; Magnum/ Fred Mayer, BL. 110 Topham Picturepoint, foreground, TM; Günter Endres, background, TM; CB, BL; Illustration Kevin Jones Associates, BR. 111 Popperfoto, TR; Image Select, MM. 112 SSPL, ML; Popperfoto, BM. 112-13 Topham Picturepoint. 113 Popperfoto, TL; Gamma/FSP, TR. 114 National Geographic Society, BL. 115 Illustration Martin Woodward/JAMSTEC/Harbor Branch Oceanographic Institution/Woods Hole Oceanographic Institution. 116 AKG London, TM; UB, LM; Illustration Kevin Jones Associates, BR. 117 Genesis Space Photo Library, T; SSPL, BR. 118 Novosti, TM; Genesis Space Photo Library, B. 119 Pictorial Press, TL; Illustration Kevin Jones Associates/Hamilton Standard. 120 SSPL, TL; SPL/Jim Amos, ML; Olympus Cameras, TR; Genesis Space Photo Library, MR; Julie McMahon, BR. 121 Superstock; Sygma, L; CB, LM; Magnum/Steve McCurry, RM; Aviation Photographs International, R. 122 UB, TR, BR; Imperial War Museum, London, ML. 122-3 Illustrations Martin Woodward. 123 Robert Hunt Picture Library, ML; CB, MR. 124 Robert Hunt Picture Library, TM. 124-5 Illustration Graham White. 125 CB, TL; UB, TR. 126 Imperial War Museum, London, TR. 126-7 Quadrant Picture Library. 127 ROC, ML; Planet Earth Pictures/Peter Scoones, TR. 128 UB, ML; Robert Harding Picture Library, R. 129 Sygma, TL, ML; Robert Hunt Picture Library, BM, BR. 130 Imperial War Museum, London, TR; Magnum/Steve McCurry, ML; Sygma, BL, BR. 131 Aviation Photographs International, B; Illustration Martin Woodward. 132 Magnum/Steve McCurry, TR; CB, BL. 133 British Library/National Sound Archive; Aquarius Library, L; HG, LM; SSPL, RM; The Ronald Grant Archive, R. 134 SSPL, TR, ML, BR. 135 Topham Picturepoint, TM, TR; Magnum/Henri Cartier-Bresson, BL. 136 Mary Evans Picture Library, ML; Superstock, BR; Illustration Michael Robinson. 137 Popperfoto, TL; HG/Martin Austin, ML; Museum of Synthesiser Technology, BR. 138 UB, TR; Aquarius Library, ML; The Ronald Grant Archive, BR. 139 The Ronald Grant Archive, TL, BR; Aquarius Library, MR; CB, MM. 140 Aquarius Library, TR; The Ronald Grant Archive, BR. 141 Pictorial Press, TL; The Ronald Grant Archive, TM, MR, BM; Disney Enterprises Inc, BR. 142 Superstock, TR; HG, BL. 143 HG, TM; SSPL, ML; Illustration Kevin Jones Associates/NTL/Yorkshire Cable. 144 The Advertising Archives, TR; Popperfoto, BL. 145 Illustration Matthew White. 146 Houses & Interiors, TM, TR; The Advertising Archives, TL; National Motor Museum, Beaulieu, BR. 147 Allsport/Didier Givois, TL; Allsport/C. Le Bozec, BL; Stockfile/F. Witmer, MR. 148 Jean-Loup Charmet, TR; ROC, BL. 149 Jerry Kearns, TR; CB, ML; ROC, BR. 150 ROC, TL; New Sulzer Diesel Ltd, TR; HG, M. 150-1 Popperfoto. 151 Mary Evans Picture Library, TM, MR; National Motor Museum, Beaulieu, BR. 152 Pictorial Press, TL; HG, MM. 152-3 TRH Pictures. 153 Jean-Loup Charmet, TR; SPL/Dr Jeremy Burgess, M; SPL/David Parker, BR. 154 CB,

background; SPL/David Parker, TR; Genesis Space Photo Library, BL. 155 SPL/Martin Dohrn, background; SPL/AlfredPasieka, TL; Network/Mike Goldwater, MR; NEC, BM.

Front Cover
Top: Laurie Platt Winfrey, Inc.
Middle: PhotoDisc, Inc.
Bottom: Corbis-Bettmann

Back Cover
Top: SPL/David Parker
Middle: Roger Viollet
Bottom: The Advertising Archives

The editors are grateful to the following individuals and publishers for their kind permission to quote passages from the books below:

Bantam Press from *Black Holes and Baby Universes and Other Essays* by Stephen Hawking, 1993
BBC Books from *Seventy Summers* by Tony Harman, 1986
Facts on File from *The Vietnam War: An Eyewitness History* by Sanford Wexler, 1992
Hamish Hamilton from *The 'Good War': An Oral History of World War Two* by Studs Terkel, 1985
Heinemann from *My Life and Work* by Henry Ford, 1922
Michael Joseph from *1914-1918: Voices and Images of the Great War* by Lynn MacDonald, 1988
McGraw-Hill from *My Father, Marconi* by Degna Marconi, 1962
Michael O'Mara Books from *ITN Book of Firsts* by Melvin Harris, 1994
Frederick Muller from *Jet* by Sir Frank Whittle, 1953
Odhams from *Three Steps to Victory* by Sir Robert Watson-Watt, 1957